THE
POLITICS
OF INDIAN
REMOVAL

THE POLITICS OF INDIAN REMOVAL

Creek Government and Society in Crisis

Michael D. Green

UNIVERSITY OF NEBRASKA PRESS
Lincoln and London

Library of Congress Cataloging in Publication Data

Green, Michael D., 1941–
   The politics of Indian removal.

   Bibliography: p.
   Includes index.
   1. Creek Indians—Removal. 2. Creek Indians—Tribal government. 3. Indians of North America—Southern States—Removal. I. Title
E99.C9G74   970.004'97   81–14670
ISBN 0–8032–2109–6   AACR2

For our children:
Dan, Tom, and Julie

CONTENTS

List of Maps   ix

Preface   xi

1. The Creek Nation: A Place and a People   1

2. The Erosion of Creek Autonomy, 1540–1814   17

3. The Politicization of the Creek Agency   45

4. Creek Law and the Treaty of Indian Springs, 1818–25   69

5. The Abrogation of the Treaty of Indian Springs, 1825–26   98

6. Creek Removal from Georgia, 1826–27   126

7. Alabama Interlude, 1827–36   141

8. Removal from Alabama   174

Notes   187

Note on the Sources   229

Index   233

MAPS

Creek Country of Georgia and Alabama   xvi

Creek Lands in Georgia   44

Upper Creek Lands in Alabama   140

PREFACE

THIS BOOK is about Creek society and government. At first a loosely organized alliance of independent and autonomous tribes, the Creek Confederacy of the seventeenth and eighteenth centuries evolved a body of institutions that gradually began to assert the powers of nationhood. The pace of change was slow, and there is little evidence to argue that it was altogether deliberate. But by the end of the eighteenth century the political science of Alexander McGillivray, a Creek leader who attempted to centralize Creek government, and the perpetual crisis in Creek relations with the United States combined to stimulate the relatively rapid and purposeful emergence of the Creek National Council as a government for the Nation. The territorial expansion of Georgia, the admission of Alabama to statehood in 1819, and the great migration of white settlers into the neighborhood of the Creeks after the War of 1812 all greatly magnified the external pressures upon the Creek nation and vastly accelerated the pace of internal social change. Threatened with the prospect of drowning in a sea of white people, Creek leaders bent to their responsibilities to guide and protect their people and to preserve from inundation all that was salvageable of their values and way of life.

The spotlight was on the leaders. Sitting in the National Council, they had little to guide them. The Council was an ancient institution, but for most of its existence it had served more as a gathering of town civil and war leaders than as a legislative body. Towns surrendered their autonomy with great reluctance, and many of their headmen were loath to experiment with political innovation. Factions formed around influential figures, their conflicts spread to involve local federal officers, and ambitious Georgia politicians fanned the flames of Creek political dissension to further their own electoral goals. Throughout this conflict ran the consistent thread of the United States government's policy—one of expansionism and, ultimately, of removal.

Creek leaders found it hard to reach a consensus on positive action. During the 1820s and '30s, the time of the most intense crisis, they lacked McGillivray's driving force and imagination. Spurning the example of the Cherokees, who were devising a constitutional government modeled on that of the United States, the Creek Council responded to the pressures of encroaching whites and to the incessant demands for land with attempts to stiffen its power to resist. The Council greatly increased its authority, at the direct cost of traditional town autonomy, but for the purpose of surviving. Unwilling to innovate to control change, the Creek Council innovated to prevent change, and, ultimately, it failed. Caught in a whirlwind of conflicting external forces, Creek society was simultaneously transforming and disintegrating at a pace too rapid to be stopped. In the following pages I have attempted to explain the social and political history of the Creek Nation in the two decades before removal; the forces, both external and internal, that shook Creek society; and the efforts of the Creek leadership, through the National Council, to come to grips with calamity.

This book has been long in coming. Through it all, my wife, Andrea Ohl Green, has been my partner. Her words and ideas are so mixed with my own that there is no way I can distinguish them now. When portions of this book first began to emerge as a dissertation, my director at the University of Iowa, Professor Malcolm J. Rohrbough, did what all good thesis advisers should do—he gave me my head. At the same time, his enthusiasm, quiet guidance, and good advice, as well as his continuing friendship, have shaped me, as well as this book, in ways for which I am deeply grateful. And his willingness over the years to read and reread drafts has helped me sharpen my ideas as well as my prose. Professor Jere Daniell of Dartmouth College expertly helped me solve a difficult organizational problem, greatly improving the manuscript. Professor Michael A. Dorris of the Native American Studies Program at Dartmouth has been my good friend. His criticisms of the manuscript and his responses to my ideas have enormously enriched the result. Doctor Angie Debo generously gave me her criticisms and encouragement, for which I am deeply thankful.

I have been fortunate to receive a good deal of financial help in the preparation of this book. The Organized Research Committee of

West Texas State University, Canyon, provided support at the crucial beginning stage. Dartmouth College, with a Faculty Fellowship and additional Faculty Research grants, provided me with a free term and funds for travel, typing, and all the rest of the unexpected costs of preparing a manuscript for publication. I am particularly grateful for Dartmouth's generosity. And the Newberry Library, Chicago, granted me a fellowship year at its distinguished Center for the History of the American Indian. The congenial atmosphere of the center; its fellows and their fellowship; and its director, Francis Jennings, provided me with one of the most rewarding experiences of my professional life.

Finally, countless librarians in Texas, Alabama, Georgia, Illinois, Iowa and New Hampshire have been universally generous of their time and skills in easing my way. Much of what is good about this book is owed to all these people. For the rest, I have no one to blame but myself.

THE
POLITICS
OF INDIAN
REMOVAL

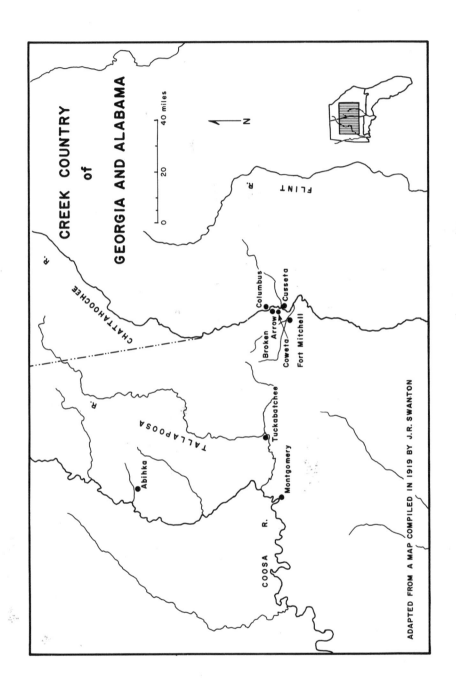

CREEK COUNTRY
of
GEORGIA AND ALABAMA

40 miles

20

0

N

FLINT R.

CHATTAHOOCHEE R.

Columbus
Broken Arrow
Cusseta
Coweta
Fort Mitchell

Tuckabatchee

TALLAPOOSA R.

Abihka

Montgomery

COOSA R.

ADAPTED FROM A MAP COMPILED IN 1919 BY J.R. SWANTON

1

THE CREEK NATION: A PLACE AND A PEOPLE

THE CREEK NATION was a land of wood and water, a place where nature cooperated with people to provide in abundance the necessities of life. A land of sunshine and warmth, rain and trees, deer and corn, it had been the Creek Nation far beyond the sharpest memory of the oldest Creek. It was hard to imagine a better place to live.

At its greatest extent, the Creeks' home encompassed what is now Georgia, most of Alabama, and the panhandle of Florida. But these political boundaries are the creations of Euroamerican politicians and quite unimportant to Creek tradition. What was important were the rivers, the piedmont, the coastal plain, and the fall line, for these natural features defined the Nation and marked its limits.[1]

The piedmont, the hilly upland plateau region between the Appalachians and the coastal plain, was heavily forested with oak and hickory trees intermixed with pine and various hardwoods. Many rivers, mostly narrow, fast-moving, and with rapids, cut gorges across the piedmont as the mountains shed their waters in a southerly direction to the Atlantic Ocean and the Gulf of Mexico. The plunge to the coastal plain, as much as five hundred feet below the piedmont, was sharp enough to create the fall line—a series of falls and rapids—as the rivers tumbled from the plateau.

The coastal plain is flatter than the piedmont and is forested mostly with pine and a mix of magnolia, live oak, and cypress trees. The rivers there are broad, sluggish, and given to overflowing their banks in spring. In the floodplains of these rivers grew enormous canebrakes, which frequently stretched for dozens of miles along the banks, extended inland for a few miles to the bluffs, and grew sometimes thirty feet tall or more. There were also dark and murky swamps.

Much of the coastal plain is agriculturally uninviting, but a fairly narrow band of this low land, abutting the fall line, is among the richest cotton land in the world. This Black Belt extends across central Georgia and Alabama and into northern Mississippi in a huge crescent. Here the Creeks located most of their towns and fields.[2]

The tree cover was heavy in the Creek Nation, but it was not a dense and impenetrable forestland. For centuries the Indians of the Southeast had modified the forests, in some places substantially, through burning. They used fire to clear grazing areas for deer herds, thereby greatly increasing the deer population. They also used fire to hunt and to burn off their fields in late winter in preparation for spring planting. In addition, the Natives developed the technique of girdling (making a deep cut through the bark around a tree to starve it to death) to make clearings around their towns for gardens. Thus the forests were interspersed with fairly large open areas, and the underbrush among the trees tended to be thin. In most seasons it was not hard to travel overland through the Creek Nation, if one was heading north or south. The many rivers and streams, on the other hand, made east-west travel by land difficult. The English traders from Charleston commemorated this inconvenience by calling the people Creeks, and no doubt they cursed the truth of the name as they wrestled their packs through the countless creeks in the nation.[3]

Rapids and falls on the rivers in the piedmont made water transport there difficult. But after the rivers fell onto the coastal plain, the character of these rivers changed and they became wide and gently flowing highways to the sea. In dugouts made by burning out cypress, pine, or poplar logs, the Creeks easily kept in touch with Florida. Any European trader with an interest in the Creek Nation had an important advantage if he located on the Florida coast.

There were six major river systems in the Creek Nation. The Savannah, the Nation's eastern boundary, has its source in the mountains of the Cherokees. The Ogeechee River drains eastern Georgia. The Oconee and Ocmulgee, flowing from the central Georgia piedmont, join to form the Altamaha. All these streams course to the Atlantic. The Flint and Chattahoochee head in northern Georgia, join to form the Apalachicola River, and empty into the Gulf of Mexico. The Chattahoochee was the heart of the Lower Creek country; situated on its banks were Coweta and Cusseta, the two mother towns of the Lower Creeks. The Coosa and Tallapoosa rivers drain northeast Alabama and join to form the Alabama River. Tuckabatchee, the most prominent Upper Creek town, was on the Tallapoosa near this junction. The Black Warrior and Tombigbee rivers flow from northwestern Alabama and northeastern Mississippi. The Black Warrior joins the Tombigbee, and the Tombigbee and the Alabama merge to form the Mobile River, which empties into Mobile Bay and the Gulf of Mexico. From ancient times the watershed between the Black Warrior and Tombigbee rivers formed the boundary between Creek and Chickasaw hunting grounds, just as the watershed between the Alabama and Tombigbee rivers separated the territory of the Creeks and Choctaws.

The rivers flooded in the spring. A ten- to fifteen-foot rise was not uncommon, and sometimes the crest rose to sixty feet above normal.[4] The floodplains were the sites for most of the Creeks' large fields, and although sometimes washed away or buried under sand, these croplands were also often enriched with silt. In addition to being fertile, the ground was soft and easy to work with hoes.

Although the Creeks were not exclusively agriculturalists, farming played a significant role in Creek life. Each season their gardens yielded two crops of early corn, which they picked green and ate immediately. Their large river-bottom fields produced one crop of late corn, which they permitted to dry for several weeks on the stalk. After picking, the dried corn was stored for use as hominy. Using the corn stalks for poles, the Creeks planted several varieties of beans with the corn. They grew well together, the beans replacing the nitrogen in the soil consumed by the corn, and together they provided the Creeks with the bulk of their vegetable protein. Along with these crops, the people planted squash, melons, and gourds.[5]

The Creeks supplemented their vegetable intake with wild plants. They knew about, and used for food and medicine, many varieties of wild fruits, berries, herbs, and roots. Women and children also gathered nuts, especially hickory nuts and acorns, which they ground and cooked with corn or boiled for oil.

The men were active and skilled hunters and fishermen. By far their most important prey was the white-tailed deer, abundant in the Southeast. Perhaps 90 percent of their meat consumption was deer, supplemented with bear (which they valued more for the oil they rendered from its fat than for its meat), small game, turkeys, passenger pigeons, and various water birds. Fish swimming upstream to spawn congregated at the fall line, making those rapids among the richest fishing sites in North America. Using nets, weirs and traps, spears and harpoons, bow and arrows, and poison, the Creeks harvested a wide variety of fish. Their techniques for bagging the larger species were dramatic. Creek fishermen wrestled the giant catfish into submission and captured sturgeon with a lasso.[6]

The riches of the Nation were vast, but the Creeks did not live in scattered isolation. They were town and village dwellers, and here an important distinction must be made. A town (*talwa*) was an autonomous political and ceremonial center that probably had once been independent. Linguists and ethnologists frequently translate talwa as "town," but it would be more accurate to think of it as "tribe." The grouping of these independent tribes created the Creek Confederacy. A Creek town was institutionally complete and was built around a square ground, the site for all local governmental and ceremonial functions. A village (*talofa*), on the other hand, was a residential community without a square ground. Villages were small, politically and ceremonially incomplete, and dependent on a nearby town; often they were an offshoot from such a town. The relationship between the two was much like that of a modern bedroom suburb to a nearby metropolis. During the eighteenth century, Creek towns ranged in population from about fifty to nearly two thousand. Before contact with Europeans, they were surely much more populous. In the 1832 census, officials counted fifty-two Creek towns. At one time or another during the eighteenth century, Europeans listed the names of over eighty towns.[7]

The people who lived in those towns have been referred to by several different names. Ethnologists called their language group Muskhogean because the people who spoke such languages had often been called Muskogees. The Shawnees probably originally bestowed this name, related to *muskeg*, because the Nation was a wet and swampy country.[8] Charleston traders named them Creeks for the same reason. A Creek might have called himself either of these, but more likely, if asked by a white, he would have given the name of his town.

For their own purposes, however, there were other important identities by which individuals located themselves within the spectrum of Creek society. The Creek Nation was not a nation of individual citizens in the European sense. It was a nation of clan members. Clan membership gave individuals identity, putting them into social perspective and determining their relationships with all other Creeks. The clan membership of a particular person defined whom he could joke with, whom he could marry, whom he must defend or avenge, and what his ceremonial and political obligations might be. Clan membership specified his duties to others and their duties to him and provided him a place where he belonged.[9]

A clan is a kinship group; all members of the same clan are considered to be related. Creek clans are matrilineal: each person is born a member of his mother's clan and nothing can change that membership. A Creek remains forever a relative of his mother and her family and is never a relative of his father. His uncles, his mother's brothers, provided the guidance, education, and discipline a Creek boy received. The biological father fulfilled the same responsibility for the children of his sisters. A Creek girl was prepared for adulthood by her mother and her aunts. Certainly, emotional ties bound fathers to their children, and in informal settings the influence of a father on his children could be strong, but at the milestones of a boy's life, it was his maternal uncle, not his father, who assumed the role of counselor, guide, protector, and adviser.[10]

The clans were also matrilocal. A young man, upon marriage, moved with his wife into the neighborhood of her mother. He built their house and assisted in the heaviest spring and fall farm work, but the house and fields were hers. It was her home, but never his. His home was the house of his mother or sister. This matrilocality meant that Creek towns were composed of several clan neighborhoods, identified by the clan of the women, influenced by the oldest and most respected clan mother, supervised by the Clan Elder (who lived in a different neighborhood if he was married), and inhabited by the related women and children and the unrelated husbands, who spent much of their time away from their families in their own clan's neighborhood.

The town council allotted farmland to the clans according to their population needs: the clan councils, presided over by Clan Elders, subdivided the clan's allotment among the various households; and the women of the households raised the crops, usually with the periodic help of their husbands. The clan neighborhoods were, therefore, small agricultural communities.

As in any community, there was a potential for conflict in Creek towns. One of the most important functions of the clans was to keep such conflict to a minimum. The social training of Creek children was primarily the responsibility of the Clan Elders. These old and wise men gathered together the children of both sexes to teach them to be thoughtful of others, to respect and obey their elders, to be loyal to their clans, to participate with devotion in the religious ceremonies, and to obey the rules of the clan and the laws of the town and nation. This teaching was done through stories, admonitions, and elaborate explanations of the frequently announced laws and regulations. These learning sessions began when the children reached the age of five or six and continued until they were in their mid-teens.

Just as the Clan Elder was responsible for their education, he was also responsible for punishing the children when they violated society's rules. For major crimes he presided over a court of clan members. In minor cases he ruled alone, forgiving and instructing the wrongdoer if the infraction was due to ignorance. The Clan Elder punished willful misbehavior by scratching the dry legs of the youthful offender with the teeth of a gar. The depth and number of scratches was determined by the severity of the offense. Although dry scratching was used for painful punishment, the Creeks thought wet scratching was a positive experience because they believed the incisions made the calf muscles supple and that the harmless flow of blood taught the child not to fear his own blood.[11]

In addition to regulating internal behavior, the clan also offered a measure of safety for its members from outsiders. The security that clan membership provided ranged far beyond the comforting realization that clan relatives in other towns, even those an individual might never have met, could be relied on to provide support and protection. Except in those towns where one's clan did not exist, any Creek knew he was never far from relatives anywhere in the Nation. Moreover, the clan structure itself shielded him from harm. The system rested on the idea of compensation; if any Creek was injured or killed, the clan of the perpetrator was obligated to compensate the clan of the victim. Such compensation could take a variety of forms. The perpetrator or his clan relatives could give presents to the victim's clan, they could pay with the life of an enemy, or they could provide a captive for adoption as a replacement. Most commonly, however, they could offer a life of their own in return, perhaps that of the perpetrator. Accidental death was compensated for in the same manner as murder. Thus, every Creek knew that his clan relatives stood ready to demand repayment for his loss. The certainty that the clan would respond to the injury of one of its members kept the incidence of such harm to a minimum in Creek society, and thus clan reciprocity served the function that formal institutions of law and jurisprudence provided in European societies.[12]

Clan attachments were strong, but the matrilocality of Creek society imposed an ambiguous and potentially conflicting set of loyalties upon at least the married male portion of the population. Ties of affection bound a husband and father to the clan of his wife, children, and most of his neighbors, introducing a secondary loyalty to compete with his clan obligations. Hypothetically, at least, a situation could occur in which he would have to demand punishment, perhaps even death, of a member of his wife's clan (even his own child) if one of her relatives injured or killed one of his. Such difficult eventualities made it likely that the Creeks kept interclan factionalism and feuding to a minimum in order to forestall such a collision of emotional attachments and clan obligations.[13]

The Creeks also developed a moiety system. The term *moiety* is of French origin, meaning half. In an ethnographic context it refers to the division of a tribe into two groups. Some tribes made the division by individual; the Creeks did it by clan, calling their two subdivisions *Hathagalgi* and *Tcilokogalgi*. The Hathagalgi were "white people," so called because white was the color of peace. Tcilokogalgi means "people of a different speech," or, perhaps, "foreigners." Tciloki clans have frequently been called red clans, partly perhaps to maintain the color analogy, because red was one of the colors Creeks used to symbolize war, and clearly the Tciloki clans had special military responsibilities. European observers often called the two subdivisions "peace" and "war" as well as "white" and "red." The Creeks also applied their moiety division to their nation by dividing the towns into white, or peace, and red, or war, groups.[14]

There may have once been some division of responsibility between red and white towns, with the red towns playing a more prominent war role than the white. Hothliwahali, a red town on the west bank of the Tallapoosa River, once had the right to declare war for at least all the Upper Creek towns. It may have been that certain of the white towns had the job of negotiating peace. Some of these towns, at any rate, were places of refuge to which persons could flee if they were foreign enemies or fellow Creeks seeking to avoid clan justice.[15]

This Hathagalgi-Tcilokogalgi division was enormously important in the affairs of both town and nation. It established and maintained a separation of public responsibility into the two conditions of Creek life, peace and war. By accepting this dualism, and by creating dual leadership institutions, the Creeks attempted to impose order without suffering the consequences of excessive concentration of power in the hands of a few. Like many native peoples, the Creeks were extremely uncomfortable with highly centralized leadership. Seeing such a structure as a threat to individual liberty, they evolved a political system which denied great power to any one person or small group. At the same time, they appreciated the need for discipline in time of war. To resolve the conflict between retaining personal liberty and the need for military discipline, they created a hierarchy of military officials but denied them power except in emergencies. In such times of crisis, however, discipline was tight, and respect for authority was strong enough to prompt some ethnologists to list the Creeks among the more authoritarian of native societies. Their moiety system was their machine for maintaining the doctrine of separation of powers.

The Creeks honored military achievement. They structured their male society into warrior ranks, which young men yearned to join. Be-

fore a youth earned his first war name, he served the men in the council and was called by the name of his mother. Only an elaborate initia-
tion ritual and some personal exploit, such as participation in a battle,
could release him from his immaturity, individualize him with a name
publicly bestowed, and admit him to the adult male world of the *tasikayalgi*.[16] But a tasikaya was just a private and was never consulted in
council by the chiefs. Therefore, for an ambitious Creek youth, becoming a tasikaya was only the starting point. Above the tasikayalgi were
two grades of *imathlayalgi*—*imathla labotke* (little imathla) and
imathla thlako (big imathla). Little imathlas served big imathlas as
messengers and assistants. Big imathlas, who might sometimes be admitted into the councils, served their superiors, the *tastanagalgi*.
These were the war heroes and leaders, the men whose bravery, skill,
and tactical abilities had earned for them the adoration of small boys
and the respect of their fellow townsmen. One, the greatest of them all,
was the *tastanagi thlako* (big warrior), their leader.[17]

The warrior progressed through the ranks as his merit permitted,
each step marked by an elaborate public ceremony, a new and more
distinguished name that bore his title, and greater ceremonial and
political responsibilities. Members of both clans could participate in
warrior training up to a point. War leaders, however, had to complete
special training under the guidance of a *hilis haya* (medicine man or
healer), and only members of Tciloki clans could receive such instruction. Therefore, only members of Tciloki clans could advance to the
highest military ranks and sit on the warriors' council.[18]

In times of peace, the war leaders met with the civil leaders in
council, but their voices were muted and their role, except in cases of
great urgency, was minor. Once the council reached its decisions, however, the warriors became the police, with the big warrior as "chief," to
enforce them.

The civil council made all decisions, including that of declaring
war, but when that step was taken, the big warrior issued the declaration and took over the mobilization. Until peace was reestablished
military rule prevailed, and the war council functioned as the effective
government. If the dual system of the Creeks worked properly, peacetime brought a return to civil government.[19]

The Creek civil government consisted of a council of administrators and professional peace advocates (*henihalgi*) and elder statesmen
distinguished by past governmental accomplishments or military fame
(*isti atcagagi*), presided over by a head chief (*miko*) and a consulting
board of chiefs (*mikagi*). In white towns, the miko and mikagi were
members of a white, or peace, clan, very often the Bear or Bird. In red

towns they were likely to belong to a Tciloki clan, commonly the Raccoon, but not invariably so.[20]

The miko presided over the town council. He called it into session and presented the questions for discussion. The councillors treated him with great respect, but he had no authority to act independently of them or to pursue a policy not previously decided upon by unanimous decision. A miko with a distinguished record of past successes and a strong following could exert great influence in his town, but his powers flowed from his personality, not from the prerogatives of his office. But mikos had certain duties that could be useful in building a power base. Each town had a public granary filled by contributions from all its residents. The town miko controlled this surplus food supply, doling it out to needy families in time of famine or personal catastrophe. He also drew from this surplus to entertain visiting dignitaries or, on occasion, to host a town feast. The town miko was also likely to be the town's representative in relations with other Creek towns or with neighboring foreign tribes.[21]

A miko rarely spoke for himself. Oratory was an art among the Creeks, and they preferred to have highly talented professional speakers make the speeches that characterized their political and religious activities. Mikos used speakers to introduce the business at hand in council and to announce council decisions to the people. Speakers accompanied mikos on diplomatic missions and did most, or all, of the negotiating. A speaker delivered the long and elaborate addresses that opened and concluded the major religious ceremonies—speeches that told the history of the town and its people and exhorted all to live moral, peaceful, and honorable lives, to obey the laws, and to respect their elders. Speakers were needed for so many occasions that most towns had several, of various ranks. The *yatika* (interpreter) spoke for the miko in council. But if the town had a really brilliant orator, it honored him with the title of *hothlibonaya* (war speaker). He spoke on special occasions and was the one most likely to be chosen to defend the town's interests in diplomatic affairs. His voice gave him great influence, and his office was likely to make him internationally known.[22]

All possible positions, by design, had their advocates in a Creek town council. The big warrior and the highest-ranking tastanagalgi, all of whom belonged to Tciloki clans, represented the large warrior class. The henihalgi were peace advocates. They had undergone the training of war discipline, but as members of white clans they were barred from the highest warrior ranks. Their regular duties included supervising the construction and maintenance of public buildings, directing the construction of homes for newcomers, and organizing the community agricultural activities. But these menial administrative duties, vital as they were to the daily lives of the people, did not alone earn them their honored seats in the square ground. Their mere presence in council served to remind the others of the essentially peaceful purpose of Creek life. In some of the red towns, Tuckabatchee, for instance, each civil officer and each of the highest ranking military officers had a heniha assigned to him who accompanied him in all his official duties. These heniha shadows (nicknamed "Second Men" by early white observers) assured all who saw of the peaceful intent of the mission. The henihalgi seem to have been the guarantee that nothing untoward would happen and that an ameliorating argument would always accompany a strident or bellicose one.[23]

The *isti atcagagi* had a foot in both camps. These elder statesmen represented both white and Tciloki clans. They had won military distinction, had held major religious or civil offices, and had accumulated too much experience and knowledge to be ignored. They knew how the ceremonies should be conducted and they remembered their past glories. The "brains" of the town, these "Beloved Men" supplied wisdom and good judgment from a position of neutrality. The miko and his "kitchen cabinet" of mikagi presented the issues, presided over the meeting, and performed such executive tasks as were needed. The clans, the white and Tciloki moieties, merit, age, ambition, war, peace —all were represented.[24]

No council or other set of institutions designed to maintain a separation of power works perfectly, but the Creeks established checks and built-in rivalries that at least sought to preclude unholy, under-the-table collusion. While males could have divided clan loyalties, there could be no question of their moiety allegiance. They referred in their common speech to the people, clans, and towns of their moiety as "my friends" and to those of the other moiety as "my enemies." The suspicion between the two groups was so strong that friendships, marriages, and even casual associations rarely crossed the line. There was no formal rule, but the suspicion was just too great.[25]

There may have been several things in Creek life that kept this intense Hathagalgi-Tcilokogalgi rivalry alive, but none was more important than the ball game.[26] The Creeks played several kinds of ball games, but the most important, the match game, was considered the "younger brother to war." This game seems to have assumed a role of major importance in Creek life after the Confederacy had grown strong enough to have absorbed or destroyed likely enemies. The match game became important for controlling the aggressive impulses of the warriors and for providing opportunities for young men to distinguish themselves and win local fame without war. The Hathagalgi and Tcilokogalgi clansmen played practice games against each other, honing their skills for the big games between rival red and white towns.[27]

The games whetted a competitive spirit that remained alive in the strong feelings of loyalty the people held for their side. When a town lost four consecutive games to its archrival, it had to join the enemy's side. This seems to have happened frequently, and any list of white and red towns reflects only the current status and fails to identify past changes. Indeed, such forced changes from white to red or vice versa were so humiliating that the townsmen often tried to hide the fact of their loss by pretending that their town had always been classed as it now was.[28]

Throughout the centuries, the Creeks played the match game, but it gradually lost much of its original political and social significance. Changing times rendered some of its functions unnecessary; different institutions emerged to absorb others. Increasingly, in inter-town relationships, the dominating factor in determining sides became geographic location. As it grew in population and power, and as its relations with whites increased, the Creek Nation found that the division into Upper and Lower towns made more political sense than the division into red and white towns. This distinction recognized the fact that there were two concentrations of Creek towns within the Nation. One lay in the Chattahoochee valley stretching to the south about seventy miles from a point just above the falls (or between the present cities of Columbus, Georgia, and Eufaula, Alabama). The other center of population, less concentrated than the one in the Chattahoochee valley, extended down the Coosa and Tallapoosa rivers to the point where they joined to form the Alabama, and then down that river about thirty miles. Within this rather extensive gathering of towns, the heaviest concentration of people was along the lower Tallapoosa and upper Alabama rivers, not far from present-day Montgomery, Alabama.

It is not clear how the people in these two regions came to be called Upper and Lower Creeks, or when. The Tallapoosa towns lay directly west of the Chattahoochee towns, so it was not a matter of one group being situated north of the other. Probably the Charleston traders named the two sets of towns. The trading road forked in central Georgia, with the left, or lower, path leading to the Chattahoochee, the right, or upper, path, branching off to the Tallapoosa River. Also, the more distant Tallapoosa towns were farther "up the road" from the Chattahoochee towns. At any rate, by the early eighteenth

century, both the English and the Creeks began to call the Chattahoochee towns the Lower Creeks and the Tallapoosa towns the Upper
Creeks. (Such terminology made no sense to the Spanish and French,
who approached the Creeks from south or west. They called the Upper
Creeks Talapoosas, the Lower Creeks Cowetas.) Distinguishing between the two sets of towns made sense to the Creeks because the geographic separation of the two had resulted in different political, military, and economic conditions. For example, the proximity of Carolina
and Georgia traders and settlers decisively affected Lower Creek policies. The Upper Towns, on the other hand, were more isolated from
English encroachment, and during the eighteenth century traded more
easily with the French and Spanish.[29]

This Upper-Lower division of towns had an increasing influence
upon Creek internal affairs. The headmen of neighboring towns gathered together in councils to discuss common problems and organize
joint action. Late seventeenth and early eighteenth century sources
document the existence of Upper Town and Lower Town Councils able
to conduct business in the name of their respective groups. For most of
its history, however, the Creek Nation remained more united than
divided. This internal harmony and cooperation, sometimes more apparent than real, provided the basis for the power the Creeks wielded
in the Southeast. The Confederacy bound the towns together.

Some sort of confederate or national Council seems to have existed for a very long time. Before the early eighteenth century, when
Europeans began to describe it, the form of the council can only be sur-
mised. It seems to have met infrequently, perhaps not even annually;
all towns probably did not send delegates; and it appears to have had
no power and only limited influence. Its function seems to have been
primarily to acquaint leaders of the major towns with one another and
with events in distant places. One thing is quite clear, however. The
Creek Confederacy was never designed to have a central government.
Beginning late in the eighteenth century in response to the Anglo-
American expansionist pressure, some Creeks tried to centralize the
government, but the Creeks had neither the traditions nor the institutions for centralization. Indeed, their history pointed in the opposite
direction, to local autonomy and the independence of towns. Little in
the collective experience of the Creeks had prepared them for such a
radical departure, and those who pushed the Confederacy toward centralization met considerable resistance.

The Confederacy had its beginnings before DeSoto's exploration
in 1540, but it is impossible to know how much earlier, for versions dif-

fer.[30] The earliest recorded Creek account, provided in 1735 by Chekilli, a Cusseta headman, tells how the earth opened up, somewhere in the West, and the Cussetas came out. The earth then tried to eat the Cussetas, so they fled to the east, crossing many rivers. On their way, they came to a mountain that thundered and had a fire on its peak that sang as it burned. The Cussetas met three other nations of Muskogee-speaking people at the mountain, and together the four groups received fire and the sacred medicines vital to their ceremonies. The sharing of this profound experience bound them together. Once joined, the four nations held a contest to decide their ranking. For four years they made war on foreign tribes. When they finished, each group erected a scalp pole and piled the scalps of their victims around it. The Cussetas brought in so much hair that they completely buried their pole, so the others called them the "eldest," or first in rank. The Chickasaws ranked next, then the Alabamas, and finally the Abihkas, who had only a few scalps and could make a pile only knee high.

After deciding their rank, the four friendly groups continued eastward, where they found the Coosas living on the bank of a large river (Coosa). A lion terrorized the Coosas by killing and eating them, but the four allies devised a trap to capture the beast. They burned his body and made his bones an important part of their war medicine. For four years the Coosas entertained their saviors, and they became permanent friends, but finally the migrants set off again, still heading east. The four nations reached another large river (Chattahoochee), on the banks of which lived people with flat heads. The friends killed all but two, who escaped along a white path. The invading Muskogees followed these two refugees south to Apalachicola. The Apalachicolas welcomed the Muskogees, entertained them with black drink, a decoction brewed from the leaves of the tea-like Yaupon holly, and urged them to give up war and killing and develop a white (peaceful) heart.[31] Some of the Cussetas agreed, but others were "too bloody-minded" to take such advice. They moved across the river and became the Cowetas.

Some legends say the Chickasaws stopped along the way and never completed the eastward trek, others tell of the Chickasaws going all the way to the Atlantic and then returning west. At any rate, the Chickasaws became separated from their friends and founded their own nation. The ancient bond between them and Cusseta was never forgotten, however, and as late as 1796, when there was war between the Chickasaws and the Creeks, Cusseta refused to participate.

Chekilli's legend explains the presence of most of the original Muskogee people in the southeast, and it accounts for their relationships with each other. Coweta and Cusseta became the two leading Lower Creek towns, "bloody-minded" Coweta heading the red side, "peaceful" Cusseta the white. Abihka became white and remained in the Upper Creek country, and along with Coosa it was remembered as an ancient and important town. Coosa disintegrated in later years, spinning off the many Tallassee and Oakfuskee towns. A refugee people from the north entered the Confederacy, founded Tuckabatchee, and gained leadership of the red side among the Upper Creeks.[32]

Not much is known about the growth process of the Confederacy except that it did grow. The survivors of many tribes entered it, either as conquered enemies or as refugees. Many speakers of Muskhogean dialects joined the Confederacy, although the differences in the languages were sometimes great enough to render them mutually unintelligible. Cusseta, Coweta, Coosa, Abihka, Hothliwahali, Hilibi, and Eufaula formed a nucleus of Muskogee towns. The Tuckabatchees, Okchais, and Pakanas, also Muskogee-speakers, joined later. The Hitchitis and Alabamas spoke more distantly related dialects. The Natchez, who spoke a Muskhogean tongue unintelligible to the Muskogees, fled to the Confederacy in the 1730s to escape a concerted French effort to exterminate them. The Yuchis and a sizable number of Shawnees, both with languages of quite different stocks, also entered the alliance. These tribes became Creek towns, spawning new settlements and increasing in size with the security that numbers provided.[33]

It seems clear that military alliance remained the first principle of the Confederacy. The original friends agreed not to make war on one another, perhaps because of the shared religious experience described in Chekilli's legend. Once allied, they agreed to make war on others. These wars led them all eastward, making them invaders. Their successes, enhanced by their alliance, made them conquerors, and their victims, voluntarily or not, became new allies. The alliance was distinctly aggressive.

The Creeks' age of conquest ended in the eighteenth century and was followed by a time of encroachment and intrusion by whites. The Confederacy continued intact, indeed it grew stronger internally, but the alliance took on a more defensive aspect. Creek warriors continued their business, but increasingly their enemies were white men, and the purpose of the warriors was the defense of their frontiers. And while the Confederacy continued to absorb new tribes, they were more likely to be refugees from white aggression, not the defeated enemies of the Creeks.

The affection of kinship bound the people of the towns and helped to unite them. A similar kind of friendship, perhaps more abstract and symbolic because it was not personal, seems to have bound the towns in the Confederacy. As new towns joined, they became friends with the others. Friends helped each other whenever and however they could, but there was no formal obligation to do so and no official censure when they did not. Thus there were no mass armies of Confederacy warriors, no central policy, and no central government. There was only good will among friends and the realization that an invading enemy was a common enemy.

The ball games knotted these ties of friendship. New tribes appear usually to have entered the Confederacy on the white side, the side of peace and diplomacy, perhaps with an especially close relationship with a particular town. Friendship with one white town led to friendship with all white towns, and games against red towns established a newcomer's legitimacy with the other side. As towns lost the required number of games and switched sides, their circle of friends changed, along with their obligations and ceremonial connections. Over an extended period of time, a new town became friends with all other Creek towns, and their interrelatedness was reaffirmed.[34]

Another phenomenon united the Confederacy—probably the most important one of all. Despite the many dissimilarities among the tribes in the alliance—in ceremonial detail, political form, ancient history, language—all shared in the Busk, a religious experience that transcended the differences and emphasized the oneness of the Creek Nation.

The word *Busk* is an English corruption of the Creek *poskita*, meaning "a fast." The Creeks fasted on many occasions (there were many "busks"), but late in the summer they held *the* Busk, a multiday celebration to commemorate the harvest, usher in the new year, and to remember with ceremony their history, their laws, their mutual obligations, and their friendship.[35]

The Green Corn Celebration, as the Busk was also called, had religious, social, political, and recreational functions. It not only brought all the people of a town together in a common ceremonial experience, but also drew in all of a town's outlying villages and attracted visitors from other towns of the same side. Attendance was mandatory, and the town council fined any iconoclasts who stayed home.

During the days of celebration (from four to eight), all the clans gathered into their own councils to hear their Elders comment on their conduct over the past year and urge good behavior for the next. The town council met to review the year and plan for the next, and, through a vigorous oration by the speaker, reminded the citizens of the town's history and proclaimed the laws. The religious leaders con ducted elaborate ceremonies to give thanks for the year ending and to prepare for the next. The fire maker built a new town fire from which the women, who had put out their home fires and scattered the ashes, took an ember to kindle a pure new flame.

The Busk was replete with symbolism. Extinguishing the old fire and lighting the new was one of the many ceremonies the Creeks used to signify the central meaning of the festival. It was a ceremony of renewal. The new fire symbolized the rebirth of each Creek person. Old sins were wiped away, crimes short of murder were forgiven, and all were made pure and innocent. The Busk celebrated life—its spirituality and its beauty—and the Creeks welcomed the new year with the solemnity of devout religious observances and the exuberance of ball games and social dances. The fast was broken with a feast that featured newly picked green corn, the first fruit of the fall harvest.

By wiping the slate clean every year, the Creeks kept their society in harmony. By remembering the sacred sources of their power, they kept their lives in spiritual perspective. And by ending the Busk with the green corn feast, they looked ahead to the living of a new year. Like the fire, the corn symbolized the renewal of life. Corn came from the ground, and through it the land nourished the people. By focusing on the produce of the land, the Creeks celebrated their past and their future life in the place where they were. They could never forget that they were uniquely the people of that place.[36]

2
THE EROSION
OF CREEK AUTONOMY,
1540–1814

F<small>ROM THE MOMENT</small> the first European set foot on the soil of the Creek Nation, the pace of natural change in life, society, and culture was accelerated. Whatever the Creeks first visual impressions may have been —and they were perhaps not particularly shocked by the Europeans[1] —the experiences which fleshed out those impressions quickly showed the Creeks how strange and unpredictable the future could be. Disease, the fellow traveler of European explorers, reached the region even before DeSoto. "Two years before," wrote the Gentleman of Elvas, a Portuguese chronicler of the Expedition, "there had been a pest in the land," and everywhere there were "large vacant towns, grown up in grass." And DeSoto's men left a legacy of illness of their own. Twenty years later, the western Creek country, which in the 1540s had been rich and densely settled, was depopulated. Further contacts with Spanish and other European explorers, settlers, and missionaries in the sixteenth and seventeenth centuries meant that small pox, measles, influenza and other diseases continued to take their toll on the hitherto unexposed Native people of southeastern North America. If the recent estimates of some scholars are correct, and nineteen out of twenty Native people died of epidemic disease within the first two centuries of contact, then perhaps two hundred thousand Creeks were alive in 1500.[2]

How does a society react when its population plummets from two-hundred thousand to below ten thousand in less than two centuries, at the hands of an unseen and seemingly invulnerable killer? In a society such as that of the Creeks, which was not literate, how much history, literature, art, ritual, and technology was lost forever? What happened to the structure of leadership, the patterns of marriage and descent, the military organizations? How profound was the panic? Creek population more than doubled during the eighteenth century, reaching some twenty-five thousand people by the 1820s, but much of this influx came from incorporating additional tribes into the Confederacy, and smallpox, measles, and other European diseases continued to be a hazard. Regional epidemics occurring in 1696–98, 1738–39, 1759–60, 1779–80, and as late as 1831 carried off large but untabulated numbers of people. At no time before removal were the Creeks free of the shadow of epidemic disease.[3]

While the full impact of disease on the Creeks in the sixteenth and seventeenth centuries can only be guessed at, other effects of the European presence on those who survived can be documented. Social, political, and economic changes, all interrelated and difficult to understand and control, occurred with increased speed and magnitude. The alterations of Creek life, occasioned in large part by the eighteenth-century slave and deerskin trade, propelled the people through a time of riches and power unparalleled in their history, only to end in a dependence so debilitating that the Nation could no longer defend its territory from the expansionist demands of its white neighbors.

After DeSoto's explorations, there was an influx of Europeans of various nationalities. By 1700 the Creeks were in direct and frequent contact with the Spanish in Florida, the French in Louisiana, and the British in Carolina. During those early years, economics dominated the relations between Natives and Europeans. Both sides actively sought trade and both benefited, at least initially, from the barter of deer hides and captives for guns, powder, and a variety of manufactured goods. For the Creeks, as for other native peoples in North America, the full ramifications of such an exchange became apparent only after a long association with it.[4]

One of the most basic changes imposed on Creek society by the acquisition of European goods related to the ways in which adult Creeks spent their time. Iron and steel utensils replaced painstakingly shaped stone tools; wearing apparel fashioned from easily worked woven cloth superseded hand-tanned leather clothing; and guns proved more efficient in hunting and war than bows, arrows, and blowguns, although the silence of these ancient weapons made them still useful in certain select situations long after the widespread adoption of firearms.

 Superficially, it might appear by these exchanges of artifacts that Creek adults were able to enjoy a massive increase in leisure time. On the contrary, however, the time released by a sharp reduction in do mestic manufacture of goods was absorbed by a major increase in the production of deer hides, the Creek Nation's prime export, and by increased warfare on neighboring tribes to acquire captives for the Charleston (known as Charles Town before 1783) slave market. When Creek men hunted only for home consumption, their hunting season was a relatively short, late fall–early winter expedition to reasonably close hunting grounds. Their escalating appetite for goods required an increased number of hides. To kill more deer, Creek hunters had to spend more time hunting and had to travel farther, thereby decreasing their time at home and increasing their contacts with Native neighbors competing with them for a finite number of deer. The profit motive also changed the character of Creek warfare. At one time, war had been waged against enemies guilty of past offenses against the Nation, but now Creek warriors made large-scale invasions into distant territories for the sole purpose of capturing prisoners to be sold to the Carolina traders. These slave-catching raids were sometimes led by Carolinians who had political as well as economic goals, but the profits of slaving were adequate enough to perpetuate the devastating business. One observer estimated that three Indians died for every one captured for slavery. Creek men became, in effect, commercial hunters and slave raiders, and were less and less involved with agriculture and other domestic affairs. The women, to fill the void, took on a greater share of the farming responsibilities (as opposed to the gardening, which they had always done), even engaging in limited commercial agriculture as the numbers of Europeans in the Creek Nation increased. Their child-rearing duties probably expanded to include many of the male obligations once undertaken by their brothers. And they continued to do much, if not all, of the tanning of the hides brought home by the itinerant men.[5]

European peddlers circulated throughout the Nation hawking their wares (mostly rum) for skins, but permanently established traders did much of the business. Most towns had a trader, and some towns had several in residence. They built stores and houses; kept herds of cattle, horses, and hogs; married Creek women; and raised bilingual and bicultural mixed-blood children. For most of the year the trader sold goods on credit, collecting payment in tanned hides in the spring. It was a diverse market, but one placing heavy emphasis on manufactured goods to replace those once made by the Indians. James Adair wrote that the Creeks, "by reason of our supplying them so cheap with every sort of goods, have forgotten the chief part of their ancient mechanical skill, so as not to be well able now, at least for some years, to live independently of us."[6] The traders had acquired a stranglehold on the Creek economy and through it an extraordinary influence on other aspects of Creek life.[7]

The trade also stimulated a socioeconomic transformation within the Nation. Deerskins and captives, the produce of individual effort, were the private property of the individual hunters and warriors who brought them home. And when the owner exchanged this property for trade goods, they too were his personal possessions. The more successful hunters and warriors, with more produce to trade, accumulated more goods and became wealthy. Success at hunting and warfare had always been the route to prestige and position for individual men. Trade introduced wealth into the equation for success and stimulated the development of a propertied class of Creek families.[8]

As European goods gained significance in the lives of the Creeks, and as the influence of the purveyors of those goods grew apace, the imperial governments and their American representatives became increasingly anxious to extend political control over the trade and the traders. It became an axiom in colonial capitals that he who controlled the trade controlled the Indians. Never absolutely true, the rule was at least correct in suggesting that if goods alone would not win Native friends, friendship was rarely won without goods. Europeans saw the Creeks as a threat and a promise. They were so powerful that their concerted hostility could be fatal. Their friendship, on the other hand, could be enormously valuable politically as well as economically.

From about 1670 to 1715, Creek trade rested almost exclusively with the English headquartered in Charleston. Theirs was a bittersweet relationship, but it was desirable enough in its early period to cause most of the Lower Towns to move, during the 1690s, from the Chattahoochee River to the fall line on the Ogeechee, Oconee, and Ocmulgee rivers, to meet the Carolinians halfway. They stayed there for twenty-five years, until the unscrupulous traders drove their abused customers to rebellion. The Yamasee War of 1715 did enormous damage on the southern English frontier, caused the Creeks to move back to the Chattahoochee, and led to the opening of important new commercial and political contacts with England's rivals. The Lower Creeks mended their relations with Spanish St. Augustine. The Upper Creeks, particularly the westernmost Alabamas and the Koasatis, made peace with French Mobile. Both the French and the Spanish responded with alacrity to the unexpected opportunity. In 1716, a garrison of French troops, with Alabama guides, built Fort Toulouse near the head of the Alabama River, and two years later the Spanish established Fort San Marcos on Apalachee Bay.[9]

All this Spanish and French activity reflected an inability to compete with the English in the marketplace for Creek affections. Only by exploiting the persistent British arrogance could they make political gains among the Natives. British influence over Confederacy policy followed the trading paths from Charleston. The French and Spanish had to counter the British as best they could with a small military presence and the diplomacy of gift giving.[10]

Three European colonies, each using the tools at its disposal to construct an alliance at the expense of the others, surrounded the Creek Nation. Irrationally confident, these tiny colonial outposts expected to dominate the much larger, more powerful Creek Confederacy. In fact, for the next several decades, it was the Confederacy which controlled affairs in the Southeast—following its own course, exploiting the jealousies and ambitions of the Europeans, and reaping the rewards of the competition for Creek friendship.

In 1775, James Adair published a colorful, much quoted description of the Creeks' response to the politics of European colonialism. "The old men," he wrote,

> being long informed by the opposite parties, of the different views, and intrigues of those European powers, who paid them annual tribute under the vague appellation of presents, were becoming surprisingly crafty in every turn of low politics. They held it as an invariable maxim, that their security and welfare required a perpetual friendly intercourse with us and the French.

More detached scholars have called Adair's "low politics" the Creek "doctrine of neutrality."[11]

The French presence on the western and southwestern borders of the Creek Nation inevitably influenced the Natives who lived there, and a pro-French faction emerged among the Alabamas and Koasatis and others of the Upper Towns. Likewise, the Spanish on the southern border of the Nation stimulated the development of a pro-Spanish faction there. The Carolina traders maintained contacts throughout the Nation—their goods opening doors even in towns with a strong political predisposition to support their rivals. A pro-British faction sprang up throughout the Nation, with its strongest adherents in the center among the northern Lower Towns and eastern Upper Towns. These three factions, partially, but not exclusively, sectional, fluctuated in size and sway as the actions or inactions of the Europeans pleased or alienated individual Creeks.[12]

For the Creeks, the challenge of this period was to maintain their autonomy and their control over the region. Surrounded by foreign powers, their strength lay in developing a national policy of response while simultaneously keeping the Europeans off balance. This was best achieved through the National Council, the only institution of the

Confederacy with a history of bringing together leaders from both the Upper and Lower Towns. The nature of the Confederacy precluded the establishment of an active central government, but despite that, the Council emerged in the early eighteenth century with a heightened national significance.

No National Council could agree on an alliance with one of the European colonies to the exclusion of the others. No Council could heed the ambitions of one to the detriment of the others. To do so would have produced schism within the Confederacy and threatened the friendship upon which it rested. With no political machinery capable of imposing the will of one faction upon the adherents of the others, the Creek Nation after the Yamasee War was caught in a state of apparent political paralysis, unable to move in any direction without the prospect of serious internal disharmony. Creek leaders made the most of this difficult situation by turning it to their advantage.

Brims, headman of Coweta until his death in the early 1730s, has been most prominently linked with the Creek doctrine of neutrality. The English and the French called him "Emperor." Brims did not exercise imperial power, but being headman of the most important Lower Town gave great weight to his advice in the Council. He recommended friendship with all the Europeans but obligations to none. "No one has ever been able to make him take sides with one of the three European nations who know him, he alleging that he wishes to see every one, to be neutral, and not to espouse any of the quarrels which the French, English, and Spaniards have with one another," wrote a Frenchman who toured among the Creeks in 1715, and who enjoyed Brims's hospitality. This neutrality only tantalized the three powers, each of which "made very great presents to the emperor to regain his friendship,. . . . which makes him very rich."[13]

What was true for Brims was true for the Creek Nation as a whole. Brims and the headmen of the other towns received presents, commissions, and much flattering recognition from the three powers. Any delegation of warriors to Charleston, St. Augustine, Pensacola, Fort Toulouse, Mobile, or New Orleans left loaded down with cloth, arms, powder, and rum. Officers in the service of European kings, leading pack horses laden with presents, made periodic visits to the Nation. More important, the Charleston trade became more stable and, under the guidance of the commissioner of Indian trade, South Carolina became generally more responsive to Native needs.[14]

Unfortunately, the Creeks were not very good at foretelling the future. Had they been better prophets, they might have become alarmed by their growing dependence on things they could not make.

Instead, over a period of time, as the luxuries they consumed became necessities, the Creeks lost much of their independence. Life was good. The French and the Spanish could be put off with promises, although the English, the most numerous of their European neighbors, were harder to handle. Many of the British wanted much more than deer hides. But until 1763, when England threw out the French and pushed back the Spanish, the Creeks' doctrine of neutrality made it possible for the Natives to grow rich and to dominate the other Southeastern nations while at the same time keeping their European neighbors at arm's length. Brims's genius lay not in his invention of this neutral policy; the nature of the Creek Confederacy made such a policy virtually certain. His accomplishment lay in his ability to turn that certainty into a useable strategy.

When established as a colony in 1733, Georgia suited the needs of the Creeks; for the Natives welcomed a nearby alternative to Charleston that purveyed the coveted English goods. There were conditions for the Georgians to meet, however. The Natives were in no mood to tolerate more of the Carolina brand of unregulated, unsupervised, and thus unrestrained traders who encouraged slave raiding, charged high prices, sold rum, pestered debtors, and otherwise treated the people with disrespect. In return for its permission to found the colony, the Lower Creek Council who negotiated with General James Oglethorpe demanded a licensed trade with a formal schedule of prices, uniform weights and measures, and one permanently established trader per town. Oglethorpe accepted the stipulations and the Lower Creeks agreed to let settlers occupy and use certain lands the Natives did not immediately need. A permanent arrangement required the agreement of the Georgia trustees, however, and to seal the bargain Oglethorpe took a small number of headmen to England. Together they produced a law, approved by the crown 3 April 1735, drafted to meet the requirements of the Creeks and thereby maintain "the Peace with the Indians in the Province of Georgia." In addition to establishing the rules for a licensed and regulated trade, the trustees set up enforcement machinery under the authority of a commissioner of Indian affairs, to which office they appointed Oglethorpe. Any abuses in the future might thus be settled without recourse to violence. Oglethorpe, the trustees, and the Creeks were anxious to prevent the development of a situation so fraught with fraud and maltreatment that an outbreak like the Yamasee War could again occur.[15]

Clearly, the Creeks were not the only people to benefit from a system of regulated trade. The established traders had lost much business to wandering rum peddlers, who were often the employees of rival

Charleston houses. And whether they were unscrupulous peddlers or sparklingly honest licensed traders, all whites were vulnerable in the Creek Nation. An outrage committed by one jeopardized the profits and security, perhaps the lives, of all. Also, in the scheme of imperial politics, any situation that attracted the natives to foreign agents was bad for England.

But the jealousies of competing trading firms and rival colonial governments prevented the 1735 trade law from accomplishing its purpose. South Carolina resented Georgia's arrogation of responsibility for the western trade that had once been exclusively hers. Charleston traders bitterly complained about having to go annually to Savannah to pay for a Georgia license. Even worse, they charged, favoritism for Georgia traders barred Carolina firms from towns they had served for years. Charleston traders and the South Carolina government joined in denouncing Georgia as an upstart latecomer that had tried to use a law to force old and experienced houses out of a lucrative market. They lodged complaints in London, voiced their objections to the Privy Council and Board of Trade, and tied up the 1735 law in litigation until finally, in 1741, the Privy Council imposed a compromise solution that was impossible to administer. The law of 1735 was a dead letter and had been from the moment of its passage.[16]

While the controversy raged over Georgia's effort to regulate trade with the Creeks, Oglethorpe turned his attention to Spanish Florida. The growing prospect of an Anglo-Spanish war gave Georgia, England's buffer on the southern frontier, an important military role. Georgia and Florida would constitute the American theater, and Oglethorpe, commander of Britain's southern forces, made preparations to strike at St. Augustine. But he could do little without ascertaining the attitude of the Creeks, who had the power to determine the outcome. Spanish emissaries had recently made new friends in the Lower Towns, and both Oglethorpe and the pro-British faction were anxious to cement the Georgia-Creek connection. Unable to do so from Savannah, the general journeyed to the Lower Towns. During July and August 1739, he attended major councils at Coweta and Cusseta and discussed with the headmen Anglo-Creek friendship, trade, and the growing influence of the pro-Spanish and pro-French factions in Creek politics. They concluded no formal military alliance, but Oglethorpe's visit strengthened the hand of the pro-British faction and thus restored the political balance within the Nation. Chekilli, head warrior of Coweta, brother of the dead Brims, and strong advocate of Creek neutrality, welcomed the correction of what he feared was a dangerous pro-French and pro-Spanish tilt in Creek affairs.[17]

The Treaty of Coweta, signed 21 August 1739, was the chief result of the general's visit. Chekilli and Brims's son Malatchi spoke for the delegations of ten Creek towns present; Oglethorpe represented the king. In return for an affirmation of British protection, Oglethorpe recognized Creek claims to

> all the Dominions, Territories and Lands from the River Savannah to the River Saint John's and all the Islands between the said Rivers and from the River St. John's to the Bay of Appalache within which is all the Appalache old Fields, and from the said Bay of Appalache to the Mountains.

This country "doth by ancient right belong to the Creek Nation." Nowhere in the delineation was there a niche carved out for Georgia. The colony had no land—its settlers had only the permission of the Lower Towns to live in places not used by the Creeks. In case Oglethorpe had any thoughts of securing a more permanent title by conquest, the headmen proudly pointed out that Creek warriors had fought "all opposers by War and can show the heaps of Bones of their Enemies slain by them in defense of the said Lands." No Native or European nation had a right to any of their country, and they would let no strangers live there save the Georgians. But the Georgians needed limits. The vague permission of 1733 would no longer suffice. In the Treaty of Coweta the Creeks carefully specified that Georgia could have "all the Lands upon the Savannah River as far as the Ogeechee & all the Lands along the Sea-Coast as far as the River St. John's and as high as the tyde flows and all the Islands as far as the said River" except "the Lands from Pipe Maker's Bluff to Savannah [Yamacraw Bluff] and the Islands of Saint Catherine's, Ossebaw, and Sapelo." To prevent any attempt to pressure or bribe individual Creeks into selling more land, the headmen concluded with an explanatory declaration that "all the said Lands are held by the Creek Nation as Tenants in Common." Therefore, no cession could legally be made except by an act of the National Council. To make doubly certain their position was clear and fully understood, the Creeks extracted from Oglethorpe a treaty guarantee and a public proclamation that the "reserved" land of the Creek Nation would be off limits to any settler, and that any intruders who penetrated beyond the bounds described in the treaty would be prosecuted.[18]

Some scholars have called the Treaty of Coweta "a stunning victory for Oglethorpe and the British." But it did not secure an alliance against England's enemies nor did it interrupt the contacts those enemies maintained with the Creeks. It did not make Georgia's land claims more secure nor did it throw open significant additional territories for occupation. Indeed, the Treaty of Coweta circumscribed Georgia with boundaries and made it a crime for settlers to pass beyond them. If the treaty was anyone's "stunning victory," it was hardly Oglethorpe's. The victory belonged to Chekilli and Malatchi of Coweta, Eneah Thlucco of Osochi, Sawmawme Mico of Eufaula, and the other headmen at the Coweta council, and to all the Creeks. But it was a short-lived victory. An imaginary line drawn from the high-tide mark of one river to the high-tide mark of another might be a boundary on a map, but it was no boundary for settlers or herds of cattle. And a proclamation from Oglethorpe was no better than his ability to find and police that line. The Creeks gave the Georgians a name— "Ecunnaunuxulgee"—which meant "People greedily grasping after the lands of the red people." The date of its first utterance is unclear, but it could well have been very early in the history of their acquaintance.[19]

Georgia began its career of expansionism almost immediately. Oglethorpe made some effort to control and direct the colony's physical growth, but he was acutely aware that as a military outpost the province needed more people. The Creeks were alarmed enough to insist in 1739 on a boundary, and it is clear from the general's proclamation, issued at Coweta under the watchful eyes of the National Council, that they expected him to enforce it. Within two years the Georgians began to look with interest at the Uchee country on the Savannah above Augusta. Because it was well beyond the 1739 border, it was clearly off limits, but the argument that the Uchees did not use the area served to rationalize the occupation of it. Oglethorpe attempted to defend the Creek point of view arguing against the position that

> because Indian land is not planted therefore there is no Hurt in taking it from them. [T]he Indian Nations have as much Right to their Woods as an English Gentleman to a Forest or Chace, and they are more necessary to them since the Venison is the Flesh that chiefly feeds them, and the Skins of the Deer is what enables them to pay the English for their Goods.

Worse, he added, any move against their lands would probably make the Uchees "go to the Spaniards."[20] Such arguments fell on deaf ears, however, and white intrusion on Creek lands continued and increased. By the 1750s, because of trade abuses, encroachment, and insults to Malatchi's sister, Mary Bosomworth, relations between the Creeks and the English had badly deteriorated.[21]

Creek leaders were sharply divided on how to respond to English encroachment. Wolf Warrior (Yaha Tustunnuggee) of the Upper

Creek town of Okchai, called The Mortar by the English, was a powerful spokesman in opposition to all European influence among the Creeks. His actions were generally anti-English because that presence was the most pervasive, but The Mortar's primary interest lay in promoting an international Native alliance devoted to blocking the encroachment of all Europeans. As other nativist leaders have done, The Mortar turned to the lesser European evil, in this case France, to underwrite his project. However, the French could not maintain a flow of supplies adequate to the needs, and The Mortar could not overcome the obstacles blocking his dream. Nevertheless, his consistently anti-English voice in Creek affairs helped to counter the attempts of Charleston and Savannah to convert their economic influence into absolute political control of the Confederacy.

The English had few consistent Native spokesmen within the Nation. The arrogance of British colonial officials, the abusive traders, and the unprincipled squatters made it emotionally hard for any Creek to support the English position despite the economic necessity for doing so. Headmen such as Gun Merchant of Okchai, Wolf King (Yaha Mico) of Muklasa, Malatchi of Coweta, and others often identified with the English were principally neutralists who, in order to preserve the factional balance within the National Council, threw their weight to the weaker group. In the name of the long-standing doctrine of neutrality they negotiated with all Europeans, hosted all the envoys, collected medals, commissions, and flags from all the countries, and made whatever promises were necessary to keep the Confederacy on a middle course. To them peace with the Europeans and an uninterrupted flow of trade goods was paramount. This did not mean, however, that unofficial parties of warriors would not respond to increased Georgia encroachment into the Ogeechee valley, or that they would not retaliate against a particularly abusive trader. The National Council had never been able to control such parties. So relations between the Creeks and their European neighbors, especially the English, functioned on two levels. While warriors did battle with traders and squatters, headmen talked with government officials, trying to reach some peaceful solution to the problems caused by unregulated traders, unrestrained squatters, and uncontrollable warriors. The Georgia government, royal since 1752 when the trustees handed the colony over to the crown, made some halfhearted attempts to establish a licensing policy satisfactory to both the Creeks and the traders. That they found it an impossible task, however, suggests that such attempts were a smoke screen designed to deflect Creek attention from encroachment and to prevent Creek attacks. The Georgia government made no effective effort to remove its squatting citizens from Creek lands. The expansionist colonial leaders seem instead to have been waiting impatiently for the right moment to demand a cession of the illegally occupied territory.[22]

The British victory over France in the Seven Years' War required major readjustment throughout North America. Within the Creek Nation, the question quickly became one of devising a new policy to protect the national interest. The old doctrine of neutrality had worked well. Living between the contending powers, the Creeks had maintained contacts with all while carefully withholding from any the ability for one to grow dominant. But events in distant places, quite out of Creek control, had decided the future of the Southeast. England gained Spanish East and West Florida, Spain took French Louisiana, and France withdrew entirely. No longer the objects of imperial competition, the Creeks in 1763 found themselves reduced to dealing with only the British.

Creek power, the threat of Creek reprisals, and the Spanish and French presence had all conspired in the years before 1763 to keep Georgia weak and small. Except for the acquisition of the three sea islands retained by the Lower Creeks in 1739, Georgia's land base had remained unchanged. With an estimated Georgia population in the early 1750s of five thousand, perhaps 40 percent of which was enslaved, the white pressure on the border had been light and scattered. To be sure, squatters had pushed up the Savannah and Ogeechee valleys, and their presence there had been an ongoing source of irritation to the Creeks, but the numbers of Georgians had simply not reached dangerous proportions.

The effect of the British victory in 1763 on the Georgia population was like pulling the cork from an upturned bottle. Governor James Wright estimated Georgia's 1760 population at six thousand whites and over thirty-five hundred blacks. By 1770, his white figures exceeded ten thousand, and in 1773 he estimated that eighteen thousand whites and fifteen thousand blacks were living in Georgia. There were probably fifty thousand non-Native people living in the colony on the eve of the Revolution.

At about the same period, various French, British, and Georgia sources guessed the Creek population to be some ten thousand to twelve thousand people. Although almost certainly an underestimation, the important fact of Creek demography during the eighteenth century was its dynamism. "All the other Indian nations we have any acquaintance with," wrote trader James Adair in 1775, are visibly and fast declining, on account of their continual merciless wars, the immoderate use of spiritous liquors, and the infectious ravaging nature of the small pox: but the Muskohge have few enemies, and the traders with them have taught them to prevent the last contagion from spreading among their towns, by cutting off any communication with those who are infected, till the danger is over. Besides, as the men rarely go to war till they have helped the women to plant a sufficient plenty of provisions, contrary to the usual method of warring savages, it is so great a help to propagation, that by this means also, and their artful policy of inviting decayed tribes to incorporate with them, I am assured by a gentleman of distinguished character, who speaks their language as well as their best orators, they have increased double in number within the space of thirty years past.

With all elements of the Georgia population increasing rapidly, growing contact and competition for the limited usable space was bound to occur.[23]

Britain hoped to mollify the Native residents of its newly enlarged North American empire with a policy of restraint. The royal government established two bureaucracies, each headed by a superintendent of Indian affairs, to administer a body of imperial laws regulating trade, land purchases, and diplomacy. This program, in conjunction with the Proclamation of 1763, which established a boundary (roughly along the crest of the Appalachians) between areas settled or open for settlement by Europeans and areas guaranteed to Native use, was designed to severely limit colonial participation in Indian affairs in favor of a dominant royal role. British officials in London expected that this centralization would bring an order and consistency to the administration of Indian relations that would please and placate the Natives. The system was begun on an experimental basis in 1755 during the war, with Edmund Atkin, a Charleston trader, as the first superintendent for the Southern District. After his death in 1761, he was replaced by John Stuart, also a former merchant from Charleston. By far the more distinguished of the two, Stuart remained superintendent until his death in 1779.[24]

In November 1763, at a conference in Augusta, Stuart formally explained the new political situation to the Creeks. Lord Egremont, secretary of state for the southern department, dictated Stuart's line: England had driven the French and Spanish out because they threatened Anglo-Indian friendship; England forgave all previous Creek misdeeds; and for the future, England promised them a prosperous trade and the redress of all Native grievances. Moreover, any forts occupied by British troops in the Indians' territory were there to protect the trade and not to intimidate the Natives. Egremont also authorized the distribution of £4,000–£5,000 worth of presents.

The grievances of the southern Indians were the same as they had been for decades—too many unlicensed, transient, abusive peddlers and not enough honest, permanently located traders, and increased encroachment on unceded land. Stuart and the governors responded to such complaints with platitudes. Land was the real issue at the Augusta Conference, as was seen by Governor James Wright's solution to the squatter problem—the Creeks should sell the lands illegally occupied by settlers. Indeed, the governor had been looking for two years for the opportune moment to demand an enlargement of Georgia's territory. In exchange for peace and quiet and Wright's promise of forgiveness for all their previous actions defined by Georgia as criminal, the headmen ceded a tract between the Savannah and the Ogeechee rivers well above Augusta and extending south from the Ogeechee to the Altamaha.[25]

The 1763 talks at Augusta were the first of six official conclaves held over a ten-year period between Stuart and the Creeks. All but one, a trade conference in Augusta in 1767, required cessions of land. A meeting at Pensacola in 1765 took land from the Upper Towns to "establish the boundary" of West Florida, another later that year at Picolata set the border between the Lower Towns and East Florida. In 1771, at a treaty in Pensacola, the Upper Creeks gave up a long strip in the Lower Alabama River valley. And in 1773, in a particularly underhanded deal orchestrated by the traders and directed by Governor Wright, the Creeks and Cherokees jointly ceded several million acres of northeastern Georgia, between the Savannah and the Ogeechee rivers, adjoining the cession of 1763. It is estimated that some three thousand squatters were living in the Creek portion of this new purchase a year before the sale was made. The two nations received in payment a sum equal to their indebtedness, which was paid directly to the traders. Each of these five cessions related in some way to the dependence of the Creek people upon their trade with Charleston and Augusta. Headmen responded to promises of lower trade prices, a competitive trade with a third base to be opened at Pensacola, threats of an embargo if they refused, and, finally, the erasure of their heavy debts. Both Englishmen and Creeks saw with increased clarity how vulnerable the Indians had become. Between 1763 and 1773, Georgia quintupled its useable space, and the area in the two Floridas open for settlement was increased by several times. The Indians' dependence upon trade, made obvious by the loss of large tracts of land, added to the collapse of the play-off system and posed an unprecedented threat to the autonomy of the Nation.[26]

During those ten years of Georgia expansion, the Creeks also learned a great deal about the differences among Englishmen. They came to know, like, and respect John Stuart as a representative of the king. He tried to institute reforms in the trading system that would have made the Creeks' deerskins worth more in the exchange for manufactured goods; he attempted to inaugurate a policy of licensing traders and locating them in the various towns where they must do business in the public eye; and he sent agents and commissaries to live in the Nation to enforce the regulations and provide some measure of protection from unscrupulous whites. Stuart and those in the Southern Indian Department who served with him earned a reputation for integrity among the Creeks—in stark contrast to the other Englishmen with whom they had contact. The Georgia and Carolina traders, peddlers, herders, and squatters were a different breed of Englishmen. Contemptuous of the Native persons and property, they were cruel, dishonest, and greedy. They did not respect the Indians nor were they respected. As purveyors of the needed guns, powder, and goods, the traders were tolerated, but the rest were enemies whose encroachments and abuses demanded resistance.[27]

The American Revolution, as it related to the Creeks, must be understood within the context of this thinking. The political decisions the towns and the Confederacy had to make between 1775 and 1783 were influenced by a wide variety of factors, but the prejudice which underlay the deliberations stemmed from the double-barrelled attitude of respect for Stuart and the king's men and hatred for the American frontiersmen.

When the war began, the Americans hoped for Native neutrality; the British expected alliance. A successful accomplishment of the aspirations of each depended heavily on the flow of goods. Gunpowder, a necessity for both hunters and warriors, was the *sine qua non*. Without it, the Creek trading economy would collapse. The side that supplied powder had an enormous advantage over the side which could not. Generally, British agents in the Southeast had more powder to spare, as well as other goods valuable to the Creeks, than did the Americans. On two counts, then, a pro-British predisposition made sense.

On the other hand, there were strong factors which militated against enthusiastic Creek support for the king. The basic one was tradition. Europeans had never permitted Native Americans to escape completely their imperial squabbles, but the Creeks had for over half a century been able to avoid a deep commitment to any side. There was neither attraction nor advantage to fighting the white men's wars for them and they had rarely done it. In addition, the Creeks and Choctaws had been at war since 1765, and after about five years of fighting, the Creeks had begun to lose. They tried to achieve an honorable disengagement, but the Choctaws refused. Stuart and his agents encouraged the Choctaws, gave them guns and powder, and talked against a cease-fire. True to his firm policy of dividing and conquering, the superintendent believed that the best way to protect the Georgia and Florida frontiers was to promote a long debilitating war between the two largest southern nations. As long as the war continued, the Creeks would have no interest in any other military adventures, and they were justifiably miffed by the support the king's men gave their enemies.

An end to the war with the Choctaws might have eased the Creeks into an alliance with the British, but the smashing American invasion of the Cherokee Nation in 1776 gave them further cause for inaction. Outraged by the penetration of their heartland by North Carolina land speculators and squatters, and embittered by a long and bloody contact with Virginians, the Cherokees took to heart British calls for alliance and struck out on their own against their American neighbors. The retaliation they suffered at the hands of Virginia and Carolina militia armies was staggering. Invaded from three directions by three large armies, the Cherokees lost heavily. The Virginia army alone destroyed forty thousand to fifty thousand bushels of corn and ten thousand to fifteen thousand bushels of potatoes in addition to burning all the towns and fields they encountered. This demonstration of ferocity, plus verbal threats from Georgia agents of similar treatment, showed the Creeks what they could expect if they became too vigorous in their friendship for the British. Neither Stuart nor the king was worth that kind of suffering. As a result, the Creeks, for the most part, remained officially inactive during the American Revolution.[28]

Pro-British and pro-American factions developed during the war, however, and maintained contacts with the representatives of the two sides. Hoboithle Mico (Good Child King), variously called the Tame King and the Tallassee King, and Eneah Mico (Fat King) of Cusseta came under the influence of George Galphin, a long-time South Carolina trader who became the chief American agent to the Creeks. For some time a major supplier of goods to Tallassee and Cusseta, he was well known in those towns and for years prominently associated with their headmen. The Tallassee King and the Fat King, along with Galphin's two Creek sons, represented a vigorous and vocal pro-American sentiment that contributed to the weakening of the pro-British position.[29]

Alexander McGillivray, a leader of the pro-British faction, was uniquely situated. Assistant British commissary until 1779, and then commissary for the Upper Creeks, he was a Koasati of the Wind clan and a native of Little Tallassee, an Upper Town on the Coosa River. Unable to gain a national Creek commitment to the British, McGillivray organized and encouraged "unofficial" warfare against American targets, harbored and supported Loyalist raiders, and worked to increase the number of Native warriors available for joint operations with British forces. Though never as useful to England as Stuart had hoped, the pro-British Creeks did considerable, if scattered, damage to their American enemies.[30]

McGillivray's wartime political experience, coupled with his official and clan connections, left him in a strong position of leadership within the Creek Nation at war's end. Between 1783 and 1793, he was so prominent, especially among the Upper Towns, that outsiders called him "dictator" of the Creeks. Though McGillivray never held dictatorial powers, he was clearly the most influential man in the Nation, and the force of his personality and intellect was, at moments, overpowering. Entitled Isti atcagagi thlacco (Great Beloved Man), he was the most prestigious adviser in council and the Nation's chief diplomatic representative.[31]

Motivated by the realization that the sovereignty of the United States posed a grave threat to the political independence and territorial integrity of the Creek Nation, McGillivray attempted to Centralize Creek government and to build a network of protective alliances against the American republic. His reading of history convinced him that a strong Creek national government with a consistent policy that could be enforced internally provided the best basis for Creek survival. Such a goal was not quickly achievable, he realized, because of the traditions of town autonomy within the Confederacy and factionalism within the National Council. Thus, McGillivray had to play for time. The British betrayal of the Nation at the Peace of Paris left the Creeks exposed to Georgia aggression, but an alliance that obligated Spain to recognize and protect Creek independence and territory would guarantee the support necessary to enable the Nation's warriors to defend their country. If Georgia could be held at bay long enough for internal Creek solidification, then a powerful Creek state could deal with the Americans unaided.[32]

The problem was time. McGillivray had much support, especially in the Upper Towns, thanks to his British service and his Wind clan kinsmen. But he had enemies as well. The Tallassee King and the Fat King resented him, denounced him as "a boy and an usurper" and conducted their own relations with Georgia, with disastrous results for the Nation. They especially opposed McGillivray's meddling with the town councils to encourage the war leaders and their military governments to continue in power in peacetime. McGillivray also worked out an arrangement with the St. Augustine trading company of Panton, Leslie and the Spanish government in Florida that gave a commercial monopoly to the firm in the Creek Nation under McGillivray's own absolute control. McGillivray then used this authority to punish recalcitrant towns by withholding trade. As Spanish Indian agent, a commission he demanded and received in 1784, McGillivray controlled the distribution of presents, particularly gunpowder, and he also used that power to reward his supporters and punish his enemies. For more immediate and personalized enforcement requirements, McGillivray had a small, privately maintained force of "constables." Backlash from the use of these techniques swelled the ranks of the dissenters, whose numbers increased in proportion to their distance from McGillivray's home at Little Tallassee on the Coosa.[33]

Still, McGillivray seldom openly violated traditional form. He did not usurp high office, he rarely issued direct orders, he avoided personalized leadership. His power lay in the National Council, in his influence over his faction, and in his command of tremendous but unofficial power. Sometimes he pushed the Nation too hard and too fast toward a destination that he, but perhaps few others, understood. For the Creek National Council to assume the role of an active, positive, centralized, policy-making and enforcing government was to violate ancient traditions deeply ingrained and tenacious. With time, perhaps, McGillivray could have achieved his goal. But Georgia gave him little time.[34]

Three unauthorized and fraudulent treaties between the Tallassee King and the Fat King and Georgia in 1783, 1785, and 1786 gave that state the spurious claim to a large parcel of Creek hunting ground. Acting on this claim, Georgians in large numbers crossed the Ogeechee River and swarmed to the illegitimately established new boundary, the Oconee River. Supported by many thousands of pounds of Spanish gunpowder, Creek warriors began in 1786 to clear the region of these intruders. Sweeping Creek success frightened the Spanish, who stopped the flow of powder and demanded that the Nation make peace with Georgia. Almost at that moment, William Augustus Bowles, an adventurer with earlier Creek connections arrived at the Lower Towns with a large present of powder. McGillivray hurried to accept it, learn ing only later that Bowles represented a rival trading company bent on breaking the Panton monopoly and undermining McGillivray's influence. Bowles and his promises were attractive to many Lower Creeks, far distant from McGillivray and groaning under high Panton prices, and a new faction emerged to threaten the slowly developing unity McGillivray was trying to establish. To add yet another crisis, the new United States Constitution vastly increased Georgia's power relative to her Native neighbors. Hitherto, Georgia had been left alone to solve the problems her abusive Indian policy caused her. The Constitutional union put at Georgia's disposal the full power of the federal government, including its army. Such an eventuality, McGillivray understood, could spell catastrophe for the Creek Confederacy.[35]

In August, 1790, McGillivray negotiated the Treaty of New York with the United States. The two nations made peace; the Creeks ceded part of the country illegally claimed by Georgia; the United States restored the balance of the land to the Creeks and promised to recognize and guarantee Creek territorial claims within the agreed-upon boundaries. The Creeks accepted the protection of United States, as spelled out in the 1790 Trade and Intercourse Act, and in a secret article, the United States granted McGillivray authority to import goods through American ports, further extending his control over all trade in the Nation. The United States also commissioned McGillivray a brigadier general in the United States Army, the first commission of that rank granted by the Constitutional government.

In most respects the Treaty of New York was favorable to the Creeks. The guarantee of Creek land claims pledged the United States to defend the Creek Nation against Georgia aggression, thus disarming that troublesome state. The trade provisions gave the Creeks an alternative source of goods in case of an interruption in Panton's business in Spanish Florida, and they provided McGillivray with an economic club to wave over Panton's head. McGillivray paid with the cession of a large slice of territory between the Oconee and the Ogeechee rivers, but he had been prepared for two years for that eventuality. Even if the Creek warriors could sweep the tract clean of settlers, much damage had already been done. Georgia hunters had destroyed thousands of animals, rendering the region useless for hunting.[36]

Despite this achievement, many in the Lower Towns resented McGillivray's cession. It had been Lower Creek hunting country, and they were bitter about its loss. Anti-McGillivray sentiment became so strong in their towns that he was forced to postpone Creek participation in the survey of the new national boundaries. To add to McGillivray's troubles, Bowles returned to assume the leadership of the dissidents. By the end of 1791, the harried McGillivray, worn out and frustrated by the difficulties of uniting the Creek Nation, threatened to quit politics and retire to the quiet of his plantation near Pensacola. There was too much at stake, however, and McGillivray spent his last year much as before, stalling for time, fighting for concessions, and trying to bridge the gaps between the many factions, interests, and sections within the Confederacy. He was by no means finished when he died at William Panton's house in Pensacola, 17 February 1793.[37]

McGillivray was only thirty-four at the time of his death. His natural talents and his education made him an unusual Creek. Well read in history and politically experienced, he tried during the last decade of his life to prepare the Creek Nation for its battle for survival with the United States. He believed the best defense for the Creeks began with domestic preparation. Factionalism, disunity, particularism, obsessive local loyalties—all these sapped the Nation's strength. McGillivray believed that the only way to defeat the Americans was to learn from their culture, especially their political organization, and make the necessary adaptations. Spanish financial and military aid was not enough. Only a strong, single-minded Creek Nation could protect its lands and block the onrushing settlers. McGillivray encouraged domestic political changes designed to unify and strengthen the Nation, and with his diplomatic genius he fought for time for those reforms to bear fruit. He won some time and many concessions for his people, but his premature death left the Nation with no one of equal education, position, and imagination to continue his work.

Scholars have been fond of arguing that Benjamin Hawkins was the man who replaced McGillivray as the dominant force among the Creeks. Some superficial comparisons seem to suggest that this might be so. Both men were educated and literate, both tried to use their knowledge to change the Creeks, and both made reforms in Creek government designed to foster unity. The striking difference between the two lies in their purposes. McGillivray tried to strengthen Creek government in order to preserve the Nation's independence. Hawkins tried to strengthen Creek government in order to control it and thereby destroy the Nation's independence.[38]

Hawkins was appointed United States agent in 1796. He succeeded James Seagrove, the first permanent federal representative in the Nation, who in the previous four years had managed to ease relations between the Creeks and Georgia. Hawkins's job was to keep the peace intact, acquire more of the Creeks' land, and encourage the natives to adopt a "civilized" white American style of life. This last goal was his greatest interest. The agent spent much of his time turning the Creek agency compound into a model farm where he could experiment in scientific agriculture and demonstrate the advantages of cattle raising, orchard growing and cotton farming, spinning and weaving.[39]

But these were preliminary goals, important only insofar as they reflected more fundamental alterations he hoped to achieve in the ways Creeks lived and thought. Hawkins was a dedicated missionary who took great pride in his victories, and he never relaxed. He wanted his gospel of massive cultural change to pervade the Nation and be the guiding influence on its people. Recognizing that the enormous size and large population of the Nation made personal acquaintance and control throughout an impossiblility, Hawkins planned to establish and gain control of a governmental system he understood, and thereby control the entire Nation.[40]

Working with the National Council, Hawkin's first move was to make it more representative through the creation of legislative districts with systematically appointed delegates. He then encouraged the establishment of an executive committee and the creation of two capitals, Tuckabatchee and Coweta, where the Councils would always meet. Those towns were the largest and most prominent in the Confederacy and the homes of two of Hawkins's subagents, Alexander Cornells and James Burgess. Thus the major business of the Nation would be conducted under the nose of an American official. Hawkins adopted the practice of delivering a "state of the Nation" address at each National Council meeting, which afforded him the opportunity in a formal setting to expound on his "civilization" program to the most important men in the Nation.

Once he had his governmental machine in operation, Hawkins demanded the establishment of a legal system patterned after European practice. He wanted laws enacted and enforced so that crime control would be removed from the clans and put into the hands of the National Council. To enforce these laws, the Council, with Hawkins's encouragement, established a body of "law menders" reminiscent of McGillivray's "constables." Law menders repaired the laws broken by individual Creeks by meting out punishments on the spot in the name of the National Council and the Nation.[41]

The law creating the law menders specifically exempted them from clan revenge for punishing a violator. This was a radical change from traditional Creek jurisprudence and a sharp blow to the ancient clan system, the legal and political foundation of Creek society. It introduced the idea of individual guilt for crime and denied clan kin the right to defend their relatives. With a diminished sense of clan community and responsibility, the door was ajar for the introduction of further "civilized" concepts which, according to the policy of the United States, would break down Creek "tribalism" and foster the spirit of individuality, thereby weakening the internal strength of the Nation.[42]

Much of what Hawkins did exacerbated the ancient Upper-Lower Creek split. As McGillivray's seat of power had been founded in the Upper Towns, Hawkins's was in the Lower Towns. McGillivray had leaned heavily on Upper Town headmen, Hawkins looked to Lower Creek leaders for support. During Hawkins's tenure as agent (1796-1816), Bird Tail King (Fushatchie Mico) of Cusseta, Little Prince (Tustunnuggee Hopoi) of Broken Arrow, and William McIntosh (Tustunnuggee Hutkee—White Warrior) of Coweta emerged as major forces in the Nation. The influence of Mad Dog (Efau Hadjo) of Tuckabatchee receded, and his successor, Big Warrior (Tustunnuggee Thlucco), fought to retain Upper Town prominence with a stillborn scheme to join his towns with the Cherokees and Chickasaws in an international coalition. Hawkins resented Big Warrior who was outside his control, labeled him as greedy, power-hungry, and generally kept him at arm's length. The Tallassee King was the only Upper Creek headman to maintain his prestige undiminished during the Hawkins years.[43]

The increasing intensity of the Upper-Lower split was visible in several areas: in the jockeying for power in the National Council, in competition for the location of Council meetings, in Big Warrior's interest in coalescing with the other southern nations, in the struggle over the distribution of the annuities, and in the attachment to Hawkins and his program. The Upper Creeks took their presents and annuities in guns and ammunition, the Lower Creeks took theirs in hoes, axes, plows, and spinning wheels. In the Lower Creek towns, accomodation and adaptation to the ways of their white neighbors was much more rapid and complete than in the Upper Towns.[44]

The Lower Towns were partly forced into their position of adopting white ways. Closer to Georgia than the Upper Towns, their lands were the first to be lost. The cession of 1790 and two additional land sales in 1802 and 1805 were of Lower Creek hunting grounds. Before the land had been sold, it had been squatted on by Georgians who destroyed the game and rendered the country useless for hunting. With access to the trading market curtailed through the depletion of the deer herds and the loss of their hunting grounds, the Lower Creeks experienced a depression in their hunting economy. In the face of catastrophe, many hunters followed the lead of their mixed-blood neighbors and the advice of Agent Hawkins and adopted some form of plow agriculture. Those unwilling or unable to make this transition attempted to live on the annuity income derived from the land sales. That the Upper Creeks shared the annuities paid for this lost hunting ground only intensified the Lower Creeks' resentment.

The Upper Creeks were anxious to avoid a similar fate. They not only opposed Hawkins's effort to make them plow farmers, they opposed anything that might put them in a position of having white civilization forced on them. Thus the Upper Creeks fought the 1805 treaty stipulation that authorized a road through their country to connect the coast with Mobile and New Orleans. Survey and construction of the Federal Road was delayed until 1811 by Upper Creek opposition. When it was built, its construction was imposed by Hawkins and an army survey team. The Upper Creeks did not want whites tramping through their country, killing their animals, cutting their trees, fouling their water, and offering tempting targets to their reckless young men. Any trouble on the road could be used by the United States to extort a land cession in compensation.[45]

The split between Upper and Lower Creeks paralleled a growing schism within the Upper Towns. The origins of the Upper Creek division remain obscure, but the enormous person and forceful personality of Big Warrior of Tuckabatchee loom large. Inheritor of the Upper Creek leadership once held by Mad Dog, Big Warrior found himself struggling for a place within the Confederacy. In his negotiations with former enemies, the Chickasaws and Cherokees, he gave offense to many. And his acquisitive nature aroused the anger of the Tallassee King, who was moving from his pro-American position to an increasingly nativist stance.

Big Warrior took full advantage of the personal emoluments which came his way—unfairly, many thought. He became rich, accumulated possessions, slaves, and property in a style that made him appear, to his more traditional fellows, more like an assimilated Lower Creek than one of them. His relationship, by marriage to Alexander Cornells, Hawkins's Upper Town subagent, probably underscored the impression that he was too closely identified with the agency. Cornells (Oche Hadjo—Mad Hickory) was also a Tuckabatchee headman. To many, however, his loyalty to the Nation was suspect.[46]

Although Big Warrior did not sign the treaty of 1805 that extracted permission for the Federal Road, he collected his share of the profitable opportunities it provided. One of the payoffs had been control over all the ferries, toll bridges, and taverns on the route. So while the road threatened the peace and calm of the Upper Creeks generally, a small number of headmen, led by Big Warrior, cashed in by monopolizing the money-making opportunities that came with the road. It was easy to charge Big Warrior and the other headmen with selling out to the Americans.[47]

Discontent emerged most strongly among the Alabamas and Koasatis. The road cut their country in half, and the rapidly growing settlements at the end of the road in the lower Alabama and Tombigbee basins—the Tensaw district—bit deeply into their hunting grounds. In 1813, when Tennessee demanded the right to free navigation of the Coosa, the penetration of whites toward the Alabama River valley and the threat of large whiskey shipments into the region further alarmed the Upper Creeks. Again, the Alabama and Koasati people seemed the most likely victims. Hawkins rebuffed the bitter protests from the Upper Town Council, which could have only intensified Alabama and Koasati anguish. Jealousy and injured pride may also have nurtured their bitterness. McGillivray had been a Koasati and during his life the Alabamas and Koasatis had been directly and intimately involved in Upper Creek affairs. His uncle Red Shoes had been recognized as one of the half-dozen most important headmen in the Nation. After McGillivray's death, the center of Upper Creek affairs swung to Tuckabatchee. The Alabamas and Koasatis, the westernmost partners in the Confederacy and the most aggrieved of all the Upper Creeks, found themselves ignored.[48]

At the same time, speculation was growing about the return of the British, or at least about a war between England and the United States in which the British would welcome Native support. It is clear that much talk of this possibility spread from nation to nation from Canada to the Gulf. The exact measure of its effect is less precise. Certainly many in the Upper Towns remembered with affection the 1760s and '70s when British presents flooded the Nation and the pro-British faction was strong and active. Such talk was far from welcome to those buoyed up and enriched by American policies.[49]

The final element in the story of how the factionalism within the Upper Towns blew into civil war is even harder to measure. It involved the great Shawnee leader, Tecumseh. His mother was a Creek, and he may have been born in the Nation. For generations a band of Shawnees had been members of the Confederacy. The exact nature of the association is shrouded in ancient lore, but Tuckabatchee always claimed a special affinity, and perhaps a blood tie, with the Shawnees. Tecumseh visited the Nation in the fall of 1811 and spent a week or so in Tuckabatchee. Mixed reports of his talks cloud what he said, but at least he brought the message of Native internationalism and the nativist word of his prophetic brother, Tenskwatawa. Big Warrior scorned his talk, and Tecumseh returned north, but accompanying him was a party of Upper Creeks (principally Koasatis) anxious to learn more, and he left behind others who had listened and believed. On their return in the spring of 1812, the Upper Creek party, led by Little Warrior (Tuskeegee Tustunnuggee), killed several settlers on the Duck River south of Nashville. Hawkins, citing provisions in the Treaty of New York and in congressional law, demanded the arrest and surrender or execution of those accused of the act. Big Warrior cooperated with the law menders, the fugitives resisted, and most were killed. The death of Little Warrior and his friends at the hands of Creek warriors doing the bidding of Agent Hawkins outraged their surviving relatives.[50]

From all sides Upper Creeks with grievances against the leadership of Big Warrior and his party, against the Federal Road, against the encroachments of squatters, against the inroads of white physical culture and their dependence on it, and now infuriated by the murder of Little Warrior and his group, coalesced. Their leadership came from a coterie of prophets influenced, in part, by Tenskwatawa and Tecumseh. They had adopted some of the Shawnee songs and the "dance of the lakes" that Tecumseh had taught them. But these prophets, the most conspicuous of whom were Josiah Francis (Hilis Hadjo) of Autauga, a Koasati town; High-head Jim (Cusseta Tustunnuggee) and Paddy Walsh, both Alabamas; and Peter McQueen of Tallassee, were responding wholly to Upper Creek problems. United States influence, especially as exercised through the actions of Benjamin Hawkins, had disrupted the lines of response that had traditionally kept headmen answerable to the needs of the people. Big Warrior and his "courthouse gang" of Upper Town leaders had become isolated from the people and their concerns. As the recipients of salaries, medals, honors, and countless other emoluments, the headmen had become more responsive to Hawkins than to their "constituents." The prophets arose from that condition of unresponsive Anglicized leadership, and their popularity in many towns was a measure of the depth of popular frustration with the headmen. Conforming to standard political practice, the people in many places transferred their loyalty and support from the old headmen to a new body of leaders—the prophets.

Through preaching and prophecy the nativist leaders gathered a large following among the Upper Creeks, perhaps as much as two-thirds to three-fourths of the total population, and declared the ancient Tallassee King their leader. In the spring of 1813, as they gained strength, they began to strike out at their Upper Creek enemies, the established leaders and those deemed corrupted by white ways. Burning plantations and killing cattle, they terrorized the region and drove those who could escape into Tuckabatchee, where Big Warrior had gathered a huge supply of corn and built a fort. Instead of deferring to the emergent spokesmen of the popular will or seeking a renewed expression of public confidence, Big Warrior and his comrades bolted from the traditional system. Surrounded and beseiged at Tuckabatchee, Big Warrior appealed to Hawkins for help. The agent, anxious to defeat the nativist reactionaries, sent warriors from Coweta and Cusseta who rescued the beleaguered refugees and carried them to safety across the Chattahoochee.[51] In the midst of armed conflict, political factionalism had become civil war. And the United States, which intervened to prop up an unpopular and unresponsive government, had become involved.

The character of the civil war changed a few months later. Late in July 1813, at the crossing of Burnt Corn Creek on the Pensacola Road, a motley collection of white settlers from Tensaw and mixed-blood Creek planters from the Little River area above Pensacola attacked a pack train of gunpowder led by McQueen and High-head Jim. The prophets' followers scattered their assailants but lost their gun-powder in the process. Some of them returned to Pensacola for more powder; the rest continued on to Autauga to plan revenge. In August the warriors of the prophet party invaded the Tensaw country. Most of the aggressors at Burnt Corn had taken refuge in a makeshift fort hastily constructed around the house of Samuel Mims, an old Georgia trader. For several reasons—lax security, the refusal of the whites to believe the reports of two blacks that Creek enemies were near, and a sand dune which blocked open the stockade gate—what began as an attack escalated into the infamous slaughter of Fort Mims. The Creek civil war became the Creek War after Fort Mims. Outraged by the bloody victory of the nativists (called Red Sticks by contemporaries) and seeing the chance to pick up much rich, free land after an easy conquest, Tennessee, Georgia, and the Mississippi Territory rushed armies into the Nation. After a bitter fight that also involved the Choctaws, Cherokees, and many nonnativist Creeks as allies of the whites, the Red Sticks succumbed.

Some three thousand Creeks (close to 15 percent of the total Creek population) lost their lives, several towns were destroyed, and in the Upper Towns the destruction of foodstuffs was overwhelming. The prophets had, in the name of their nativist doctrine, supervised the slaughter of all the cattle and hogs they could find, few crops were planted during the war years of 1813 and 1814, and stored grain was either confiscated or destroyed by one or the other of the contending parties. Peace left much of the Upper Creek country a scarred and smoking ruin.[52]

Victory belonged to Andrew Jackson, commander of the Tennessee army, and he dictated a conqueror's peace. In addition to crushing the enemy, his goal was to take as much Creek land as could be justified under his authorization to force the Confederacy to pay the costs of the war. Deciding what land to take on the basis of his understanding of the defensive needs of the United States, he demanded territory in the western part of the Confederacy to separate the Creeks from the Choctaws and Chickasaws and in the southern area to divide the Creeks from the Seminoles and the Spanish. Jackson left three isolated islands of Native people in the southeastern United States surrounded by a sea of politically organized and rapidly growing white settlements. Some of the country Jackson demanded had belonged to the prophetic towns, and as they were the agreed-upon guilty party in the war, their losses might seem just. But much of the land west of the Coosa and in southern Georgia belonged to the friendly towns, Jackson's allies in the war and the targets of prophetic wrath.[53]

The headmen heard Jackson's terms at his headquarters at Fort Jackson, built on the ruins of the old French Fort Toulouse. They did everything in their power to modify the harsh terms of the document. One after another, they pointed out that virtually all of the headmen had fought with the United States. They had suffered greatly at the hands of their mutual enemies, and they thought it unfair to lose their lands to their friend and ally. When reason failed, they gave Jackson a large and valuable gift of land, hoping he would reciprocate with the gift of sympathetic understanding. But to Jackson the protests of the Creek national leaders were of less moment than his definition of the security needs of the United States. Left with no alternative save bloodshed, the headmen signed the Treaty of Fort Jackson on 9 August 1814 and parted with over twenty million acres of southern Georgia and central Alabama land.[54]

The state of dependence, nurtured over a century and a half of intensive contact, had become one of weakness. Brims and his successors had tried to defuse the dangers of dependence by balancing relations with all sides; McGillivray had attempted to use Creek dependence as a device for creating a state; Hawkins encouraged dependence as a tool to fracture the Nation; the prophets tried to end dependence by destroying its representatives. But the nation remained dependent. Divided by civil war, invaded by foreign armies, subjected to a humiliating defeat, the Creek nation faced an uncertain future. Weakened by these experiences and caught in a whirlpool of cultural change, the Creeks could never again act with their old confidence, and they could never again use their power to force concessions for themselves and their country.

CREEK LANDS IN GEORGIA

Chattahoochee R.

Savannah River

Augusta

Indian
Springs

Milledgeville

Macon

Old
Creek
Agency

Broken
Arrow

Columbus

Ocmulgee R.

Oconee R.

Ogeechee R.

Coweta

Cusseta

Fort
Mitchell

Flint R.

Savannah

| 1790 | 1802 | 1805 | 1814 | 1818 | 1821 | 1826 | 1827 |

ADAPTED FROM ROYCE, INDIAN LAND CESSIONS IN THE U. S.

3

THE POLITICIZATION
OF THE CREEK AGENCY

THE GREAT MIGRATION west after the War of 1812 ensured that Indian policy would remain a high priority in Washington. Before the war, the northern tribes had sold title to most of their land to William Henry Harrison, and the country north of the Ohio was, theoretically, open to settlement. In the Southwest, however, the big southern nations still held their domains relatively intact. Incorporated within the boundaries of several states and territories, and surrounded by white communities, the southern tribes, unlike those in the North, could not simply be bulldozed out of the way. Removal west of the Mississippi seemed the only means to put southern Indian land into white hands. During the rest of the decade, Washington began to shape a policy designed to encourage removal. Because this policy required the voluntary emigration of the southern tribes, the government depended on its Indian agents to persuade them to go. With the power and influence of the office greatly augmented, the attraction of an agency appointment grew apace. Politicans attached the agencies to their lists of patronage plums, and during the fifteen years following the war, Indian policy and its local administration became politicized as never before. This was nowhere more evident than at the Creek Agency in Georgia.

The War of 1812 was a turning point in United States history. The "second American Revolution" produced a nationalistic spirit unlike anything seen before. Andrew Jackson's smashing victory at New Orleans, the destruction of Tecumseh's northwestern Indian alliance, and the reduction of the Creek Nation removed the immediate threats to American security and triggered the great migration into the Old Southwest. The United States Indian policy of the postwar years reflected accurately the new spirit of nationalism and self-confidence. "The neighboring tribes are becoming daily less warlike, and more helpless and dependent on us," wrote Secretary of War John C. Calhoun in 1818. "They have, in a great measure, ceased to be an object of terror, and have become that of commiseration. . . . The time seems to have arrived when our policy towards them should undergo an important change. . . . Our views of their interest, and not their own, ought to govern them." This statement of policy is inconceivable in a pre-War of 1812 context.[1]

During the administration of President James Monroe, the primary goal of federal Indian policy remained the acquisition of most, if not all, of the natural resources owned by Native Americans. It became increasingly clear to federal officials, considering the general collapse of Indian military strength, that the use of force to influence the decision-making process of Native nations had become inexpedient. It thus became the special task of the secretary of war, the chief administrator of Indian policy, to devise peaceful solutions to the problem of imposing the federal will on the Indians. Calhoun had several options —some more useful than others—at hand: the factory system was one; influencing the missionaries among the Indians was another; redefining the legal rights and status of Native nations was a third; but in the end the most effective technique was to alter the position and purpose of the Indian agents.

Congress had established the factory system in 1795 in response to the widespread belief that the political control of Native nations followed the lines of trade. President George Washington had argued that a federally owned and operated network of trading houses dispensing high-quality goods at fair prices would lead to a United States victory in the contest with Spanish Florida and British Canada for the loyalty of the border tribes. The lawmakers had agreed that the abusive business practices of the private traders were driving Native Americans into the arms of the enemy. With the Trade and Intercourse Acts apparently unable to provide a private trade satisfactory to the Indians, a government trading system had seemed the best alternative.

Over the next twenty years, the factories proved more useful than anyone had expected. Some cited their "yardstick" value of forcing private companies, through competition, to adopt fairer standards of trade and pricing. Others claimed the factories encouraged the "civilizing" of Native people by selling primarily "useful" goods and by refusing to sell liquor. President Thomas Jefferson used the factories to force land cessions from deeply indebted headmen. Calhoun, alert to all these benefits, had more political motives. He planned to exploit the dependence on trade goods of eastern Native people for national policy purposes. Rather than allowing private traders to influence Native decision making, he used his own subordinates to control the policies and dictate the actions of Native nations by threatening to withhold trade if they refused to do his bidding.[2]

In 1822, Congress repealed the factory system. Calhoun had tried desperately to keep it alive, but other considerations prevailed. Although denied a valuable tool for controlling Native actions, he held others. The terms of several treaties and an 1802 act of Congress obligated the president to distribute looms, spinning wheels, various types of agricultural implements, domestic animals, goods, and money "in order to promote civilization among the friendly Indians."[3] "Civilization" meant, in this context, plow agriculture practiced on small, individually owned plots of land. "The earth was given to mankind to support the greatest number of which it is capable," President Monroe informed Congress, "and no tribe or people have a right to withhold from the wants of others more than is necessary for their own support and comfort."[4] Excited by the prospect of training Native people in plow agriculture, an achievement which, it was confidently expected, would release countless thousands of acres of "surplus" land for white occupation, Congress enacted the Civilization Fund Act of 1819. The lawmakers, in conformity with Calhoun's recommendation, provided ten thousand dollars annually for the instruction of Native people "in the mode of agriculture suited to their situation; and for teaching their children in reading, writing, and arithmetic."[5]

The civilization law made it possible for Calhoun to expand his program to educate Native people off their land. For over a year before its passage, he had been providing funds to missionary societies to help underwrite the construction and maintenance of schools and to pay the salaries of teachers. In return for this aid he expected from the missionaries "a proper support of all [government] measures, growing out of our relations with these tribes, and prompted by our best policy." With the clear implication that the flow of money would stop if the societies failed the political test, most compromised their independence and conformed.[6] Ten thousand additional dollars simply enlarged the fund at Calhoun's disposal and made it possible for him to encourage the establishment of more schools (twenty-one opened in five years), to accelerate his program of land acquisition, and to influence more missionaries. The secretary succeeded in making the mission societies semi-official agencies under his strong direction, if not control.[7]

Much to Calhoun's surprise, the "civilization" policy worked both too well and to his disadvantage. As Native people became educated according to Anglo-American standards and grew more interested in participating in the market economy of their white neighbors, they also became more sophisticated in resisting the dictates of the War Department. "Civilized" Indians, it often turned out, knew the true value of their lands and refused to part with them. Clearly, the "civilization" policy that Calhoun supervised was a tool too flawed to be fully effective.

Andrew Jackson suggested the third alternative—to deny the sovereignty of Native nations, scrap the treaty system, impose full congressional control, and condemn Indian land through the exercise of eminent domain. Jackson, whose immediate concern was the military security of the Southwest, believed that the region could best be protected by a "permanent population, able to defend it." But in the face of Indian resistance, United States policy was both unrealistic and impossible to administer. "The Indians are the subjects of the United States," Jackson asserted, "inhabiting its territory and acknowledging its sovereignty, then is it not absurd for the sovereign to negotiate by treaty with the subject." Native people were "entitled to the protection and fostering care" of the government, but no more so than American citizens. Citizens were subject to the laws of Congress.

> I ask can it be contended with any propriety that [Indian] rights are better secured than our Citizens, and that Congress cannot pass laws for their regulation, when it is acknowledged, that they live within the Territory of the United States and are subject to its sovereignty and would it not be absurd to say that they were not subject to its laws.

Jackson was well aware that his proposals constituted a revolutionary change in federal Indian policy. "I beg you will not be astonished at the ground I assume until you examine it well." The policy of conducting relations with Native nations by treaty

> grew out of the weakness of the arm of Government; and the circumstances under which the nations were placed, and not from Rights acknowledged to be possessed by them, by the confederated Government. The arm of Government was not sufficiently strong to enforce its regulations amongst them, it was difficult to keep them at peace, and the policy of treating with them was adopted from necessity.

Jackson had no argument with this ancient fact of Native strength and the United States' weakness. His objection lay in continuing the practice of concluding treaties after the power relationship had changed. While the policy of treating Native nations as sovereigns had once been expedient, it no longer made sense. "Circumstances have entirely changed and the time has arrived when a just course of policy can be exercised toward them." And, Jackson proudly reminded the president, "the arm of government [is] sufficiently strong to carry [the new policy] into execution."[8]

Jackson's recommendations met with mixed reactions in Washington. President Monroe remarked cautiously that the general's views were "new but very deserving of attention." He offered little encouragement, however. Past practice had been to "purchase the title of the Indian tribes, for a valuable consideration," and Monroe showed no disposition to break with that tradition. Secretary Calhoun, on the other hand, shared little of the president's aversion to Jackson's argument. He quickly embraced the circumstances-have-entirely-changed theme of the general's letter, and before too much time had passed, he adopted the more extreme treaties-are-absurd notion. In late 1818, Calhoun urged Congress to act on this interpretation. Indian tribes "neither are, in fact, nor ought to be, considered as independent nations," he argued. The lawmakers disagreed, however, and United States Indian policy for the next half century rested on the assumption of tribal sovereignty and its corollary, the treaty system.[9]

Almost immediately after the War of 1812, Georgia and Tennessee began to demand that Congress negotiate treaties with the Creeks, Cherokees, and Chickasaws that would remove them beyond the state borders. Early in 1817, Congress recommended that lands in the West be given to eastern nations in exchange for their home country.[10] Later that year, the Cherokees signed a treaty that provided a tract on the Arkansas River for several thousand of their fellow tribesmen who had migrated west in small groups over the previous decade. The pact also provided for the continued movement of easterners from Tennessee and Georgia to the West.[11] In his first annual message, President Monroe pointed with pride to the doctrine of removal. By the end of 1817, Monroe and Calhoun had resurrected the old Jeffersonian concept and within the next year removal had become "the great object" of the Monroe administration.[12]

The removal policy rested on the assumption that the Native nations would willingly sell their eastern holdings and migrate to the West. This principle of voluntary cession was as old as the treaty system, and lawmakers and government spokesmen had repeatedly pledged that "just wars" were the only exception to the rule. The implication of Native sovereignty that accompanied the treaty concept buttressed the notion of voluntary cooperation. The "tribes have been recognized so far," explained the Senate Committee on the Public Lands in 1817,

> as independent communities, as to become parties to treaties with us, and to have a right to govern themselves without being subject to the laws of the United States; and their right to remain in possession of the lands they occupy, and to sell them when they please, has been always acknowledged. [Therefore], the removal of the Indian tribes . . . can only take place with the voluntary consent of those tribes, and must be effected by negotiation and treaty in the usual manner.

As long as the Native nations agreed to sell their land, the principle of voluntary cooperation was a safe and creditable one upon which the United States could depend.[13]

The southeastern nations had their own sense of destiny, however, and there was no place in it for the voluntary abandonment of their homeland for an uncertain existence in the wild and distant West. Without congressional cooperation, Calhoun could not scrap the treaty system and legislate removal. Thus, during the latter half of the second decade of the 1800s and into the third, the secretary encouraged the increased use of ruse, subterfuge, circumvention, and outright fraud to achieve through chicanery, under the cloak of voluntary cooperation, a continued stream of land cessions leading inexorably to the final surrender and the wholesale removals of the 1830s.[14]

Such activities, in order to be useful, had to be practiced in conjunction with the ongoing and less dramatic administrative activities of the Indian agents, the federal officials who, because they were on the scene, enjoyed the greatest opportunity to influence directly the individual and national behavior of Native Americans. Having its origin deep in the colonial past, the system of maintaining political representatives within Native communities became an institutionalized part of the federal bureaucracy in the 1790s. As presidential appointees, many of the agents for Indian affairs chosen during the first decades had broad backgrounds of public service performed in parts of the country different from where they were now stationed. Benjamin Hawkins, agent for all the southern Nations from 1796 to 1802, and from then until 1816 agent for the Creeks, was a North Carolinian with extensive congressional experience. Silas Dinsmoor, a native of New Hampshire and a navy veteran, served as a special Cherokee agent between 1796 and 1799, and from 1802 to 1813 was agent to the Choctaws. Return J. Meigs, Cherokee agent from 1801 to 1823, had a distinguished military career during the Revolution and was afterwards a member of the legislature of the Northwest Territory. These and others of the period were honest men, generally fair in their dealings with the Native people in their agencies, and reasonably divorced from the political and economic affairs of the surrounding states.[15]

This final attribute was essential. The agent's duties were complex and difficult enough without his being vulnerable to the many pressures of the surrounding white communities. As officials of the federal government, agents served in a quasi-diplomatic capacity as representatives of the United States and local administrators of U.S. Indian policy. An important part of their duties, however, also made them the servants of the Native people among whom they were stationed. Quite apart from the "civilizing" labors demanded by federal policy, agents were expected to protect the Native people in their jurisdiction from the encroachment of pioneers, from attacks on their persons and depredations against their property, and from swindlers, dishonest traders, and charlatans of all varieties. Agents were the conduits for tribal communications with Washington, and as such they were frequently called upon to represent the interests and give voice to the demands of the Native people of their agencies before the federal bureaucracy. Clearly, these duties were often in conflict; and at best, a conscientious agent could balance them off on a situational basis. At worst, he could deny his obligations to serve the Indians and instead participate fully in the many official policies and private adventures designed to destroy the Indian societies, rob them of their lands, and expel them to distant and unknown places. These latter options were the goals of the surrounding states.[16]

Southern postwar expansion held great economic promise, and the political leaders of the states and territories of the region saw land development as both a public responsibility and a personal opportunity. Local citizens and government leaders looked longingly at the rich country occupied by the large Native nations. Legal access of the states to that land, however, lay only through the indirect route of appeal to Washington for the negotiation of treaties of cession. The successful completion of such arrangements was threatened by countless obstacles, many of which could be found within the walls of the Native council houses. Influencing the decisions made in the sanctity of the council required careful advance preparation, and included both direct and immediate bribery and more subtle, long-term persuasion requiring months of effort. This last was the overriding function of the agent. But federal employees from distant parts of the country could stand aloof from local political pressures and block the many schemes advanced to defraud the people of their property. In 1813, when Benjamin Hawkins refused to help Georgia governor David B. Mitchell wring compensation from the Creeks for every piece of property allegedly lost, destroyed, or stolen in the state since 1775, the outraged governor could only complain of Hawkins's "over-zealousness . . . in the interest of the Indians."[17]

It was in the obvious interest of local politicians, boomers, developers, and expansionists to gain control of the influential agency positions. During the second decade of the 1800s and into the third, they largely succeeded in accomplishing this objective. As one of his last official acts as president, James Madison appointed Governor Mitchell agent to the Creeks to replace the deceased Benjamin Hawkins.[18] Doctor William Baldwin, a navy surgeon stationed in Georgia and an acquaintance of both Hawkins and Mitchell, was astounded by the appointment. *"I know him well,"* Baldwin wrote of Mitchell to a friend in Congress, "and cannot entertain a doubt but that in all his decisions he will lean to the side of Georgia—the State in which he is *popular,* and where the *popular* cry is—*exterminate the savages."* Fully appreciating the terrible injustice to the Creeks of such an appointment, Baldwin warned that "it will be no difficult matter, under such a state of things, to produce disturbances among the Indians which will lead to their destruction,—and the Government sanction the horrid deed, from the want of real knowledge of the *infamous causes* which would alone produce such an event."[19]

Baldwin innocently believed the choice of Mitchell was a terrible but thoughtless accident. On the contrary, it was the quite deliberate act of William H. Crawford, who was James Madison's last secretary of war, the Republican caucus presidential candidate in 1816, secretary of the treasury in the cabinet of James Monroe, a vigorous contender for the presidency in 1824, and one of Georgia's most powerful political bosses. In partyless Georgia, two factions did constant battle for political control of the state. One element followed a dynasty founded by James Jackson, the "hero" who in the 1790s had led the fight in the Georgia legislature against the Yazoo land swindles. A string of able politicians had allied with Jackson, and for the next several decades John Milledge, William H. Crawford, David B. Mitchell, and George M. Troup supplied the machine's leadership. Elijah Clarke and his son John Clark were the standard-bearers of the opposition. Class distinction partially explains the difference between the factions. Support for Crawford came mainly from the older, settled, and more prosperous plantation country of east Georgia; boosters for Clark tended to be yeoman farmers and frontiersmen. But for the most part, Georgia political contests were unrelated to socioeconomic differences or public philosophy. They were preeminently personality battles, fought with few holds barred.[20]

In his race to the White House, Crawford early saw the value of federal patronage. He worked to put his allies in the coastal customs-houses, in the marshals' and attorneys' offices, and when Hawkins's death created an opening in the Creek agency, he was anxious to gain control of it as well. The clear importance of the agency to the growth of Georgia magnified Crawford's interest in its occupant.

There is no suggestion that anyone in Washington wondered if Mitchell would make a good agent for the Creeks. Rather, the pressing questions were: Was Mitchell the most prominent available Crawford-ite; could he appoint a Crawford man to fill his unexpired gubernatorial term; and could the agency position be made attractive enough to entice him from the statehouse? Upon receiving assurances that "the appointment is not incompatible with the rank of chief magistrate," that the "job would be easy," and that he need not be in the Creek Nation more than half the year, and with the promise from President Madison that he could delay taking office until the governor's chair was properly filled, Mitchell accepted. It may be no coincidence that he agreed to fill the vacancy shortly before Congress appropriated eighty-five thousand dollars to indemnify "friendly" Creeks for losses suffered at the hands of the prophet party during the Creek civil war. Mitchell withheld thirty-five thousand dollars of that sum for several months, and unsupported allegations were made that he used the money to finance a series of unethical and illegal business schemes. During his four years in office, Mitchell located for future speculation valuable town sites within the Creek Nation, established a large trading concern adjacent to the agency, and became involved in a smuggling operation by which slaves were imported across the international border from Spanish Florida to the United States through the Creek Nation.[21]

Mitchell was a purely political appointee, and his job was to run the agency so that Crawford could take credit for whatever Georgia might gain at the Creeks' expense. Mitchell expected support and, perhaps, some political reward from Crawford. But their bitter political enemy, John Clark, became governor of Georgia, Andrew Jackson came to hate Crawford, and Calhoun began to have presidential ambitions himself. For political reasons of their own, Clark, Jackson and Calhoun joined to destroy Crawford's political aspirations. Smeared by charges of financial complicity in Mitchell's slave-smuggling adventure and embarrassed by Mitchell's clumsy attempts at cover-up, Crawford sacrificed his foolish friend. Attorney General William Wirt read the bundles of evidence and concluded that Mitchell, "the most impudent rascal" that he had "ever had any knowledge of," was guilty. Monroe fired Mitchell.[22]

Mitchell had been appointed and dismissed for reasons quite unrelated to the needs of the Creeks, and his tenure in their agency represented a new kind of indignity. He sneered at the petty favors and gifts Hawkins had dispensed to his friends and the influential headmen and brought hard-core corruption to the Nation. Under his practiced guidance, embezzlement, bribery, and betrayal were introduced into the National Council and permanently changed the character of United States-Creek relations. Mitchell's partner, co-conspirator, and front man in the looting of the Creek Nation was William McIntosh (Tustunnuggee Hutkee, White Warrior), a leading Coweta headman and sometime-speaker in the Lower Town and National Councils. Old acquaintances and kindred spirits, they became congenial henchmen.

William McIntosh was the son of Captain William McIntosh, a loyalist officer during the Revolution. His mother was a Coweta woman of the prominent Wind clan. His biographer has estimated his birth year as 1778. Probably raised in Coweta, he first appeared in the written record in 1797 as the vendor of some beef purchased by Benjamin Hawkins for provisions for a public meeting. The details of his subsequent emergence in the public affairs of Coweta are unknown, but events rapidly propelled him forward. In 1805 he was one of a six-man delegation sent to Washington to negotiate the sale of a strip of country between the Oconee and Ocmulgee rivers. He made the principal reply to President Jefferson, and on the treaty document his was the second Creek signature. McIntosh's prominence was established. For the next twenty years, he was a leader to be reckoned with.[23]

The attributes which enabled McIntosh to move to the forefront of Creek affairs were not unlike those which paved McGillivray's way. Both Wind people, they had high-ranking relatives throughout the Nation. Although probably not as fluent in English as McGillivray, McIntosh could converse in English, and as an adult he learned to write, which made him an extremely useful member of the Creek Council. More significant, perhaps, McIntosh had a number of white relatives who were prominent in Georgia affairs. William R. McIntosh, a half brother, served in the Georgia legislature during the late part of the second decade; John McIntosh, another half brother, was the Crawfordite Treasury Department collector for the port of Savannah; and George M. Troup, United States senator, Georgia governor, and stalwart Crawfordite friend and ally of Mitchell, was McIntosh's cousin. Given the history of Georgia's aggression against the Creek Nation, it could hardly have escaped the notice of the headmen that a man with important Georgia relatives would be a valuable member of the Council.

William McIntosh was more than just well placed. Seeing the advantages that flowed from an alliance with the agent, he became, fairly early in his career, an important part of the agency entourage. In 1811, when Tecumseh visited the Nation, Hawkins used McIntosh to spy on the Shawnee's activities and report his speeches. During the next two years, Hawkins further entrusted McIntosh with the onerous and socially unpopular task of arresting and executing those Upper Town warriors charged with murdering whites on the Federal Road and at the Duck River settlements in Tennessee. Many of the outraged friends and kinsmen of those punished by McIntosh and his law menders joined the prophet movement and carried their enmity into the civil war. McIntosh was equally committed to the "friendly" side. He led the force of warriors that broke through the seige of Tuckabatchee and rescued Big Warrior, and during the next year, first as a major and then as a brigadier general, McIntosh commanded the Creek warriors in alliance with Jackson. The continuation of the Creek War into Florida during 1816–19 kept McIntosh intermittently on the march, and by the time peace was established, he was easily the most well-known Creek in the United States, acquainted with the political and military leaders of the Southeast and the favorite of all those who preached the "civilization" of the Indians. In late 1818, General McIntosh was the guest of honor at a public dinner hosted by the citizens of Augusta. He was, according to the press coverage,

> prepossessing, . . . dignified, . . . entirely devoid of the wild, vacant, unmeaning stare of the savage. . . . We have seen him in the bosom of the forest, surrounded by a band of wild and ungovernable savages—we have seen him too, in the drawing room in the civilized walks of life, receiving that meed of approbation which his services so justly merit. In each situation we found him the same, easy and unconstrained in his address, and uniform in his conduct.[24]

This reporter inadvertently but correctly identified what made McIntosh invaluable to the National Council. He could function easily in both worlds. Like McGillivray, McIntosh was equally comfortable and equally adept in the Creek Nation and in Georgia.

During the years following the War of 1812 and into the early 1820s, McIntosh occupied two important Council posts. His prominence in Coweta, one of the two leading Lower Towns, and his ability to deal with the whites in English, made him speaker of the Lower Towns. This appointment put him into the highest levels of regional decision making and established him as the public spokesman of Lower Town policy. The headman of the Lower Towns, Little Prince (Tustunnuggee Hopoie) of Broken Arrow, a Coweta daughter town, was one of the two chiefs of the Nation. Because there were two national chiefs, the National Council met alternately in each of their towns. When the Council sat at Broken Arrow and Little Prince played host, McIntosh, as his speaker, became speaker of the whole Council.

McIntosh's most visible national role during these years was as a leading Creek spokesman in the relations of the Nation with the United States. Three times between January 1817 and January 1820 he led delegations of Creek headmen to Washington to press the government for recognition of their claims to Florida, for promised compensation for losses suffered at the hands of the prophet party during the civil war, and for protection from the harrassment of lumber poachers, cattle herders, hunters, and squatters illegally within their borders. McIntosh and his friends had limited success in Washington.[25]

In the Nation, McIntosh's function as speaker put him in the forefront of several treaty negotiations. On 22 January 1818, Agent Mitchell and the Creek headmen concluded a sale of two tracts adjacent to Georgia. One was a small, irregularly shaped piece in the far northeastern corner of the Nation; the other was a parcel situated between the Ocmulgee and Altamaha rivers and the Fort Jackson cession line in the southeast.[26]

Washington was disappointed by the small size of the cession, but the Creeks' unwillingness to sell made any cession extremely difficult to obtain. McIntosh had hinted to Acting Secretary of War George Graham the previous March, however, that he could break down Creek resistance if his demands were met. McIntosh wanted all private white traders excluded from the Nation. Graham demanded a large cession. As the talks proceeded, Graham agreed to omit from the official minutes his request for land and accepted, in principle, the ouster of private traders. In return, McIntosh agreed that a cession, smaller than Graham had asked for, might be obtained. The minutes of the 1818 treaty negotiation are lost and McIntosh's role therein is unknown. He was, however, well established as a major trader in the Nation, he operated a large store in partnership with Agent Mitchell, and his interest in using the government to remove his competitors is clear. By 1818, it seems, McIntosh had begun to serve his own interests at the expense of those of his people.[27]

Speaker McIntosh and Agent Mitchell, whose children were married 14 August 1818, combined their political power to gain control of the wealth of the Nation. No longer large-scale commercial hunters, the Creeks had become dependent on the annual payments the United States made for past land cessions. The Council headmen administered the annuity income, which was paid in cash, as a national fund to meet the expenses of government and to pay the collective debts of the people. Because the annuities of 1815 and 1816 were delayed, the sum paid in 1817 was $48,547. In 1818 the payment figure returned to its normal level of $15,500, increased in 1819 to $35,000, and leveled off for 1820 and 1821 at $25,500. Totalling nearly $150,000, the Creek annuity was a tempting target.[28]

The swindlers devised two techniques for defrauding the Creeks of their money, both of which involved the McIntosh-Mitchell store. Free from competition and stocked with vastly overpriced goods, the store did a brisk credit business. Claiming that his accounts receivable constituted a national debt, at annuity time McIntosh carved off the top the sums necessary to pay the bills of his credit customers. Although it had long been standard practice for the Council to pay the debts owed traders, that policy had emerged at a time when the traders were whites with political influence in their home states and unpaid debts had been commonly used to justify demands for additional land cessions. McIntosh and Mitchell perverted the policy, now outmoded, for their personal gain.

The second scheme was more innovative. After the national debts had been paid, mostly to McIntosh, Mitchell used the balance of the annuity to buy merchandise from the store. He then distributed these items to the Creeks. The headmen preferred to receive cash and successfully protested to Washington. An order from the War Department forbade Mitchell to continue the practice. Arguing that the Indians were unable to manage their own financial affairs, the agent claimed he was simply trying to protect their interests from the fraudulent schemes of the Council headmen. Mitchell ignored his instructions from Calhoun, and he and McIntosh managed to pocket virtually the entire annuity income of the Nation.[29]

Treaty negotiations provided even greater opportunities for making money. In 1820, responding to the renewed demands of the Georgia delegation, Congress appropriated thirty thousand dollars to open talks with the Creeks. Georgia particularly desired a cession in the north that would separate the Creeks from the Cherokees and reduce the possibility of their uniting in resistance to her ultimate goal of expelling all of them. If that effort should fail, the state desired the country between the Ocmulgee and the Flint rivers.[30]

McIntosh hosted the talks, which began late in December 1820, at his newly built tavern at Indian Springs, a mineral spring of great medicinal repute, situated west of the Ocmulgee River. No influential Upper Town headmen attended the negotiations, which were conducted under the immediate auspices of Little Prince. McIntosh dominated the proceedings. He spoke for the assembled Creeks and worked behind the scenes to arrange a special deal for himself.

The Lower Town delegation had to respond to two sets of demands. Commissioners for the United States pressed for a cession of land and tried, unsuccessfully, to interest the headmen in removing west of the Mississippi. At the same time, Georgia sent a team of politicians to present claims for property allegedly stolen or destroyed by the Creeks since the Revolutionary War. The Georgia commissioners demanded some $350,000 supposedly due their fellow citizens under the terms of various treaties that required the Creeks to return stolen property, primarily slaves and horses. A blatant attempt at fraud, it unnerved the headmen and "embarrassed" the United States commissioners. On the other hand, the demand was a useful technique to put the headmen on the defensive, and the federal officers fully exploited it. The two sets of commissioners agreed to a $250,000 compromise and together pressed the Creeks for payment. Because they had no such sum of money, the headmen were forced to agree to an arrangement whereby the quarter million would make up part of the consideration they would receive for the cession they were induced to make, and would be paid by the United States directly to the Georgia claimants. So Secretary Calhoun would not be alarmed when he saw the treaty, the commissioners assured him that a careful audit would reduce by well over half the amount actually due the Georgians. In fact, that total was ultimately evaluated at $100,589.[31]

The headmen refused to be isolated from the Cherokees, but they did agree to part with the tract between the Ocmulgee and the Flint rivers. In addition to offering to pay the spurious $250,000 to cover Georgia's claims, the government offered $200,000 more for the nearly five million acres, to be paid over fourteen years. Of this sum, the commissioners paid $10,000 on the spot and promised $40,000 more "as soon as practicable." There was an additional sum distributed under the table. McIntosh's immediate cash profits from the Treaty of Indian Springs are unknown, but shortly before the treaty was signed two of the Georgia commissioners wrote Governor John Clark:

> Our prospects of obtaining land from the Indians upon our first arrival were gloomy, but they now begin to brighten. . . . General McIntosh is very unwell, but if his health should improve and the treaty be effected, he will pay you a visit in a few days for the purpose of obtaining money, and we are in hopes the fine opportunity of obtaining a vast acquisition of territory so highly beneficial to our State and fellow citizens generally, will not be neglected for the want of a little money, even if it should amount to forty thousand dollars.[32]

McIntosh also received two reserves of land in the cession, one thousand acres surrounding Indian Springs, and a square mile, including his plantation, on the west bank of the Ocmulgee. Several additional reserves of one mile square each went to the many members of the influential Barnard family, and Efau Imathla, one of the ranking leaders at the negotiations, received a similar tract.[33]

McIntosh's predominance at the 1821 treaty negotiations demonstrates the extent of his influence in Creek national affairs. This was due, in part, to his obvious talents. But it was also because in the post-War of 1812 world of supercharged politics and intensified outside expansionist pressures, the burden of Creek national leadership fell on the shoulders of two aging headmen. Big Warrior (Tustunnuggee Thlucco) of Tuckabatchee had occupied the position of Upper Town headman for a decade at least. Recipient of the mantle as well as of the youngest wife of the distinguished Mad Dog, Big Warrior became increasingly interested in wealth and the appurtenances of power. While his rumbling voice continued to carry weight, his corpulence and age combined to render him inactive, and for a time during the late teens and early twenties the full force of Upper Town influence in national affairs was rarely felt. Little Prince (Tustunnuggee Hopoie) was Big Warrior's Lower Creek counterpart. He was older than Big Warrior and, at least by the mid-1820's, reputedly senile.[34]

Big Warrior's inactivity and Little Prince's age combined to create a political vacuum that suited McIntosh perfectly. Speakers tended to acquire greater authority than their office warranted because of the mistaken belief of federal officials that they were the decision makers of the Nation rather than their spokesmen. McIntosh's ambition and his relationship with Agent Mitchell simply accelerated his rise to power. The opportunities were right for McIntosh to exploit, and he was not hesitant to do so.

McIntosh's dominance was soon challenged. Mitchell's successor, John Crowell, had his own plans for the Creek agency, and there was little room in them for the liberties McIntosh had enjoyed under his predecessor. Born in Halifax County, North Carolina, 18 September 1780, Crowell moved to Mississippi Territory in 1815 where he settled at St. Stephens, a "thriving healthy" town of fifteen hundred people on the Tombigbee River north of Mobile. He was a prolific public correspondent, but his private character remains a mystery. Handsome, enterprising, and politically successful, Crowell resigned his seat as Alabama's lone congressman to accept President Monroe's appointment, tendered in March 1821, to the Creek agency. The reasons why Monroe chose him and why he left Congress to take the post are unclear. There were two candidates challenging Crowell for his seat; perhaps he feared to lose. Although he served four years in the House (he had been Alabama Territory's only appointed delegate preceding statehood and his election in 1819), Crowell left behind no legislative record. Still, he was a well-known local figure and, having survived Calhoun's screening, clearly no supporter of Crawford. Perhaps he was a daring Calhounite sent out to beat the bushes in Crawford's home state. Whatever the private arrangements or unspoken assumptions may have been, Crowell, no less than Mitchell, was a political appointee sent into a situation for which he had no apparent experience. He may simply, like Mitchell, have arrived at that time in his life when it was important to settle down to the task of making money. That the Creek agency could attract both a governor and a congressman suggests that, in addition to its political importance, it promised suitable profits.[35]

In one of his first official acts as Creek agent, Crowell issued a license to his brother Thomas to establish a store at Fort Mitchell, an abandoned Georgia militia post on the Chattahoochee River, close to Coweta and near the McIntosh-Mitchell emporium. John and Thomas Crowell had long been in commercial partnership. A second brother, Henry, soon opened a tavern adjacent to the agency on the Flint River boundary of the Nation. Agent Crowell hotly denied all charges of financial interest in his brother's enterprises and successfully dodged the accusations that he was, in violation of the Trade and Intercourse Acts, illegally trading with the Creeks. It was "common knowledge," however, that he received an income from Thomas's store.[36] On a salary of fifteen hundred dollars per year, Crowell lived like a lord on the agency reserve,[37] dispensing hospitality with legendary generosity. Horses were his special passion. He raised thoroughbred racers, worked them out on his private one-mile oval, and won purses and tropies throughout the South. He had six of his favorites immortalized on canvas by Thomas Troye, "famous throughout the world for his pictures of animals in oil." After the Creeks were removed to the West, Crowell bought several tracts of the recently vacated land, including the 1,280-acre agency compound at Fort Mitchell, and settled down to a life of genteel retirement. His will disposed of twelve slaves (ten of whom were emancipated and sent to a free state) and sixteen thousand dollars in investments in addition to an undisclosed amount of land and personal belongings. This was no measly legacy for a man who had spent the last two decades of his employed life in public service.[38]

Before the Crowell brothers arrived in the Nation, the McIntosh-Mitchell store controlled the trade of the surrounding Creek towns.

The annuity-payment swindle the two had devised guaranteed a handsome income for the two families. Crowell was accused of running a swindle that was equally slick. He paid in cash, the complainants charged, but in bills of large denomination. When the headmen sought small bills to distribute to their townsmen, they allegedly found that only Thomas Crowell could make change. But he would allegedly give only five to ten dollars in exchange for a one hundred dollar note, insisting that the headmen take the rest in goods at prices even higher than McIntosh charged. Whether or not these charges were true, Crowell controlled the money and there was no place in the distribution process for McIntosh. The irate McIntosh, once in profitable command of the Nation's annuity, found himself shoved aside by the new order.[39]

McIntosh did, however, enjoy one competitive advantage over Thomas Crowell. The Trade and Intercourse law stipulated that traders be licensed, post a bond, and operate from a permanent store, its location fixed by the agent. As an Indian, McIntosh was exempt from the law.[40] He outfitted his brother-in-law, a white man named George Stinson, and sent him around to the Creek towns as a traveling salesman. With this ploy, McIntosh could bite deeply into Thomas Crowell's market by saving his customers a trip to Fort Mitchell.

Agent Crowell demanded that Little Prince dispatch the law menders to find and arrest Stinson. "If six men is not enough, send six hundred," Crowell thundered, "& take him by force if [you have] to destroy McIntosh and his whole establishment to effect it." When McIntosh tried to protect Stinson, Crowell announced that his conduct was "quite sufficient to break him as a chief" and threatened Little Prince with reprisals so dire that he would make his "whole nation suffer" for McIntosh's action. "I can get men from Geo. that will take him by paying enough for it," Crowell warned, "and rather than not have him I will pay every dollar of the annuity for him."[41]

Such outbursts rarely found their way into Crowell's correspondence, and a simple trade violation can hardly account for this tirade. Clearly, there was more involved. If Crowell shared in the profits of his brother's store, McIntosh's competition threatened financial loss. More important, however, McIntosh was challenging Crowell's authority. Flaunting his special status, McIntosh defied Crowell to match his power. And the agent, to maintain his credibility, had to answer the challenge.

Crowell managed to arrest Stinson, confiscated his goods and presented him for trial in the United States district court at Savannah. The grand jury indicted him in August 1824 and released him on three hundred dollars bond, to be tried in November. McIntosh and former agent David B. Mitchell directed the defense, despite the prosecution's efforts to disqualify Indian witnesses. Testifying that Stinson was married to a Creek woman and therefore an "adopted . . . citizen of the Creek Nation" as well as an employee of a Creek, the defense argued that he was exempt from the federal laws regulating trade. Replying to Crowell's denial of this argument, the defense counsel asserted that "the Creek Indians were a sovereign & independent nation and were competent to naturalize this Deft. a citizen of that nation, with full powers and authority to do all & every act which the Indians themselves could do." The district attorney, nonplussed by this line of argument, cited Article 3 of the Treaty of Fort Jackson which stipulated that no one could trade in the Nation who had not received a "license from the President or authorized agent of the United States."

Judge Jeremiah Cuyler instructed the jury that the defense argument was false. "Indian Tribes within the limits of the U. States were not sovereign and independent," he said, and he was "surprised to hear gentlemen at this day contend for such a doctrine." The judge then charged the jury to find Stinson guilty. To Crowell's chagrin and Judge Cuyler's surprise, the jury acquitted him.[42]

The defense had presented a truly amazing argument. Although federal Indian policy rested on that assumption, it would probably be safe to say that no non-Indian in Georgia in 1824 believed the Creek Nation was sovereign. Crowell was flabbergasted by the notion. How, then, does one account for the jury's unexpected verdict? The influence and popularity of the two star defense witnesses, David B. Mitchell and William McIntosh, were probably crucial. Savannah was strongly pro-Crawford, and Mitchell had been the faction's standard-bearer. He had also been sacrificed in 1821, and his successor, anti-Crawfordite John Crowell, had pressed the charges and was the key prosecution witness. In the highly charged atmosphere of Georgia politics, such distinctions were important. On the other hand, the jury may have concluded that McIntosh's exemption from the trade regulations applied to his employees as well. Humiliated, Crowell returned the goods confiscated from Stinson and predicted "it will [now] be worse than useless to attempt the execution of the laws of the U. States in this Nation."[43]

McIntosh had proved a dangerous and powerful adversary, and it was risky for Crowell to become involved in a running feud with him. It was also impolitic. If he was to influence the Creeks, push the National Council along the path determined in Washington, and serve the people according to his instructions, it was important for the agent to build bridges—not burn them—between the agency and the important men. But the factionalism within the Creek Nation made it virtually impossible for Crowell to maintain cordial political relations with all sides. It may not have been possible for Crowell to have avoided becoming entangled in the labyrinth of Creek politics. The agency was, after all, a political institution. A more sensitive, alert, thoughtful, imaginative, disinterested man, on the other hand, might have handled the agency more skillfully.

The dispute with McIntosh concerning the store and control of the annuity distribution and the deeper conflict over who was to dominate the agency not only determined Crowell's Creek enemies, it also chose his friends. There is evidence that William McIntosh and Big Warrior had been rivals for a long time. Though not of equal rank, they were competitors. Proud and ambitious men, sensitive to any slight, they were jealous of each another and anxious to gain at the other's cost.[44] Sometime between 1821 and 1823, Crowell and Big Warrior discovered in each other a useful ally. The strength that Crowell found in this alliance gave him the courage to pursue his vendetta against McIntosh, and Big Warrior's aid was decisive. Their partnership goaded on the proud and stubborn McIntosh in his determination to resist the agent's aspirations.

If the moment of the birth of the alliance between Big Warrior and Crowell is cloudy, the issue that conceived it clearly emerged from the controversy over the right of Christian missionaries to preach in the Nation. The Reverend William Capers, formerly of Savannah, first entered the Creek Nation in September 1821 as a representative of the Missionary Committee of the South Carolina Conference of the Methodist Church. His purpose was to win the approval of the National Council for him to "sit down among their red brothers and teach their children to read and write, and teach them other good things." Seeking out William McIntosh, he presented letters of introduction and endorsement from former agent Mitchell, McIntosh's Savannah half brother John McIntosh, and other prominent Georgians. Together they attended the meeting of the National Council. Crowell explained to Capers that the Creeks were suspicious of missionaries. They had two major objections: missionaries worked their children too hard in agricultural and mechanical courses, which the Creeks interpreted as an effort to make slaves of them; and missionaries wanted too much land and the right to maintain herds that were too large on Creek lands. As Crowell had predicted, Big Warrior questioned Capers at length on these points.[45]

At the conclusion of the Council session, Capers, Big Warrior, Little Prince, and George Lovett signed the extraordinarily detailed "Articles of Agreement," which authorized Capers to establish two schools, one near Coweta, the other near Tuckabatchee, by May 1822. By this agreement, any Creek could send his children to school, the schools would provide the children "comfortable lodging and suitable food," and the teachers would "at all times, treat the children committed to their care with becoming tenderness and regard." In a postscript, the signatories agreed that "whensoever either of the above named schools, or any teacher of said schools, shall have become offensive to the nation, such school, or teacher of a school, shall be withdrawn from the nation." There was no reference to religious instruction or preaching.[46]

In the spring of 1822, in anticipation of the June National Council session, Reverend Lee Compere, representing the Georgia Baptists, arrived in the Nation to apply for a school. Capers welcomed him. The Baptists could open the second school that the Methodists had promised but lacked the resources to establish. Compere had heard that the Creeks objected to preaching, to which news Capers affected surprise, and together they appealed to Crowell. By this time, however, the ministers had formed a negative impression of the agent's character. He was, they huffed, addicted to cock fights and profane swearing and had been overheard to say, "Preaching is fudge."[47] At the Council meeting, Big Warrior, in Crowell's presence, forbade the ministers to preach, insisting that they restrict their activities to educating Creek children and suggesting that if the restriction was intolerable the missionaries could leave. "At Some length and with Some Warmth," Big Warrior complained that "when any privileges were given to White men in the Nation, and a line drawn beyond which they were not to pass—that they would, so soon as they reached the line, put their foot over it and claim it as their right." When presented with Compere's application, the exasperated Big Warrior fumed, "The Missionarys is Coming here like Bees to the hive—for as fast as one flyes out an other flys in."[48]

And they came with McIntosh's encouragement. He applied for a school in the neighborhood of his Acorn Town plantation, fifty miles up the Chattahoochee from Capers' Asbury Mission. He was pleased, he told Reverend A. Hamill, at how well the schools were succeeding. "Some of our old men would not have preaching," Hamill quoted McIntosh as saying, "but I think the missionaries ought to preach to the children, as well as teach them to read and write." There is no evidence that McIntosh had become a believer in Christian education, but he may have seen the school as a money-making opportunity. His old friend Mitchell had written the previous May to introduce Reverend Compere and had suggested that McIntosh have the Baptist school built near his home where he could "furnish all the boys and the towns can pay you for their board."[49] With McIntosh agreeable to preaching and Big Warrior opposed, one more issue was added to the conflict between them.

Strangely, Reverend Capers and his fellow missionaries labored for eighteen months without "that dearest prerogative of freemen, *the liberty to worship God according to the dictates of our conscience*" before they complained to the government. They were restrained, they said, out of fear of Crowell. He had persuaded the Council to forbid preaching, they charged, and a man who opposed religion was capable of anything. "If the Agent of the United States' Government, so against all right, both civil and moral, against his country and against religion, has done this," Capers quivered, "what may he not do?"[50]

The true outrage of the Council's decision to prohibit preaching, Capers claimed, was that Crowell had instigated it. Arguing that the agent controlled the National Council, the missionaries believed the headmen would follow his orders on this as well as other matters. Crowell had not criticized preaching in the Council meetings, Capers admitted, but he suspected that the agent had denounced the ministers in secret meetings with the headmen. When asked to use his influence to win Council approval, Crowell refused. He did not want to press the headmen to reverse a decision, he explained, and advised the missionaries to be patient for a year or two. When the Creeks learned to know and trust them, they would probably relent of their own volition.[51]

Capers, though confident of Crowell's depravity, offered more worldly explanations for the agent's behavior. He quoted the agent as citing fear of "insubordination, or insurrection . . . among the negroes," as his reason for objecting to evangelizing. The vast majority of those who attended services at Asbury were indeed black, but Capers defended his gospel as one "which commands the obedience of servants." More likely, Capers suggested, Crowell feared "our preaching in the neighborhood, might injure some interest to the store at Fort Mitchell." What that interest might be Capers dared not guess, but it was strange that Big Warrior and Crowell had become so friendly. There "has been much ill feeling" between Big Warrior and McIntosh, Capers confided to Secretary Calhoun, and there was also a well-known dispute between Crowell and McIntosh. "Now it is notorious that Big Warrior's interests lie quite out of the way of the Agent," Capers explained, while McIntosh and his son may, perhaps, regard the store and tavern of the Agent, or his brother, as taking away a large income from them. Hence, any difference between the Agent and McIntosh may be agreeable to Big Warrior, by gratifying his ambition; and the disagreement between the two Chiefs may not be discouraged by the Agent, because it might bring the influence of Big Warrior to support the store and tavern establishment, near Fort Mitchell.

Capers was not certain of this turn of events, "but it agrees with what I have heard."[52]

Capers had probably heard correctly. Crowell's feud with McIntosh inevitably brought the agent and Big Warrior together. Once in agreement, they could serve the interests of each other by dealing McIntosh a public defeat. If the Coweta headman chose to support the preachers, then Crowell would do nothing to block Big Warrior's antagonism. And in this situation, a laissez-faire policy was probably also the best policy. Crowell was politically astute enough to understand that he could not endlessly challenge Council decisions. Although whites tended to think agents enjoyed unlimited power over their charges, they actually had limited influence, and it would have been foolish for Crowell to dissipate it frivolously. Moreover, it is clear that Crowell did not believe that Capers's and Compere's desire to preach was important.

An additional letter of complaint went to Washington in the packet of charges lodged by the missionaries. George M. Troup, governor of Georgia and a master of the verbal hysterics which frequently characterized Georgia politics, introduced the missionary to Secretary Calhoun. Troup at that time dominated the political scene in Georgia. The son and grandson of British Army officers and the first cousin of William McIntosh of Coweta, Troup had roots deeply implanted in Georgia history. He was college-educated and wealthy, a seaboard planter, and an attorney who emerged in the late 1790s as James Jackson's brightest young protégé. In 1806, his preparation for office complete, Troup won election to Congress. After serving in Washington for a dozen years, he returned to Georgia in 1818 on account of his wife's illness. He arrived at the right time to take up the Crawfordite party standard relinquished by David B. Mitchell. For the next ten years he led the fight against John Clark.

Before 1824, the Georgia general assembly had had the power to select the governor. In that year, however, the people ratified a reformist constitutional amendment that made the office subject to the direct suffrage of the people. Clarkites, identified with the socioeconomic interests of the yeoman farmers and frontiersmen, claimed credit. Troup, the planter head of the "aristocratic" Crawford faction, needed desperately to counteract Clarkite influence among these people and to win their votes in 1825 if he was to retain control of the state government. And Troup had good reason to be worried about the 1825 race. Clark had defeated Troup in the 1819 and 1821 contests, and Troup's narrow (84-82) victory in 1823 had been due primarily to the absence of Clark's name from the ballot.[53]

By the end of 1824, the Creek agency had become more politicized than anyone could have predicted a few short years before. David Mitchell and John Crowell owed their appointments to their high-placed friends and had been selected with an eye to the national political scene. Their task was to influence the behavior of the Creeks in ways that would reward their mentors as well as further the policy goals of the federal government. Unexpectedly, Georgia's volatile factional politics intruded. As Clarkites and Troupites fought each other for control of the state, the Creeks became a central issue. Both groups sought their removal and both desired the credit for accomplishing it. George Troup needed a Creek land cession to remain in office; John Clark needed to block Troup's victory. With the election approaching, Creek-United States relations had to be made to conform to Governor Troup's timetable. Troup believed that Crowell controlled the Creeks and that with that power Crowell, a Clark partisan, held the key to the election.

When Troup took up the pen on behalf of the preacher, he did so less in the cause of Christianity than to gain political advantage for himself, his friends, and his state, in that order of importance. Troup wanted to get rid of the man who replaced the discredited, "sacrificed" Crawfordite Mitchell. "Why have you a man in a confidential place, without morals, without dignity, without even the exterior of religion, forcing by insolent authority the peaceful ministers of the gospel from their hallowed places, and pursuing the idol mammon, with a zeal which never tires, in all places and among all men." Troup's complaint was unabashedly political. He did not know Crowell. "My general impression of his character," he blandly admitted, was "collected from rumor." But Crowell had campaigned for Troup's Clarkite opponent in the 1823 gubernatorial selection "in the most open, public, and grossly indelicate manner." As a federal employee, such political activism (on the part of his competitor) endangered "no less . . . than the freedom and independence of the elective franchise."[54]

Crowell had to go to make way for a substitute more pliable, more Georgian, more cooperative, more Crawfordite. The missionaries, particularly Capers, were willing abettors. Perhaps they had Troup's assurance that the new agent would force the National Council to accept preaching. William McIntosh was an enthusiastic cohort, for Crowell interfered with his business, disrupted his annuity swindle, denied him control of the agency, and gave his patronage to Big Warrior. McIntosh bragged about their plan to get rid of Crowell. Along with his half brother, John McIntosh, a Crawfordite wheelhorse from Savannah, he had prepared a bill of complaint against Agent Crowell that was circulated in the National Council and was supposed to have been included in the packet with Troup's and Caper's letters of accusation. When Big Warrior refused to sign the petition, the Council suppressed it. By this simple act, Big Warrior protected Crowell and defeated McIntosh. John McIntosh was slated to replace Crowell, "which would do," McIntosh was quoted as saying, "because he could do with his half brother as he pleased." At least four "Indian countrymen"—white residents in the Creek Nation—were also a part of this "combination to remove the Agent." Demanding "free trade and sailor's rights," they resented Crowell's refusal to permit them to trade without licenses. They, along with Stinson, looked to McIntosh and his friends to create an atmosphere in the Nation more conducive to their wishes.[55]

The emergence of the Big Warrior–Crowell alliance marked a new era in Creek public affairs. Crowell was no less a political appointee than Mitchell had been, and it was his job to keep the Creek agency out of Crawfordite control. Secretary Calhoun, interested only in removing the Crawfordite Mitchell, wrecked the very lucrative Mitchell-McIntosh machine and left McIntosh exposed, alone, and bitter. Crowell's appointment, presumably a fairly simple political holding action, unexpectedly precipitated a host of problems in the Nation, the most troublesome of which soon became the power struggle between Crowell and McIntosh.

Big Warrior was waiting for the chance to beat McIntosh at his own game. When Crowell refused to take Mitchell's place in partnership with McIntosh and instead offended the powerful Coweta headman, Big Warrior moved to make his own alliance with the agent. Each needed the other, and together they pushed McIntosh to the periphery of Creek affairs. Isolated, McIntosh found a useful ally in Georgia's Governor Troup. Together they might regain control of the agency, each for his own purposes. Despite their failure to secure Crowell's dismissal, the McIntosh-Troup conspiracy gained momentum, and during the winter of 1824–25 the politics of the Nation and the politics of Georgia were inextricably combined.

4

CREEK LAW
AND THE TREATY OF
INDIAN SPRINGS
1818–25

It is clear that Native customs, law, and government influenced, and sometimes determined, both the form and the substance of Anglo-American relations with Indian nations. That was true from the time of the first entry of Englishmen into North America, most visibly in the evolution of the treaty system, and it became even more prevalent as the range of relationships widened and Native understanding of European ways improved. At the same time, Native people adapted to their own purposes an increasing variety of European concepts. Experience taught valuable lessons about English ideas of law and government. Early in the nineteenth century, after military defeat and in conjunction with continuing acculturation, the Creeks incorporated aspects of Anglo-American law designed to protect both individual and national property rights. The novelty of personal wealth and national weakness raised problems that seemed to demand increasingly nontraditional solutions. In working toward an accommodation between the present and the past, Creek leaders reinforced their conceptions of self-government by reserving the functions of law making and administration for the National Council. Although the acquisition of these powers seemed innovative in form and purpose, they rested on the very firm foundation of Creek political independence.

Benjamin Hawkins's "reform" of 1799 had been a significant step in the early stages of the Creeks' institutional response to contact with whites. Creek councils on all levels had long made decisions for the guidance of the people, and the clan system, functioning as a judicial mechanism, had adequately and efficiently met the needs of Creek society. But the neighboring presence of people with a European jurisprudential tradition interrupted the efficacy of these traditional institutions. The assumption of most whites that all things European were superior to those of their Native counterparts motivated Hawkins to encourage among the Creeks a nontraditional system for identifying and enforcing the law. As the assimilative pressures increased, guidance no longer seemed adequate, the clan system became weakened, and the foreign judicial concepts gained strength. By 1818, it was but a short step to the decision to draw a written code of laws and also an enormously important step. Because it was the first legal document of the Creeks, the social and political significance of the compilation lies nearly as much in its codification as in the laws themselves.

Four of the first five statutes restated the principles of the earlier Hawkins effort. In the case of murder, only the murderer was liable for punishment, and no one was held responsible for an accidental death. By reiterating the concept of individual guilt, and by interjecting the Nation between the victim and the perpetrator, the laws in this code went far in continuing the process of undermining the judicial purpose of the clans. Indeed, by declaring that accidental injury could not be punished, the law disallowed a clan response. And furthermore, the law permitted killing in self-defense, stating, "He shall be forgiven, as he killed the man to save his own life." An additional law sought to regulate fatal conflict between Creeks and blacks by stipulating that if a black man killed a Creek, he should be executed, but if a Creek killed a black, he must pay the owner the value of the victim. A recognition of the prevalence of slavery among the Creeks, this law assumes that to be "a Negro" was to be a slave.

Except for the final act, the balance of the laws written in 1818 relate to personal property, which suggests the significance of possessions to those responsible for the code. One law regulated trading; another provided that any white man who married into the Nation and accumulated property must leave it behind for the benefit of his Creek family should he depart; still another imposed strict punishments for theft, escalating from whipping to cropping to death upon the third conviction, and any person who gave false evidence was to receive punishment similar to that meted out to the victim of his perjury.

The eighth law was the most portentous. "It is agreed that when a man dies, and has children living, his children shall have his property. His other relations shall not take the property to the injury of the children." By institutionalizing the concept of patrimony in a hitherto matrilineal society, this law, if strictly adhered to, carried the prospect of major social change. In part, the enormity of its impact flows from its tendency to break the ties between maternal uncle and nephew and to establish in their place an official bond between father and children, a vital step in the development of the nuclear family and in the further erosion of clan ties. The law also encouraged the accumulation of an estate, thereby protecting the economic interests of prosperous Creeks and permitting through inheritance the concentration of wealth. It recognized the existence of a nontraditional socioeconomic elite and it established the vital machinery whereby that elite could be protected and allowed to prosper. Written by and for the acquisitive element in the Creek Nation, this law, along with the code generally, illustrates both how weak the ancient clan system had become and how serious the threat was to its future.

The final law in the code recognized the dangers inherent in the attempt to impose a new legal system upon a people, many of whom were culturally unprepared for its innovations. The success of the code depended on the ability of the law menders to enforce it, but to do so required that they violate the much older and still respected clan law and thereby render themselves liable for punishment, even execution, under its provisions. Therefore, the eleventh law forbade any person to threaten or interfere with a law mender in the legal performance of his duty. Violators of this provision were to be punished "at the discretion of the chiefs of the town they may belong to." The code was equally concerned with controlling the actions of the law menders, stipulating that any who abused his power must pay restitution to his victim and be dismissed from office.[1] This last provision suggests that there was anxiety about giving so few people so much power. The headmen no doubt remembered McGillivray's constables.

Except for the law on inheritance, there is evidence that most of the provisions in the 1818 code had some precedent in at least the recent history of Creek law. And if the inheritance law was new, the concept of sons assuming the positions (political and economic) of their fathers certainly was not. For a generation, at least, the matrilineally correct relationship between nephews and maternal uncles had been eroded significantly. So if William McIntosh was especially responsible for the legal transformation in 1818, as the evidence suggests, and if he had his eye on his son Chilly as the inheritor of his estate, he was still not introducing a concept completely devoid of precedent.[2]

It also appears that McIntosh was concerned with more than the preservation and proliferation of his personal estate. The code was an attempt by some Creeks to proclaim their "civilization" in a way that was recognizable to the United States. McIntosh submitted the document to Mitchell for his approval and requested that the agent send it

on to Secretary Calhoun. The code gave Calhoun "much satisfaction."
He interpreted it, he wrote, "as another evidence of their progress towards civilization, and as an effort to form for themselves something
like a regular government."[3]

An anglicized code of law could not alter the reality of Creek social and political life, however. Factionalism continued unabated. Indeed, the jealousy between McIntosh and Big Warrior, exacerbated by
the presence after 1821 of John Crowell, simply gave new vigor to an
ancient phenomenon. But such a factional contest was manageable.
Strong men had always vied for influence, and the National Council
had long since learned how to accommodate their ambitions. That Big
Warrior and William McIntosh represented the Upper and Lower
Towns simply put their feud into context. The two major divisions of
the Nation had always been separated physically, and the distance between them had often given them distinctive points of view. The pressures they felt were different, and since the Creek War, the difference
in pressures was significant. The Lower Creeks were much closer to
white settlements than were the Upper Creeks. More mixed bloods and
more white "Indian countrymen" lived in the Lower Towns, and the
assimilationist influences on the Lower Creeks were more intense.
More Lower Creeks spoke English, were plow farmers, planters, and
ranchers, more owned black slaves, and more participated in the market economy of western Georgia.[4]

The Upper Creeks were more isolated. The Federal Road bisected
their country, and they were not immune to assimilationist pressures,
but more of them clung to the traditions of the past. In the Lower
Towns growing numbers of Creeks were moving out of the settlements
and establishing themselves on farmsteads in nuclear families. Among
the Upper Creeks, few were leaving the security of town life. They remained in their communities along the rivers, gardened in the ancient
ways, and tried to hunt. It was increasingly difficult to survive in the
face of rapidly shrinking deer herds and encroachments from Alabama,
but during the early 1820s it was still possible, and the devotion of
most Upper Creeks to this traditional way of life was stronger than
among the Lower Towns.

This cultural bifurcation, following as it did the ancient Upper-
Lower division, was also politically manageable. Interests had changed
with the decades, but the need and the experience required to harmo-
nize the differences remained. The only cement necessary was a uniform dedication to the land. Each side could tolerate how differently
the other chose to use the land as long as they could agree that the
land was the patrimony of all. Then they could agree on the only other

truly important issue—to preserve the Nation as a separate and distinct entity, located where it had always been, the home for all the people who had become Creeks.

The National Council was the forum in which Creek leaders, united in their commitment to the Nation, debated and decided on how the commitment was to be administered. Petty or large, the questions of concern to the people came before the councillors. They considered matters of domestic concern and, with the aid of their agent, forged a foreign policy. Cloaked in the mantle of United States government power, the agent had a major influence on the Council's decisions. If he commanded the respect and affection of the people, his authority might appear supreme. But the Creeks responded to their agent in much the same way as they responded to their own leaders. If he proved himself worthy of their devotion, they might obey him implicitly. If he failed or consistently disagreed with them, his was a voice in the dark. John Crowell seems to have had an instinctive political sense. He understood when and how to disagree and when to acquiesce. While his first three years were stormy, his relations with the Council were good. With their agent's help the Creek headmen were learning new ways to defend themselves, their country, and their interests from the attacks of their neighbors.[5]

Georgia and Alabama put heavy pressure on the Creeks to give up their land and leave for the West. Unlike the old days of armed incursion, however, the states increasingly resorted to political pressure to achieve their goal. Well armed with the 1802 Compact, an agreement with the United States that obligated the government to remove the Indians from Georgia "peaceably" and "on reasonable terms," Georgia led the way in a barrage of demands to Congress and the executive branch that the government keep its promise to acquire the Indians' land. The state demanded the territory of both the Cherokees and the Creeks, but the rich agricultural potential of the Creek Nation made their country the primary target of the cotton-planting Georgians. The Georgians had no tolerance for assimilated Lower Creek farmers as neighbors and citizens, and they demanded more than the simple acquisition of Native-owned land. They would accept nothing less than the complete physical removal of the people. The Creeks faced, therefore, a concerted assault. Not only was their national domain in jeopardy; the individual improvements they had made, the option of assimilation if they wished, their very residence in their homes was at stake.[6]

The conflict escalated during the early 1820s as the Creeks tightened their grip on their remaining land. The Treaty of 1821, signed by

William McIntosh and other Lower Town headmen at McIntosh's tavern at Indian Springs, had cost the Nation the last of its "disposable" property. Situated between the Ocmulgee and Flint rivers, the cession was one primarily of hunting grounds. As had happened so often in the past, this border area had been frequently invaded by Georgia hunters, stockmen, and squatters, so that the value of the tract to Creek hunters had sharply declined. With the subsistence value of the land already lost, the Creeks who used it were convinced that a long-term annuity income from its sale to the United States was worth more to them than the remnant game population. There were few towns east of the Flint, so the numbers of dispossessed people were small.

Remaining in the hands of the Creeks was a roughly circular territory bounded on the east by the Flint, on the west by the Coosa, and bisected by the Chattahoochee. The heartland of the Nation, this ten-million-acre tract contained virtually all the Upper and Lower Towns. Except for the brief 1690–1715 sojourn on the upper reaches of the Ocmulgee and Ogeechee rivers, the basins of the Chattahoochee, Tallapoosa, and Coosa rivers had been home for the Creeks since their legendary migration from the West. Their ancient town sites and burial grounds were there, along with their fields, gardens, and current towns. This remaining territory was the irreducible minimum needed to maintain life in the East. There was, therefore, a strong sense that this was where the line must be drawn. The Creek Nation would part with no more land.

The National Council underscored this determination by promulgating a law defining the remaining territory as national domain and placing it under its sole jurisdiction. Reversing the ancient but not always followed tradition of permitting the leaders of each region to dispose of surplus lands independently, the law reflected the Council's claim to national authority that it was prepared to enforce with the death penalty. The date of the promulgation of this law cannot be determined with precision, but the evidence suggests it was in 1817 or 1818. Several headmen testified that the law was first enacted on the west bank of the Ocmulgee when the Creeks owned that land, putting the date before 1821. The Council suspended the law in 1821 for the cession of that year because the Nation was in debt but reinstated it following the treaty. The law was reaffirmed at least three times in 1824, and in 1825, several headmen called it an "old law." The law was binding on everyone with no exceptions. Only a formal repeal by the Council, as occurred in 1821, could save a violator from the death penalty.[7]

In his capacity as speaker of the National Council, William

McIntosh was the first to proclaim the law against land sales. As commanding officer of the law menders, he was primarily responsible for its execution. Ironically, it was also he who was its first potential violator. Despite the suspension of the law in 1821, there was much anti-McIntosh resentment following that cession. The Council considered executing McIntosh, "and it was with considerable difficulty that he was forgiven." The Council did so because McIntosh persuaded the headmen that the Creeks' debt to Georgia had to be paid. Thereafter, however, "any man should die who should . . . offer to sell."[8]

Well schooled by Mitchell, in close contact with and encouraged by Georgia politicians anxious to win the financial and political rewards that would accompany the acquisition of Indian lands, and willing to betray those who trusted him for money, William McIntosh walked a tightrope in the early 1820s between riches and death. Close to execution for his role in the 1821 Treaty of Indian Springs, he purchased his life and the renewed trust of the Creek Council by becoming the loudest to proclaim the law forbidding further land sales. His new devotion to the Creek national domain, however, did not prevent him from attempting to sell out the Cherokees.

For some years the Cherokees and Creeks had exchanged ambassadors. Major Ridge, the Cherokee representative, attended meetings of the Creek National Council with the right to participate fully in debate. William McIntosh enjoyed the same privilege in the Cherokee Council. In October 1823, after repeated refusals, the Cherokees agreed to meet a commission composed of federal and Georgia officials to discuss a cession of their lands lying within Georgia's claimed bounds. "Gentle, brilliant, and forceful periods of eloquence, strongly backed by large sums of money as presents, were spent in vain."[9] Duncan Campbell and James Meriwether, Georgians serving as commissioners for the United States, unsuccessfully tried all these techniques. During that impasse, McIntosh arrived. It is uncertain if he was under contract to the commissioners before he arrived or if their arrangement was made after he joined the Cherokee Council. At any rate, he soon began to argue that the Cherokees should sell out and move west. McIntosh wrote a private letter to John Ross, president of the Cherokee National Committee, saying that he was authorized to offer him two thousand dollars to agree to a cession plus ten thousand dollars more to spread among his friends. For his troubles, McIntosh would receive seven thousand dollars. When asked to explain, McIntosh told the stunned Ross that his offer was made with the approval of the United States commissioners and went on to describe how he had taken money in the past to sell Creek lands.

In a ceremony characterized more by sorrow than by outrage, Ross exposed McIntosh before the Cherokee Council. One after the other, his old friends "set him aside." Stripped of his position and sent away in disgrace, McIntosh rode his horse to death in his haste to return to the safety of his own nation. Hard on his heels came a letter from the Cherokee Council to Big Warrior and Little Prince describing McIntosh's corruption and advising "you as Brothers to keep a strict watch over his conduct, or if you do not he will ruin your Nation."[10]

The Creeks were wary. Now under a cloud, McIntosh worked to regain the trust of his fellow headmen. Throughout 1824, while he battled Crowell for control of the agency, McIntosh raised his voice in vigorous support of the Council's policy of refusing any further cession. In a particularly dramatic demonstration at a ball game near Coweta in August 1824, McIntosh got up on a wagon and, extending his feet, proclaimed, "Any man who should offer to sell the first bit of land as large as that between his feet, should die by the law; the National Council had made the law, and a man who violated it should die by the law."[11]

The timing of McIntosh's announcement is significant. The same two Georgians who failed so miserably with the Cherokees in October 1823, Campbell and Meriwether, had received President James Monroe's appointment in mid-July 1824 to represent the United States in dealings with Creeks. Armed with fifty thousand dollars, they were to extinguish Creek title to all their lands "lying within the limits" of Georgia. Given extremely broad authority, they were limited only by a plea for economy and their "sound discretion." Calhoun was confident they would get as much Creek land as possible at rock-bottom prices. Two months later, in response to Campbell's request, Calhoun authorized the commissioners to offer a tract in the West if the Creeks would agree to remove beyond the Mississippi. By early August, Crowell knew of the proposed negotiations, and shortly thereafter the Creeks also knew. With the pressure on, McIntosh no doubt felt compelled to appear one more time as the public defender of the national domain.[12]

Quite apart from McIntosh's pronouncements, the National Council was preparing its own response to the demands of Georgia and the United States. In late May 1824, a Council at Tuckabatchee drafted a policy statement explaining its decision that "on no account whatever will we consent to sell one foot of our land, neither by exchange or otherwise." Signed mostly by Upper Town headmen, but also by Little Prince, chief of the Lower Towns, the Tuckabatchee document explained that in the "time of our forefathers we had a large bound of country, and went through the woods after game as if there never was to be an end to that mode of life." But times had changed. Their "crazy young men made a war," won by Andrew Jackson, that taught the Creeks "that they can be conquered." They had to give up large tracts of land as a result of the war and were now left with just a little. There was enough "to support ourselves upon," but only with "the greatest economy." The Creeks had taken up large-scale farming and, the headmen announced, "We are happy to say we are making advances towards civilization to an extent that gives us encouragement." But success was possible only by retaining all their remaining lands in common ownership. The councillors therefore reminded their people of their law: "We have a great many chiefs and head men but, be they ever so great, they must all abide by the laws. We have guns and ropes: and if any of our people break these laws, those guns and ropes are to be their end."

One of the striking features of this document is its similarity in wording and argument to several statements drafted by the Cherokees over the preceding six months. Indeed, the Tuckabatchee Council noted, "On a deep and solemn reflection, we have, with one voice, [decided] to follow the pattern of the Cherokees." It is not known if any Cherokees attended the meeting. It is clear, however, that the councillors possessed copies of the 1823 negotiations as well as much of the correspondence that had taken place between the Cherokees and the United States during the winter and spring of 1824. And when the Tuckabatchee document was presented to and accepted by the full National Council at Broken Arrow in July 1824, it was discussed in conjunction with a message from the Cherokees, quoted as beginning: "We speak thus to you in Council; we wish you to live like the Cherokees, and not sell your lands, or a foot of them."[13] The Cherokees and the Creeks were well along in the development of an anti-Georgia alliance which could, if permitted to mature, unite their talents and treasuries in a campaign to defend their homes and lands. The prospect of such a combination was only one of the many factors that contributed to Governor Troup's impatience to gain removal.[14]

On 29 October 1824, many of the same headmen, including Big Warrior, Little Prince, and Hopoie Hadjo, the three most influential national leaders, drafted a second document. Formulated at Pole Cat Springs (not far from Tuckabatchee) at the house of Big Warrior's son-in-law, William Walker, also Crowell's subagent, this statement was designed for immediate publication. "We deem it impolitic and contrary to the true interest of this nation," they announced, "to dispose of any more of our country." Recalling the 1821 cession and the events of October 1823 at the Cherokee Council, the headmen went on with a warning obviously aimed at McIntosh and his friends, commissioners Campbell and Meriwether: "Any authority heretofore given to any individual, either written or verbal, has long since been revoked and done away." Closing with a description of the speed with which the Creeks were "progressing in the arts of civilization" and a statement of confidence in the "fostering hand" of the president, the seventeen signatories laid their case before the people of the neighboring states. "Being perfectly aware that our feelings are drawn from a proper source," they concluded, "we have a right to expect justice from our white and christian brethren, and nothing more do we ask or require."[15]

These are two enormously important documents. The first described with precision what had happened in Creek history over the past generations. The original "possessors . . . of the whole island, . . . no title can be equal to ours." They had been careless with their riches and had squandered their domain, but the time had come to change their way of life. They had given up hunting and become plow farmers; they were spinning and weaving; they had reorganized their government and had written a code of laws. Their thoughts now were on their children. This land "is to descend to our children, and them that come after us." Fully understanding the change that had occurred in their relations with the United States, the headmen had to admit that they could no longer defend their interests with power. "Our nation was strong; and never met a nation that was equal to us in war fare;" now

> our situation is not a desirable one! but, on the contrary, it is a very deplorable one. . . . The only difference [between Indians and whites] is the color of our skin, for we are of the same shape, but we have been born in the woods, and, in great degree, wild, and in a low and inferior situation. We, therefore, earnestly admonish our white brethren not to take advantage of our weak and unlearned situation; but treat us with tenderness and justice.[16]

The new time had come. If the Creeks were to survive the pressures imposed by their neighbors, expressed, organized, and applied in a political arena, they would have to respond in that same forum. McGillivray had been able to negotiate from a position of commanding power. Big Warrior, Little Prince, and the other headmen of the National Council, as they approached the United States commissioners late in 1824, had only their law and the hope of just treatment, and their wits, to depend on. There was no more Creek power.

The United States commissioners opened negotiations with the Creek Council at Broken Arrow on 7 December 1824. Campbell and Meriwether had been there for over a week making various prepara-

tions for feeding the several thousand Creeks in attendance and deciding on a workable strategy. Agent Crowell was under orders from the
secretary of war to help them in any way he could, but he was not directly responsible for the talks. His job was to supervise local arrangements and to influence the National Council to agree to the demanded
cession.[17]

The talks began with a ceremonial greeting by the Creek Council
and an opening statement by Campbell that called on the Creeks to
sell their eastern domain and move west of the Mississippi to lands set
aside for them. Campbell explained that their removal was necessary
under the terms of the Georgia Compact of 1802. The Creeks replied
on December 8 with a statement of trust in the president. They knew
nothing about the 1802 Compact, they said, but they were sure the
president would not do anything that would ruin them just to "ag-
grandize" Georgia. As for moving west of the Mississippi, they were
quite opposed.

On the ninth, the commissioners changed their tactics. Denouncing the Creeks as foreign invaders who had come into the area and conquered its people, the commissioners declared they had no ancient
right to claim the country as their own. Georgia, on the other hand,
had a legal charter that gave that state absolute dominion over the
territory in question. As allies of England in the Revolution, the
Creeks were conquered enemies whose rights depended solely on the
generosity of the United States. Now the president expressed his wish
that they remove. As foreign invaders and conquered enemies with no
legal claim to the land, they had no right to refuse.

Most of what the commissioners said was either untrue or based
on a policy long since discredited and abandoned. There was no land
set aside in the West for the Creeks, and any arrangement they might
make to remove would have to await an effort by the United States to
buy them a tract from a western tribe. The reference to the Creeks as
invaders and conquered enemies was misleading. Whether or not ancient Creek origins were in some other place, they had been in the region claimed by Georgia long before the first English colonists arrived,
and to claim otherwise was unfounded. The conquered-enemies formula, federal policy during the 1780s, had been abandoned by the United
States in the early 1790s and expressly repudiated in the 1790 Treaty
of New York. The use of such an argument in 1824 can only be seen as
a frantic attempt by Campbell and Meriwether to deliberately mislead
a people they considered so innocent and so stupid that they did not
know their rights and would believe anything.

Viewing the Creeks as fools, and failing to persuade the councillors with their specious arguments, the commissioners tried to attach the blame for Creek stubbornness to the outside influence of the Cherokees. In an effort to break the bond between the two nations, Campbell and Meriwether warned the Council that the Cherokees had no "right to interfere with the affairs of this nation." The time would soon come when they too would have to move west; any statements of policy resting on Cherokee advice, such as those made at Tuckabatchee and Pole Cat Springs, were therefore ill advised. Overlooking the fact that the Tuckabatchee position paper had been endorsed at the Broken Arrow Council in July, Campbell and Meriwether also argued that the policy expressed therein was the work of a few individuals and "not binding upon the nation." Finally, resorting to scare tactics, the commissioners tried to insinuate that there was a connection between the "designing individuals" who had met at Tuckabatchee and Pole Cat Springs and the "false prophets" who had "once led [the Creeks] into a dreadful war" with the United States.

The National Council held rigidly to its position. Point by point the headmen refuted the assertions of the commissioners, citing provisions in the 1790 Treaty of New York and the 1814 Treaty of Fort Jackson, which guaranteed to the Nation all its unceded territory, and brushing aside the notion that the Creeks were either foreign invaders or conquered enemies. The 1802 Compact, they argued, was irrelevant to the situation because it obligated the United States to acquire Indian land only "peacefully and on reasonable terms." This proviso, the headmen pointed out, was a federal recognition of their right to the land and of their right to refuse to sell it.[18] Then, after a brief description of the hardships such a removal would entail, the Creek delegation closed with a decisive refusal.

> Considering, then, our now circumscribed limits, the attachments we have to our native soil, and the assurances which we have, that our homes will never be forced from us, so long as the Government of the United States shall exist, we must *positively decline* the proposal of a removal beyond the Mississippi, or the sale of any more of our territory.

This declaration, for all practical purposes, ended the talks. What followed could better be called acrimony than serious negotiations. The exchange had been carried on in writing, the commissioners requested the form be changed to oral discussion, the Creeks agreed, but the Council flatly rejected a further request that the talks be conducted with a small delegation of headmen and behind closed doors. There was another discussion, on the sixteenth but it was perfunctory. In response to the commissioners' final offer, which contained references to the discredited treaties of the 1780s with Georgia, Little Prince impa-

tiently declared that his warriors had already given the Council's answer many times and he would now add his own voice. He would listen
to no old treaties, he announced. He knew his rights under the "treaty
with Washington" and he "never intended to spare another foot." Two
days later, in one final try, Big Warrior's speaker told Campbell and
Meriwether, "He would not take a house full of money for his interest
in the land; and we might take this for a final answer." The commissioners did just that and formally broke off the talks.[19]

The story told in the official treaty journal is only the veneer
which overlays the making of gigantic fraud and bitter political conflict. Campbell and Meriwether, with the aid of several relatives and
employees, offered bribes with a startlingly generous hand. Creeks,
whites living in the Nation who might have some influence over the
headmen, government officials, nearly anyone who would pause to listen, had money or the promise of land thrust at them. But McIntosh
was the object of the commissioners' special attention.[20]

One of McIntosh's duties as Lower Town speaker was to express
the opinions of the National Council when it met at Broken Arrow.
The councillors were reluctant to trust him to speak for them during
the December talks because of his performance at the Cherokee negotiations, and they agreed to make him their speaker only when Campbell perjured himself by denying that McIntosh had attempted to
bribe the Cherokee Council. To the written replies of 8 and 11 December, McIntosh, along with Little Prince, Big Warrior, and Hopoie
Hadjo of Osweechee, the three leading headmen of the Nation, signed
their names.[21]

While McIntosh was arguing publicly against a cession, he was
holding private nighttime talks with Campbell and Meriwether. These
not-so-secret conversations aroused the suspicions of the Council, and
on 11 December, out of fear that he was betraying the Nation, the
headmen "broke him" as speaker. Outraged by his dismissal, McIntosh
threatened publicly to sell the Creek lands and asked a friend to keep
his gun ready in case anybody tried to kill him in the name of the law
against unauthorized cessions. Instead of fighting it out, however,
McIntosh escaped out the window of his lodgings in the middle of the
night and fled to Coweta to the home of his son, Chilly. The next day,
Campbell and Meriwether went to Coweta to visit him, and for two
days they talked. The commissioners returned to Broken Arrow on the
thirteenth, and during the next five days the three conspirators met in
further midnight rendezvous.[22]

From the evidence of succeeding events it is clear that McIntosh,
Campbell, and Meriwether roughed out the Treaty of Indian Springs

during these midnight meetings at Coweta and in the woods between there and Broken Arrow.[23] But no amount of urging could persuade McIntosh to speak out in favor of a cession. He would sign a treaty, he promised, but only in his own house. If he signed in the Broken Arrow square ground, he would be killed under the law. To secure his cooperation, the commissioners agreed to pay McIntosh twenty-five thousand dollars for his two reserves granted under the 1821 Treaty of Indian Springs plus fifteen thousand dollars "for his trouble."[24] With McIntosh thus secured, all that remained was to figure out some way to get the negotiations moved to his place at Indian Springs—and to figure out a way to cover the scheme with the appearance of legality.

Governor Troup proved to be of enormous help. Indeed, the plan may well have been his. Even before he knew the details of the Broken Arrow negotiations, he was laying the groundwork for a second assault on Agent Crowell. Nothing if not imaginative, Troup seized upon the publication in November of the Creeks' statement drafted at Pole Cat Spring. Because the document had been agreed to in Subagent William Walker's home, and written by him, Troup concluded it was an official act to block the cession for which Agent Crowell was responsible and probably had ordered. On 9 December, in an apparent fishing expedition, the governor sent a letter by messenger to Campbell and Meriwether asking leading questions about Crowell's involvement with the Pole Cat Spring meeting.[25] The commissioners were anxious to blame all their problems on the "proceedings . . . at Tuckabatchee and Pole Cat Spring, [which] were evidently intended to forestall us. They have in great measure had the effect of spreading alarm throughout the nation, by the miserable farrago of threats which they contain." While the alarm was perhaps not so widespread as they claimed, the documents had certainly alarmed McIntosh, and the commissioners could already see their efforts at Broken Arrow defeated. Hesitant to charge any individual with direct complicity in the "conspiracy," Campbell and Meriwether preferred to complain of the Cherokees, who "have exerted a steady & officious interference in the affairs of this tribe . . . most active & insidious."[26]

When, on 18 or 19 December, the commissioners left Broken Arrow, they headed directly to the governor's office at Milledgeville. By the twenty-third, with their scheme decided, Campbell was on his way to Washington, carrying letters to President Monroe from Troup, armed with iron clad assurances from McIntosh that a cession could be had at Indian Springs, and primed with an argument for Secretary of War Calhoun.

Troup blamed Crowell for the Broken Arrow failure. Moreover, he promised that the second round of talks, the plan for which would be revealed in person by Campbell, would also fail if Crowell participated. Without explicitly demanding the agent's dismissal, Troup reminded the president that a year before he had made that request and had predicted then that if Crowell were retained in office he would sabotage Georgia's efforts to remove the Creeks. Trying to maneuver the president into relaxing his instructions to the commissioners, Troup insinuated that Monroe shared the blame for the unsuccessful negotiation.[27]

Campbell would not charge Agent Crowell with anything more than being "neutral" at Broken Arrow. On the other hand, he was fully satisfied of Walker's guilt. But Campbell was less interested in smearing the agents than in persuading the government to change its instructions. The plan worked out with Troup was to isolate McIntosh, magnify his influence, and sign the agreed-upon treaty with him alone. Campbell was absolutely certain, he assured Calhoun, that a treaty for the Georgia half of the Creek Nation could be secured. Half the Creeks lived there, and a cession of their country would remove ten thousand Indians, at least, to the West. The headmen on the Georgia side were willing, even anxious, to sign if their safety could be assured. That would require a negotiation in Georgia, away from the threats of the headmen of the Alabama side. Being less than candid with Calhoun, Campbell did not admit that "the Chiefs within the limits of Georgia" amounted only to McIntosh and a handful of his toadies. Permission to treat with these men for the Georgia side of the Nation was all he asked and, if granted, Campbell guaranteed quick success.[28]

President Monroe denied Campbell's request to treat only with the headmen on the Georgia side. Campbell's reply was to suggest submitting such an arrangement to the full Council for its assent, after the treaty was signed. Monroe rejected that idea too. McIntosh and the other Georgia chiefs lacked the authority to sell part of the Nation, he instructed. Campbell should reopen the talks, but any arrangement with McIntosh and his friends must be within the context of full Council participation.[29]

Campbell thought he had won. While his request to negotiate separately with McIntosh "was not expressly granted," he confided to Troup, the commissioners' "instructions [were] so extended and liberalized as to authorize the most sanguine expectations of success." In addition, they had succeeded in getting Subagent Walker fired and Agent Crowell reprimanded. Crowell is now "completely under our control," Campbell crowed.[30]

While Campbell was in Washington, McIntosh apparently panicked. The knowledge that his name on a treaty would constitute his death warrant had kept him quiet at Broken Arrow, and his later actions suggest that he had begun to have second thoughts about his private agreement. Shortly after the commissioners left, the National Council convened at the Broken Arrow square ground to affirm, one more time, its opposition to a cession. And again the Council repeated the law, already announced many times in the past several years, that an unauthorized cession would be punished by death. McIntosh, not present at the Council session, later wrote that the language of the Council's resolution specifically referred to himself "and any other of his chiefs who would make any proposition to the United States in favor of selling any part of the country which we now claim."[31] The Council may well have been so specific, given its practice in the past of emphasizing the strength of the law by saying that no one, not even Big Warrior, Little Prince, or McIntosh was exempt. That, plus McIntosh's obviously suspicious behavior, would have been enough to cause the Council to remind McIntosh once again of his danger.

In any event, McIntosh and his friends drafted a petition to the president with the full knowledge that their lives would be forfeit if they signed a treaty. The document was, therefore, a request for presidential protection. To strengthen their claim for United States intervention in their behalf, McIntosh referred to the Creek civil war. The current "distressing difficulties" within the Nation, McIntosh claimed, were "owing entirely to the existence of two parties in the nation, known and designated by the red sticks, (or hostile party,) and the other party friendly to the United States, and who were the warm supporters of the American war against said party of Indians, and also against the British." A clear oversimplification that did more to distort the truth than reveal it, McIntosh's argument depended on rekindling the animosities of a dozen years before. By implying that the Creek headmen who resisted the cession at Broken Arrow were members of the "Red Stick" supporters of the prophets and thus enemies of the United States in the Creek War, McIntosh was suggesting that that conflict still existed and that now, still resenting his alliance with Jackson, they were plotting to destroy him and his "friendly" friends. They could do so, McIntosh complained, because Big Warrior and the "hostiles" had control of the National Council. But it was an illegal Council. "McIntosh and his chiefs have the superiority in the grand council of the nation" because "they were the only supporters and defenders of the nation in the last war. . . . A number of Big Warrior's chiefs forfeited their rights to the country which they previously had, by their hostility to the United States during the last war."

Thus McIntosh argued that the Creek Nation was divided again along the lines of the civil war of 1812-14, with him and his friends still "friendly" to the United States and willing to sell the Nation for the benefit of Georgia to Campbell and Meriwether. On the other side stood Big Warrior and the "hostiles," opposing the cession, illegally speaking through a commandeered National Council, and "passing orders and decrees" which, if executed, would renew the civil war and give final victory to the enemies of the United States through the "destruction" of the "friendly party." "Our agent's partiality to the Big Warrior's party" encouraged their "hostility," gave the appearance of legality to the National Council and its acts, and threatened the lives and property of the McIntosh group. Only the protection of the president, McIntosh and his friends predicted, would avert disaster.[32]

On the same day, a number of obscure representatives of five Lower Towns—Broken Arrow, Taladega, Hitchiti, Cusseta, and McIntosh's Coweta—posing as the National Council signed a second document which authorized McIntosh and seven others to travel to Washington to consult with the president.

> Should our father the President give it as his opinion that the claim of the State of Georgia to the land within her limits would prevent a fee-simple title from vesting in our people, then, in that event, General William McIntosh, with the other delegates our chiefs, are duly authorized

to sign a treaty for an exchange of land west of the Mississippi. As if that was not authorization enough, the instructions went on to promise that

> any thing which the said delegates may do on the occasion will meet the approbation of the National Council in general, inasmuch as there are six of our principal council, with General William McIntosh, who are authorized to sign any treaty of that kind which our father the President and our delegates may make upon the subject.[33]

While Governor Troup had no demonstrable hand in the drafting of these instructions and allegedly saw them only after they were written, he could not have been more pleased than if he had dictated them himself. No president, under any circumstances, would tell any Native people that they could have a fee-simple title to a tract, no matter how small, that was vigorously claimed by a state. The certainty of that view was powerfully underscored by the Compact of 1802 by which the United States acknowledged Georgia's interest in the land claimed by the Creeks. The only imaginable purpose for even including such a proviso in the instructions lies in its possible later value as a screen behind which McIntosh might hide if the National Council sent out warriors to execute him. He could claim, on the basis of those instructions, that he went to Washington with an open mind and was persuaded by the president that cession and removal was the only hope for the preservation of a national domain. Two things were inevitable—there would be a treaty and there would be a negative reaction from the National Council. It was therefore necessary to persuade the government that the sitting council was illegitimate and that the McIntosh council really spoke for the Nation.[34]

Armed with these two documents, McIntosh and the other delegates stopped off at Milledgeville for a conference with Troup before proceeding on to Washington. The governor told them that Campbell was already in Washington and there would be no point in their going. Indeed, Troup dared not let them proceed. Such a visit would have ruined the Troup-Campbell scheme. McIntosh would have learned that both President Monroe and Secretary Calhoun had forbidden the commissioners to negotiate a treaty privately with him and his friends, and that information would certainly have ended his cooperation. He could expect no protection from the president if he acted in defiance of the president's very specific orders. Fearing defeat in the coming election, Troup desperately needed the Creek cession. To get it he deceived McIntosh, his cousin. With promises to rush the documents to Washington and assurances that all would be well, Troup hustled McIntosh and the erstwhile delegates home to prepare to meet again with Campbell and Meriwether, this time safely outside the Creek Nation.[35]

Campbell dashed back to Georgia. The plans for a second round of talks already under way, negotiations began 10 February 1825 at McIntosh's tavern at Indian Springs, some sixty miles east of the Creek Nation in Central Georgia. About four hundred headmen made the journey. Former Creek agent David B. Mitchell also attended. His "intimate" association with Campbell attracted much interested observation and comment. Such bitter political enemies that they would not speak on the streets of Milledgeville, the two roomed together at Indian Springs, and Campbell saved Mitchell the chair next to him during the talks. Exactly what Mitchell did to earn such treatment is unknown, but his friendship with McIntosh and his four years of experience as Creek agent were no doubt useful. He may also have been Troup's representative. Whatever his tasks, the impression of witnesses was that Mitchell was an active and important force in the negotiations.[36] Campbell requested an exchange of the land of the entire Nation for a tract of similar size in the West plus five hundred thousand dollars to pay for abandoned improvements and transportation costs, but it was only a gesture. The treaty had already been drafted. That evening, at a council of the representatives of eight of the fifty-six Creek towns, a nearly unanimous vote was taken in favor of removal.

On the next day, 11 February, the council heard a statement delivered in Big Warrior's name by his speaker, Opothle Yoholo. The chiefs present, he said, had no authority to sell any land. If part of the Nation wished to remove they were free to do so, but without the consent of all the Nation, in full council, they could not sell what they left behind. The land was not theirs—"it belongs to the nation,"—and McIntosh knew it. Willing to appear concilliatory, Opothle Yoholo admitted that maybe it would be best for the Creeks to remove. The arguments made the day before by the commissioners were compelling, and even Crowell had urged them to go. But there could be no such arrangement made here. The Creeks would need time to think it over and debate the idea in the National Council. His orders were specific. "I have received a message from my head chief, Big Warrior, telling me to listen to the Commissioners, to meet them friendly, but not sell land. I am also to invite you to meet us at Broken Arrow in 3 months when a treaty may possibly be made." Opothle Yoholo even offered that the Creeks pay the costs of the meeting. Campbell replied by telling Opothle Yoholo, who was one of the highest ranking officials of the Nation, that he was being "impudent."[37]

That night the delegations of Cusseta, one of the two most prominent Lower Towns, and of Sawokli, another influential Lower Town, left Indian Springs and headed back to the Nation. Among their numbers were Tuskeneah, the headman of Cusseta and the fourth-ranked chief of the Nation, and John Stidham, headman of Sawokli, one of the Lower Town leaders and a member of the National Council. The other influential delegations, including those from the Lower Towns of Broken Arrow (headed by Tuskeegee Tustunnuggee, son and representative of Little Prince), Osweechee (led by Powasee Emathla, nephew and representative of Hopoie Hadjo), Uchee (with William Barnard, a member of the National Council), and Eufaula, along with several Upper Town headmen, including Opothle Yoholo, Tuskeneah (son of Big Warrior), and Yoholo Mico (a very prominent national councillor) remained but refused to sign. This group, representing several Lower Towns, the Upper Town Council, and including the four highest ranking national chiefs (or their spokesmen), clearly outranked McIntosh, the fifth national chief, and his friends.[38]

But Campbell, Meriwether, and McIntosh were not to be stopped. Claiming that the chiefs in favor of a cession were "vastly superior in grade and numbers," a clear falsehood, they proceeded on 12 February to sign the Treaty of Indian Springs.

The treaty was enacted in the name of the United States policy of removal of the eastern Indians to the West and in conformity with the Compact of 1802. Cloaked in a half-truth, the preamble of the treaty declared that "the Chiefs of the Creek Towns have assented" to remove, *"those of Tokaubatchee excepted."* Next came the heart of the treaty, the cession by which McIntosh and his cronies sold the national domain in Georgia, the country covered by the 1802 Compact and demanded by Grovernor Troup. It was also the territory most directly related to the Lower Towns. While it would be a gross error to believe that the conflict over cession and removal was an Upper-Lower division with McIntosh at the head of the Lower Creeks (the vast majority of both groups opposed him), it remains true that all of his few followers were from the Lower Towns. None of his identifiable supporters were Upper Creeks; thus the shocked amazement in the Upper Towns when the full extent of the cession at Indian Springs was revealed. In addition to all of the Creeks' land in Georgia, McIntosh also sold to the United States the northern two-thirds of the national domain in Alabama. Carefully drawn to keep some important Upper Towns (Tuckabatchee, for example) intact, the deal was for the upper Tallapoosa and all of the Coosa drainage. This was Upper Creek country, heavily used, occupied by many towns and several thousand people, and quite beyond the most elastic interpretation of McIntosh's pretended power to sell any Creek land. Even if it were possible for the National Council to accept McIntosh's independent authority over Lower Creek country, which it categorically and repeatedly denied, there was no conceivable way to justify such an exercise of illegal authority over the country of the Upper Creeks. To the National Council and the Creek people generally, therefore, the Treaty of Indian Springs was an iniquitous document grounded in fraud and chicanery and acted out in treason.[39]

As McIntosh moved to sign the document, which had been prepared in secret and divulged to the assembled Creeks only moments before, Opothle Yoholo stepped forward to remind him of the consequences of his act. Spoken in Muskogee and not translated to the commissioners, Opothle Yoholo's message was later quoted as: "My friend, you are about to sell our country; I now warn you of your danger!"[40]

McIntosh did not need to be warned, and he was worried. During the negotiations at Indian Springs, he demanded a provision be added to the treaty guaranteeing him protection. The commissioners complied, adding Article 8, by which the United States was obligated to provide the "emigrating party" (meaning McIntosh and his friends) with "protection against the incroachments, hostilities, and imposition, of the whites, and of all others."[41] Thus reassured, McIntosh, as "head chief of Cowetaus," signed the treaty. Then came Etomme Tustunnuggee, second chief of Coweta, Roly McIntosh, brother of William, and a procession of others. In all, six headmen from eight of the fifty-six Creek towns signed, only one of whom, McIntosh, was a member of the National Council. Several of the fifty-two signatories were of such obscure stature they could not be identified by members of the Council. Thirty of the total were from McIntosh's town of Coweta.[42]

"The long agony is over," wrote Campbell and Meriwether to Troup the next day. The treaty was done, concluded "with what we consider the nation, for nearly the whole country." Georgia would gain four to five million acres, about one-third of which was "good" land, and within eighteen months the Georgia Creeks would be removed. Concluding with their thanks to Troup for his "ardent" help, the commissioners turned their attention to the problem of securing ratification of their dishonest work. No one knew better than they the falsity of their assertion that "the nation" had approved the treaty, and only through quick action could they hope to see the document, acquired in direct violation of their instructions, approved. The treaty would crumple like a water-soaked tissue if it were subject to the slightest senatorial scrutiny.[43]

The ink was barely dry on the document when Campbell and Meriwether rushed it off to Washington to be presented to the Senate for ratification before its early spring recess. They had less than a month, but if all went according to plan, the shortness of time would be an advantage. Breathlessly dropped into the Senate's lap in the last frenzied days of the session, the treaty was reasonably certain to be considered, and doubtless ratified, without inquiry.

In their cover letter to Secretary Calhoun, Campbell and Meriwether continued their campaign of misrepresentation and distortion. The treaty enclosed, they wrote, had been recently "concluded . . . with the Creek nation of Indians." "The attendance of the Chiefs was a full one: much more so than is usual when *Chiefs only* are invited," a half-truth further distorted by the concealed fact that most of the chiefs present opposed the treaty and had refused to sign. But not content with supplying the implication of widespread Creek approval, the commissioners went on to assert that "the opposition was feeble, and seems to have been dictated by the Big Warrior." By isolating him as the mastermind of the opposition, Campbell and Meriwether concluded with the false claim that he was now dead and with his death

"all opposition will now cease," and "the dissenting party will now
treat and reunite themselves with the majority, I have no doubt."[44]
Counting on Calhoun's predisposition to accept a signed treaty as
valid, the commissioners were confident that by disguising it with
falsehoods and misrepresentations, their handiwork could skulk
through the confirmation process unchallenged.

Even before the treaty and its accompanying documents could be
prepared for submission, Agent Crowell lodged with the War Department the first of many protests denouncing the treaty as a fraud. The
treaty signed yesterday "by M'Intosh, and his adherents, alone,"
Crowell complained, "was in direct opposition to the letter and spirit
of the instructions." The signatures on the document, "with the exception of M'Intosh and perhaps two others . . . are either of chiefs of low
grade, or not chiefs at all." Compare their names with those on the annuity receipts, Crowell instructed Secretary Calhoun, and the absence
of headmen would be obvious. Crowell believed that a treaty could be
negotiated "in conformity with the instructions," but this document,
"if ratified, . . . may produce a horrid state of things among these un-
fortunate Indians."[45]

Smarting under Calhoun's rebuke for his "neutrality" at Broken
Arrow, Crowell had not dared to speak against the treaty at Indian
Springs. Indeed, he had urged the Creeks to sell out and move west
and had offered to go with them and be their agent in the new country.
At Campbell's insistence, he had even signed the treaty as a witness.
He had not read it, but he had heard it read by Campbell and interpreted by William Hambly, United States agency interpreter. A few
days later Crowell read the treaty and found an article that had not
been read or interpreted. The offending provision, Article 5, authorized
Campbell and Meriwether to exercise control over two hundred
thousand dollars, the sum stipulated to be paid immediately to the
"emigrating party" (McIntosh and his friends) for their abandoned improvements and their removal expenses. Interpreting this as an additional bribe cooked up by the commissioners and McIntosh, Crowell
decided to hurry to Washington and argue against the ratification of
the treaty in person.[46]

Big Warrior followed Crowell to Washington carrying a letter of
protest signed by the National Council at Broken Arrow. The headmen described "the base treachery of one of our chiefs, Gen. Wm.
McIntosh," in whom they "had placed confidence" but who "has
abused it." Describing the negotiations at Broken Arrow and
McIntosh's secret sessions with the commissioners, headmen pointed
out that in combination the three scoundrels, in opposition to "the

known wish of the people of our nation, publicly and in full council expressed," had succeeded in their "nefarious scheme." By "pretending to make for the purpose Chiefs who have never before been known, and who are not, now recognized," the trio assembled a group willing to pose as the leaders of the Nation and sign the fraudulent treaty.

As proof of the dishonesty and injustice of the treaty, the Council cited the unmentioned Article 5 and its provision for paying two hundred thousand dollars to the tiny McIntosh group. This sum represented half of the entire amount authorized to compensate for abandoned improvements and transportation costs; the headmen complained that if the Nation were forced by the treaty to remove, this division of money was unfair. "After deducting [the $200,000] from the whole sum [of $400,000] promised to take us away, it leaves but a small pittance to defray expenses." Several thousand emigrants would have to share a sum equal to the amount divided among the few hundred McIntosh people. "In fact," the headmen concluded, "we cannot think that a treaty made under such circumstances, by a small minority of our people, will be ratified." "Defer the ratification," they begged, "give us time for deliberation. It is a great undertaking for a people to leave a country that has been endeared to them by the strongest ties. If we must remove, give us time for preparation." Frustrated, disappointed, victimized, confused, fearing the worst, the headmen closed on a pathetic note. "That justice may guide, and mercy direct you, is the fervent prayer of your children."[47]

The Creeks were not so pathetic as they sounded. Stunned by the enormity of McIntosh's treason and reeling momentarily, they quickly regained their composure. The National Council met twice in the six weeks between mid-February and late March 1825, first at Broken Arrow and then at Tuckabatchee. Unable to believe that such a patently illegal document would be ratified by the Senate, the councillors debated the situation before them and considered what action they might take against McIntosh. The law was clear and he was obviously guilty of its violation, but McIntosh was a powerful man, speaker of the Lower Towns, fifth ranked in the Nation, and the pet of influential Georgians. It would be an extreme step to order his execution, one fraught with great dangers from Georgia, and perhaps unnecessary. The Council stripped him of his national rank and offices but deferred a decision on the ultimate punishment, depending instead on the force of Crowell's and Big Warrior's arguments in Washington to prevail and block the ratification of the Treaty of Indian Springs. But there was no mistaking the sentiments of the Council, and McIntosh began again to fear for his life.

McIntosh, his son Chilly, and others of his close friends traveled to Milledgeville with Campbell and Meriwether. Between 17 and 20 February, the frightened Creeks and Governor Troup held three recorded conversations. McIntosh stressed his ancient friendship for the United States, his recent cooperation in furthering the interests of Georgia, and his danger now at the hands of Big Warrior and Little Prince, whom he continued falsely to accuse of being "hostile" in 1813. Speaking words which must have been symphonic to Troup's ears, McIntosh named Crowell as his "worst enemy" who, along with other "bad whites" in the Nation, would "stir up" the "hostiles" against him and his friends. Having no hope for protection in the Nation, McIntosh begged protection from Troup.

Troup was more than happy to comply. The only thing better than getting rid of Crowell and replacing him with a political ally was to meddle in the Creek Nation's affairs himself. Taking McIntosh's charges against Crowell and his plea for protection as his justification, Troup entered more directly into Creek affairs.[48] He began with a threatening message addressed to the "Chiefs of Tuckabatchee and Cusseta." Citing McIntosh's fears, the governor informed the National Council that if the Creeks did him and his friends any harm, "I will pursue you until I have full satisfaction." He would, he warned, chase them into Alabama if necessary.[49]

To see that there was no misunderstanding, Troup entrusted his warning to Colonel Henry G. Lamar, his aide-de-camp. Lamar delivered Troup's message, had a long conversation with Little Prince, which resulted in Lamar's mistaken impression that the National Council harbored no ill will toward McIntosh (Little Prince said the National Council felt no animosity toward white people), and came away convinced that all the opposition to the Treaty of Indian Springs was designed to prevent its ratification. Once the treaty had been confirmed by the Senate—and he had no doubt that it would be—Lamar was sure all bitterness in the Nation would cease. The Creeks had, he reported to Troup, an "unlimited confidence . . . in the wisdom and virtue of the President, [which] is a sure guaranty of the successful accomplishment of his wishes." With this, Lamar advised Troup to leave the Creeks "to themselves." They could and would do as the government wished.[50] While Lamar was meeting with the Creek headmen, Troup repeated his personal assurance to Chilly McIntosh that those who signed the treaty had nothing to fear. He would send the militia, he promised, if that was necessary to preserve peace in the Nation.[51]

Troup received word sometime in mid-March that the Senate had ratified the Treaty of Indian Springs. Campbell's and Meriwether's documents and Crowell's letter had reached Washington simultaneously. Secretary Calhoun, on his way out of office, and the Senate, in the last moments of its session, chose to ignore Crowell's protest. On 3 March 1825, the Senate confirmed the treaty without examination. One of John Quincy Adams's first acts as the newly installed president was to sign the document, 7 March, and authorize its proclamation. The next day Crowell, in Washington by that time, received the letter of protest from the National Council. In hopes that a problem would not develop, the new secretary of war, James Barbour of Virginia, put it aside and began to draft instructions to Crowell for the proper execution of the treaty.[52]

Ratification presented Troup with both an urgent political challenge and a magnificent political opportunity. Georgia had a land policy which, unlike that of any other state, made the acquisition of new tracts of Indian land a direct benefit to her citizens. Beginning in 1803, Georgia gave away its public land in 202½-acre parcels by lottery.[53] Any politician, particularly one like Troup with a reputation as an "aristocrat" heading an "aristocratic" party, and who was facing the suffrage of the masses, would be excited by the chance to pose as the man responsible for making five million acres available for distribution to the "common folks."[54]

Troup sprang into action. On 21 March he issued a proclamation announcing ratification, asserting Georgia's complete legal authority over the cession and its inhabitants, and prohibiting entry into the region by Georgia's citizens.[55] A week later, the governor sent a copy of the proclamation to William McIntosh, along with a request that he permit Georgia's surveyors to enter the cession and survey it ahead of schedule. This request was not intended to hustle out the Creeks, Troup assured, but he wanted to hold the lottery the moment they were gone, and "surveying takes time." Impatient for an answer, Troup wrote McIntosh a few days later, repeating the request and adding that he would appoint only honest men for the job. At about the same time, Troup informed the president of his plan.[56]

Troup's request was an embarrassment to McIntosh. According to the treaty, the Creeks had until 1 September 1826, nearly eighteen months, to evacuate the cession. In the meantime the United States, under Article 8, pledged to protect the emigrants from the "incroachments, hostilities, and impositions, of the whites, and all others." Apparently realizing that Georgia's surveyors had no right, by the terms of Article 8, to enter the cession, Troup was demanding from the "emigrating party" a special permission that could cover his plan in case of complaint. But the last thing McIntosh needed was another reason to come to the attention of the outraged National Council. His only hope of remaining alive was to keep a very low profile. On the other hand, McIntosh's vulnerability placed him in Troup's hands. With no federal troops close by and alienated from Crowell, McIntosh's only source of help in time of trouble was the Georgia governor, and he could hardly afford to anger him.

McIntosh delayed answering Troup until mid-April. He wanted, and received, the governor's assurance that the surveyors would buy their supplies from Creeks, presumably at his store, but mostly he wanted time to figure out what to do and consult his friends. The strain McIntosh was under is evident in his reply, dated 12 April from Lockchau Tolofa (Acorn Town), his plantation on the Upper Chatta-hoochee, in present-day Carroll County, Georgia. He fully understood his danger, he recognized his dependence on Troup, and he was ex-temely uncomfortable at having to entrust the governor with his life. McIntosh's labored words show less than full confidence as he re-peated Troup's promises that all "bad men" would be under control and no "bad passions" would be permitted. As to the survey, McIntosh wrote, "I have been . . . at some loss in making up my mind, and must confess to you the embarrasment I have labored under." The proper channel for such a request was through the agent, but McIntosh had no confidence in his advice. Therefore, "the nation who signed the treaty" agreed to permit Troup to begin his survey early. But, McIntosh unexpectedly went on, their consent was not enough. Hav-ing become a stickler for protocol, McIntosh told Troup that he would also have to get permission from the United States, Agent Crowell, and the National Council.[57]

Troup was more than a little annoyed by the way McIntosh had hedged his consent for an early survey. Using the terminology of the civil war learned from McIntosh, Troup blustered, "We have nothing to do with the United States, or the Agent or the Hostiles in this mat-ter all we want is the consent of the friendly Indians who made the Treaty. If we wanted the consent of the United States we could ask it."[58] Without pausing for an explanation, Troup announced that the Creeks had consented to an immediate survey and called the general assembly to a special session, to meet 23 May, to organize the ceded country and launch the survey. A week later, a chastened William McIntosh withdrew the condition to his approval.[59]

McIntosh's anxiety was well founded. Rumors had been flying through the Nation since the Indian Springs negotiations that McIntosh was about to be executed, along with six or seven others who were his closest associates. Perhaps lulled into a false sense of security by Troup's repeated promises of protection, McIntosh did not flee the

country, but his plantation on the Chattahoochee had taken on the atmosphere of an armed camp under seige. His correspondence with
Troup was carried by special messenger from the governor's office, and
McIntosh rarely strayed far from the premises. As time went on and
the news filtered into the Nation that the unbelieveable had happened
and the treaty was ratified, the tension became excruciating.

About mid-April, Crowell returned alone from Washington—Big
Warrior had died there. While McIntosh struggled with Troup's request to survey early, the agent called the National Council to hear his
news from the capitol and receive the annuity payment. Assuming sole
leadership, Little Prince sent McIntosh a pointed invitation to attend
the meeting, but McIntosh, who was planning to travel out west to
look over the land he had traded for, pleaded ill health. He sent a representative, however, who delivered to Little Prince the correspondence with Troup and the news that Georgia surveyors were coming.
Had he attended, McIntosh might not have left the Broken Arrow
square ground alive, which probably explains his indisposition.[60]

At this Council, Crowell formally told the headmen of the ratification, urged them to accept the money provided, and remove quietly.
Their reaction was "sorrow"—it was a "national calamity." With one
voice they rejected the money. The Creek Nation had sold no land, the
headmen declared, and to take the money would make it appear that
they had. Pledging no hostility toward the United States, one after another the councillors pledged to resist passively. They would die on
their land, they vowed, and the world could see how much they loved
it.[61]

McIntosh was a different matter. The Council had before it, in the
form of his correspondence with Troup, further evidence of his chicanery. The outraged headmen ousted Crowell from the Council and
began a long and private debate. Ignorant of what transpired, the
agent relayed to Washington their public sentiments. He described the
governor's request and McIntosh's consent, the "melancholy and distress" of the Council, and the "decided objection" of those who lived in
the cession to any surveying before they removed. The Creeks now
depended on the United States to "put a stop to this unjustifiable
design" of Troup's, Crowell explained, and if the survey was not prevented, it "will be impossible to prevent the encroachments and
impositions of the whites, which the United States have stipulated for
in Article 8 of the treaty, without a strong military force." The Council
asked permission to send a delegation to Washington to discuss their
situation "and future prospects," but in the meantime, Crowell urged,
"justice and humanity require that the protecting arm of the Government should be extended to these now helpless and dejected people."[62]

Filled with "melancholy and distress" assuredly, the National Council was not quite so "helpless" as Crowell believed. In great secrecy, the headmen agreed that under the laws of the Nation McIntosh was a traitor whose guilt was so manifest that he must die. Citing the law McIntosh himself had proclaimed many times in the past, the Council passed the death sentence on him, Etomme Tustunnuggee, and Samuel and Benjamin Hawkins, two of McIntosh's sons-in-law. Menawa, Council chief from the Upper Town of Okfuskee, whose lands had been sold by those condemned, was appointed to carry out the execution. On the last night in April, Menawa led a force of one hundred twenty to one hundred fifty warriors (all residents of the ceded region) and one white man (who could calm any whites with McIntosh) to McIntosh's plantation on the Chattahoochee. They surrounded the buildings, set fire to them, and waited for McIntosh to appear. He shot at the executioners from a second floor window, but after a few minutes the fire drove him down to the porch. A volley tore into his body, he stumbled into the yard, one of the law menders stabbed him in the heart, and the rest filled his corpse with bullets. Etomme Tustunnuggee was present and he, too, was executed. Later in the day the executioners found the Hawkins brothers. Samuel was hanged. Benjamin, though shot, escaped.[63]

The Council's execution of William McIntosh was no rash act. His behavior had been such as to provide the headmen of the Nation ample opportunity to consider his fate. The fact that his execution was seriously considered after the 1821 Treaty of Indian Springs suggests, in addition, that the justice of the Nation was tempered with considerable mercy. This was no savage act of uncivilized barbarians, Governor Troup's self-serving accusations to the contrary notwithstanding. It was the fully considered and legal act of a self-governing people whose ancient right to regulate their internal affairs had always been recognized and respected by the United States. It was an extreme act, clearly made with great reluctance, but McIntosh's was an extreme crime. Treason hardly defines the enormity of the 1825 Treaty of Indian Springs. Fraudulent by the standards of any society, concluded in violation of the clearly expressed orders of both interested governments, riddled with bribery, chicanery, and deceit, the treaty illegally acquired for Georgia and Alabama, through the offices of the United States, an enormous extent of land. In the selling of this tract McIntosh sold the country of his people and the legacy of their children. Much more than real estate changed hands—McIntosh sold the Nation.

Aside from the repeated explanation of the Council that McIntosh was executed "by the law," one can only guess at the emotions and arguments felt and expressed at the Broken Arrow square ground. There was no precedent for the decision. On a small number of previous occasions the Council had ordered the execution of warriors guilty of murdering whites, but then only at the insistence of the agent, and such acts were required by the treaties and the Trade and Intercourse laws. There was no known occasion when the Council ordered the execution of a Creek for the violation of its own laws. That the headmen did so in April 1825 shows how much Creek law and the authority of the National Council had changed. The Code of 1818 had done more than provide the machinery for protecting the private estates of individuals. Along with the formalization of the law menders as a national police force, it set the stage for the definition of crimes against the Nation by a centralized government.

Calhoun, Benjamin Hawkins, and David B. Mitchell had promoted what had happened. Seeing the absence of written law, they had assumed there was no law. Failing to understand the machinery of the Council, they had thought there was no government. And certain that civilization stood on law and government, they had concluded that there was no civilization. Driven by the desire to "civilize" the Creeks, these officials of the United States government encouraged and applauded the changes that occurred. But they had failed to anticipate the outcome. While the Creeks had adopted certain Anglo-American legal concepts, they had welded them to their own assumptions of political independence and used them to serve decidedly Creek purposes. The execution of William McIntosh for the treason of the Treaty of Indian Springs was the pivotal moment in the history of Creek Council government.

5
THE ABROGATION OF
THE TREATY OF
INDIAN SPRINGS, 1825–26

Mc Intosh's execution was the first of several steps taken by the newly assertive National Council to preserve its domain. Struggling to resist removal and overturn the Treaty of Indian Springs, the Council launched a campaign of political persuasion and passive resistance that put the Council into direct confrontation with the governor and the anxious citizens of Georgia. A crisis atmosphere settled over the state.

Chilly McIntosh, son of the executed headman, had been present at his father's plantation when Menawa and the law menders came. In the confusion, he made a desperate escape across the flood-swollen Chattahoochee and dashed to Milledgeville and Governor Troup, followed by a tide of wild rumors and hysterical reports of impending massacre. Alexander Ware, a planter on the Georgia frontier and a brigadier general in the state militia, reported to Troup, "the road is covered" with refugees, and "upwards of 400 warriors of hostile party" are feasting on McIntosh's cattle and would be "marching toward the settlement of whites in 3 days." He added that while he suspected some of the rumors to be exaggerated, he was preparing (just how he neglected to say) for an invasion of perhaps as many as four thousand warriors. Within a few days, even more ominous news arrived at the governor's office: "Whites, who have lived among Creeks a long time and know them, are sending their families out of the Creek Nation."[1]

Troup reacted swiftly. He counseled the surviving friends of McIntosh to be patient and "peaceable" and leave everything to him. "Depend on it," pledged the governor to Joseph Marshall, a Coweta headman and close McIntosh associate, "my revenge I will have. It will be such as we have reason to believe the Great Spirit would require; such as our Christ would not think too much; and yet so much that I trust all red and white men will be content with." Then, in letters to five militia generals, Troup ordered mobilization. To General Ware the governor indulged in a particularly bloodthirsty hope: "I sincerely trust if these infuriated monsters shall have the temerity to set foot within our settled limits you may have the opportunity to give them the Bayonet freely—the instrument which they most dread and which is most appropriate to the occasion."[2]

Troup lusted for vengeance against those he termed the "hostile" Creeks, but it is clear that from the beginning he had plans to kill more than one bird with his stone. During the next several weeks the Georgia governor, with an eye toward finally replacing Agent Crowell with a political ally, carefully orchestrated the thoughts and acts of Chilly McIntosh and the surviving followers of his father. When Chilly first arrived in Milledgeville on 2 May, his explanation to interested Georgians was that his father had been executed by order of the National Council according to Creek law. After conversations with Troup, however, he began to implicate Crowell in his father's death.[3] Shortly thereafter, Chilly, his uncle, and two friends of his father set off to Washington to carry news of the execution to President John Quincy Adams. The trip was probably Troup's idea. The delegates carried a letter from the governor to the president describing how "this Chieftain whose virtues would have honored any country . . . met the stroke of the assassin, and . . . fell by the hands of the most treacherous and cowardly" assailants, and hinting broadly that Crowell was responsible.[4] To drive the point home, Chilly and the others handed Secretary of War James Barbour a bill of complaint charging that the agent had always been "opposed to," "offended at," and "incensed against" William McIntosh and predicting, "If Col. Crowell is continued agent, we fear that the friends of general McIntosh will be sacrificed."[5]

Barbour had been carefully, though inadvertently, prepared for the charges against Crowell carried by McIntosh's survivors. Early in May, Duncan Campbell, then in Washington and therefore ignorant of the recent events in the Creek Nation, assured the secretary that "accounts of [Creek hostility toward McIntosh], if not wholly unfounded, have, at least, been greatly exaggerated. They disclaim the feeling themselves, and I regard as criminal all attempts to excite it, or to establish its existence." By equating Crowell's February report that trouble was likely to follow the signing of the Treaty of Indian Springs with attempting to incite violence, Campbell, partly to hide his own culpability and partly in connivance with Troup, was already trying to discredit the targeted agent.[6]

Official Washington first learned of the execution early in the morning of Sunday, 15 May 1825, when Chilly McIntosh and his delegation paid a before-breakfast call on President Adams. Troup's letter, which they delivered, announced that the government of Georgia held the United States responsible (because it should have fired Crowell long ago when Troup first demanded it) both for the recent "catastrophe" and for the general border war that Troup predicted would follow "unless the most ample satisfaction and atonement shall be made promptly for the death of McIntosh and his Friends." The governor informed President Adams that he had urged upon McIntosh's friends the necessity for peace and patience, but he hinted that they might not remain patient long. Exactly what steps Georgia might take were not yet decided, but Troup indicated that a special session of the legislature would meet soon to consider what "measure either of retaliation or protection" Georgia should embrace. Coupled with his mobilization of the militia, it seemed clear in Washington that Troup's intentions were violent. Crowell also gave this interpretation to Troup's statements and actions. "If Governor Troup puts into execution his threats," the agent warned Secretary Barbour, "the whole Creek Nation will be overrun by his troops, before this reaches you."[7]

Adams and Barbour, agreeing that "Governor Troup [is] a madman," prepared to head off the predicted war. But they did not want to become too embroiled in Creek affairs. Both believed the execution of McIntosh, though tragic, was legal and did not justify any meddling by outside forces. They therefore decided to send a special agent to Troup to explain their position and restrain him from "acts of violence for retaliation, or protection, [and] to inform [him] that the United States never have interposed, and cannot interpose, in transactions of internal feuds in an Indian tribe." They agreed as well to dispatch a spokesman to the National Council to "warn against further violence" and to invite a delegation to Washington to negotiate their grievances.[8] With Troup and the Creeks taken care of for the moment, Adams and Barbour turned next to the more embarrassing question of McIntosh's followers. Chilly's charges against Crowell were linked with demands for United States military protection for his friends in Georgia, for a full investigation, and for compensation for property destroyed by Menawa and the law menders. It thus became necessary to consider sending a special agent to probe into Crowell's conduct and possible complicity, as charged by Troup and Chilly McIntosh, in the execution of McIntosh and the others.[9]

Within five days of the arrival of Chilly and his friends, the Adams administration had made its decisions. It had done so reluctantly, driven to action by what President Adams considered to be Troup's "exceedingly hasty and intemperate" statements. The president for the first time fully appreciated the entangling character of Article 8 of the Treaty of Indian Springs that obligated the United States to protect the McIntosh faction from the rest of the Creek Nation. This provision, Adams fumed, was "very insidiously introduced, and the purport of which was certainly not considered by the Senate when they advised to the ratification of the treaty." But he had no choice. In addition to the special investigators Adams and his cabinet had decided to send south, Article 8 called for troops. The president was thus forced to commit the United States in a far more vigorous way than the situation seemed to him to warrant.[10]

Major Timothy P. Andrews, an officer stationed in Washington in the office of the Paymaster-General of the Army, was one of those specially appointed agents. Ordered to investigate the charges pressed against Crowell by Governor Troup and Chilly McIntosh, he had the authority, if his discoveries so warranted, to suspend the agent from office. The other special agent was Brevet Major General Edmund Pendleton Gaines, commanding officer of the Eastern Department of the U. S. Army. An old soldier with service on the Florida border, General Gaines was both familiar with Georgia and well known by many Georgians. Secretary Barbour instructed General Gaines to protect the Georgia settlers from whatever threat "hostile" Creek warriors might pose and to restore peace between the two Creek factions. Once peace was assured, the general was to hold councils with representatives of both groups, persuade the Nation to accept the Treaty of Indian Springs, and aid in every way the emigration of the McIntosh group.[11]

President Adams was fighting for time. Under the terms of the treaty, and to ensure peace, he needed to keep Georgia's surveyors out of the Creek cession until the stipulated date of 1 September 1826. Even though he had become convinced that the treaty was an "iniquity," he still hoped to persuade the Creeks that they had no alternative but to abide by its provisions. The president accepted Agent Crowell's view that the Council had finally been persuaded to execute McIntosh because of his decision to permit Troup's survey of the cession before the removal date. It thus seemed to him that the surest guarantee of peace between the Creeks and Georgia was to stall Troup long enough to get the Indians out of the state. To this end Adams and Barbour drafted a patient and conciliatory plea to the governor, explaining the duties of Gaines and Andrews and concluding with a statement, expressive more of hope than of certainty, that "the President expects from what has passed, as well as from the now state of feeling among the Indians, that the project of surveying their territory, will be abandoned by Georgia, til it can be done consistently with the provisions of the treaty."[12]

Adams's plan failed to work. Governor Troup was a stubborn and determined man whose standard tactics were to press a vigorous attack, catch his opponent off balance, sweep to his goal too fast to be stopped, and present his adversary with an accomplished fact. The governor's natural aggressiveness had served him well in the rough-and-tumble theater of Georgia politics, and in the spring of 1825 his style continued to pay dividends. The special session of the Georgia legislature opened on 23 May, and Troup outlined to the lawmakers his plan of attack. Heaping praise on Campbell and Meriwether for their successful negotiation of the Treaty of Indian Springs and upon Georgia's delegation in Congress for shepherding it unscathed through to ratification, Troup reminded the assembled legislators how close the treaty had come to failure. "Officers in the pay and confidence of the federal government" and conspiring in "perfidious plots and devices," he charged, had defeated the negotiations at Broken Arrow and had very nearly prevented the signing at Indian Springs. And official Washington, aware of the activities of its agents, "permitted [them] to escape but with little observation, and certainly without merited punishment." The War Department's failure to chastise properly these conspirators left the way open for a continuation of their sabotage. As a result, "the active and malignant interference" of these "evil-minded white men" had split the Creeks into two conflicting factions; had led directly to the "massacre of McIntosh," a hero "whose whole life had been devoted to Georgia, as faithfully as to his own tribe;" and threatened to delay Creek emigration. But for the "insidious practices" of these miscreants, Troup thundered, "the entire nation would have moved harmoniously across the Mississippi." The governor left no doubt that John Crowell was the leading white villain.[13]

In case the assembled lawmakers failed to understand exactly what the emigration of the Indians would mean for Georgia, Troup rhapsodized at length about the rosy future of the state in full possession of its territory. With the removal of the Creeks Troup promised, in addition to free land for twenty thousand lucky lottery winners, lower taxes, better state services, and internal improvements. In the midst of a deep national depression, no legislator (or voter) could scoff at that. The key to this magnificent future lay in Crowell's dismissal. With him removed, Troup reasoned, there would be no opposition to the survey, no internal division within the nation, and no possibility of the tribesmen resisting emigration. All he needed, the governor urged, was the legislative authority to continue.[14] In this frame of mind Troup replied to Adams's wish that he delay the survey: "If the president believes that we will postpone the survey of the country to gratify the agent and the hostile Indians, he deceives himself."[15]

The special session complied with Troup's requests. The state senate's standing committee on the State of the Republic investigated the governor's charges against Agent Crowell and reported that although there was no evidence that he had ordered the execution of McIntosh, it was likely that he knew of the Council's decision, and his failure to prevent the deed made him an accessory to it. The committee also found Crowell guilty of obstructing Georgia's efforts at the negotiations at Broken Arrow and Indian Springs. For these offenses the committee demanded that Agent Crowell be dismissed from office. Even more useful politically to Troup, however, was the committee's recommendation of the appointment of a special gubernatorial commission to continue the investigation. Such an ongoing effort would enable the governor to keep his campaign against the agent before the public indefinitely.[16]

By substantial majorities the legislators also authorized the governor to begin the survey and organize a land lottery. The lawmakers also provided for the establishment of Georgia law in the territory ceded at Indian Springs by dividing the region into five parts and attaching each parcel to a neighboring county. Georgia jurisdiction meant sheriffs, posses, magistrates, and courts, as well as laws. As long as the Creeks clung to the country they insisted had never been legally sold, they were subject to these foreign institutions. This act provided Governor Troup with a cloak of legality with which he could cover over and hide from view any step deemed useful in dispossessing the Creeks. Given the charges of fraud at Indian Springs brought by the National Council and the widespread predisposition of the Creeks not to remove from the cession area, the law supplied the justification for armed invasion to protect surveyors and lucky lottery winners and crush any Creek attempts to defend themselves and their interests. If war did not occur in the summer, this law seemed to guarantee its outbreak in the fall.[17]

Indications were, however, that armed conflict would not be slow in coming. Major Andrews arrived in Milledgeville the last of May, while the legislature was in special session, and the atmosphere was filled with tension. There were alarming rumors, added to by hysterical and well-publicized messages (worded suspiciously alike) from the militia officers of two frontier counties describing "threats, . . . sullen countenances, and insulting conduct" of the Creeks and calling for "a sufficient force stationed on this frontier to annoy the Indians to peace." Until such a force could be assembled, these frightened officers announced, they and their neighbors would remain in great danger because they were "destitute of arms and ammunition." Troup sent these appeals to the legislature with a covering letter calling for a "sufficient force for the protection of our inhabitants." The assembly responded with dispatch, authorizing the governor to press into service additional militia companies and to send to "the present theatre of alarm" the necessary weaponry. The shipment to one militia officer included "one hundred and sixty muskets, five thousand and fifty flints, one hundred pounds of buck shot, and one hundred and sixty cartridge boxes."[18]

All this military activity doubly alarmed Andrews because he learned from several sources that Chilly McIntosh and some friends of his father planned to trick the Georgians into taking their revenge for them. Their plan, as Andrews heard it, was to disguise themselves as "hostile" Creeks and harass the exposed settlements, perhaps even kill some settlers. Counting on the excitability of the frontier population and Governor Troup's well-known penchant for rash action, the McIntosh people hoped to flood the border area with frightened, well-armed militiamen. That combination would be explosive, and Troup seemed to be playing into their hands. Indeed, Andrews implied that Georgia's governor was privy to their scheme.

Major Andrews had strong evidence to support his suspicions. The governor's messages to the Georgia legislature's special session were deliberately inflammatory. In an address delivered 9 June he predicted "the most unpleasant tidings may be daily expected." In what amounted to a war message, the Governor announced,

> It is my deliberate opinion, that the United States' Government will be directly answerable to Georgia for every drop of blood shed upon this occasion; and I further say to you, what has been more than once said, that no State, having pretensions to even limited sovereignty, ought to be dependent on another for the protection which is due from a Government to its citizens, much less for that which, from the information communicated, seems to be urgently demanded for our frontier inhabitants. It is scarcely necessary to add, that there are no measures which you may constitutionally authorize, which I will not execute with promptness and energy.

These words impressed Andrews as a part of an elaborate preparation for a full-scale attack on the Creeks.[19]

The uproar in Georgia came as an enormous surprise to the

Creeks. From the outset there had been "no hostility or unfriendly feeling . . . entertained toward the Government or any white person whatever." The Council's sole purpose had been to enforce Creek law against offending Creeks and nothing more. Pressed for clarification, the Council submitted to a question-and-answer session in which it explained the law and absolved Agent Crowell of any prior knowledge or complicity in its decision. Indeed, the headmen stated most emphatically that Crowell could have had nothing to do with the execution. In response to the question, "Had the Agent have directed you to kill McIntosh, would you have done it?" they replied, "We would not, for he was not placed here for that purpose."[20]

These assurances had little effect in Georgia. Troup's political ambitions were best served by defending his state from the threat of "hostile" Indians. The McIntosh people, gathered in refugee camps established by the governor, had little incentive to return to the Nation, and Troup saw no advantage in returning them. Their presence in Georgia kept the crisis alive and nourished the atmosphere of emergency upon which Troup depended. So while the objective of the United States was to cool the air and heal the Nation, the governor preferred to fan the flames of fear and suspicion and point to the homeless innocents whose lives were spared only by his bold and decisive action.[21]

General Gaines's task was to keep the peace and reunite the Creeks. As the ranking United States official in Georgia, he was also the chief spokesman of federal policy in the state. A proud and stubborn man, Gaines had no predisposition to permit Troup to push him around.[22]

Gaines and Troup met on 13 June, the first day the general was in Milledgeville. It was, no doubt, inevitable that when the "excitable" Gaines and the "madman" Troup collided, the result would be explosive. Their disagreement arose over the question of the survey, and Governor Troup stood firm. In reply to the general's urging that the survey be postponed, Troup announced that he would press on with it "disregarding any obstacles which may be opposed from any quarter." Angered by this rebuff, Gaines reported to Secretary Barbour that although the Creeks seemed anxious to preserve the peace, his mission had just begun. "War will be avoided," Gaines predicted, "unless it is produced by a union of the worst men, *white* and *red,* who we view as our friends." Clearly, the general referred to Chilly McIntosh and his friends and the officers of the government of Georgia.[23]

Gaines was anxious to prevent the McIntosh people from sabotaging the uneasy peace on the Georgia frontier. To that end, and in compliance with his instructions, he immediately ordered the convening of councils with the McIntosh party at Indian Springs and the National Council at Broken Arrow. The first of the two sessions began 19 June when the general, recently arrived at Indian Springs, received a written statement from Joseph Marshall, Chilly McIntosh, and thirty-seven of McIntosh's followers. The document told of the anguish caused by the execution of McIntosh, the feeling of helplessness occasioned by the loss of his leadership, and the fear of his survivors that their lives were also in danger. Marshall and Chilly demanded protection for themselves and their friends, but they also demanded restitution or compensation for the property and valuables taken by the law menders and the lives of the national leaders who had authorized McIntosh's execution. "Blood for blood is the law of the land," they wrote, "and a law which Christ himself has tolerated. This is what we demand; and a restoration of all damages."[24]

The general responded the next day, 20 June, with a reasoned statement composed of about equal parts of commiseration for their past suffering, praise for their current peaceful restraint, and a warning that any future attempt at violent revenge would be vigorously crushed. If the "hostiles" were as peaceful as they were reported to be, Gaines announced, nothing more would be done.

> As the Government of the United States has, in no instance, deemed it proper to interfere in the intestine feuds of our red neighbors, in cases like the present, when their hostilities have not continued or extended to the white inhabitants, I am not authorized, under these circumstances, to sanction the measure of revenge proposed by you.

If the Council was "willing to restore the money and property" confiscated or destroyed, "it is expected that you will . . . moderate your demands." Adding insult to injury, Gaines also told of a change in the plan to pay the four hundred thousand dollars promised in the Treaty of Indian Springs to the "emigrating party." Rather than give it all to the McIntosh people, as they expected, the funds were to be distributed to all those living in the ceded territory, thereby increasing the number of recipients from roughly five hundred to perhaps as many as fifteen thousand.[25]

Gaines's message was a heavy blow to the McIntosh party. Expecting more than sympathy, they looked for the profits they had bargained for at the treaty talks in February plus compensation and revenge for their recent losses. In his private correspondence with Barbour, the general had already mentally reversed the identities of the "hostile" and "friendly" groups, and now the McIntosh people were beginning to learn what that reversal meant. Troup's darlings were not

Gaines's. Under orders only to restore and keep the peace, he would neither support nor tolerate any attempt at revenge, no matter how "legal."

Joseph Marshall and Chilly McIntosh responded to Gaines's message with a tightly reasoned legal argument. The authors of McIntosh's execution must be "given up to be tried by our laws." If Little Prince and Opothle Yoholo had murdered white men, "the President, would have called upon our nation to give [them] up . . . to be punished as the law said. We expect and demand the same in this case." Denying again the existence of the law under which the Council claimed to act, the McIntosh party wove an argument for punishment of the headmen that assumed that their order for execution was somehow divorced from Council deliberations and that they were individually culpable for what they decided in Council. Thus the execution was murder and punishable under the same law that forbade the taking of human life.

Gaines had told them that punishing the killers would not bring McIntosh and the others back to life. Therefore his survivors should not seek revenge. With proper indignation, Chilly and Marshall rejected that patronizing remark. "We knew that before," they pointed out, but it did not follow that the killers should not be punished. "That is not the way our white brothers talk to one another. When one of them murders another, he is tried by your law, and, if found guilty, you punish him. This is all we ask."

The McIntosh people were in a difficult position. Too few in number to take their own revenge, they had to depend on the aid of others. With Gaines on the scene and federal troops on the way, Troup could not help them with Georgia's militia. It all depended on Gaines, and he was unwilling to interfere on their behalf. The only way to win his support, it seemed, was to deny the legality of the Council's act and pin responsibility on the National headmen as individuals. Should they fail on that score, they were helpless and they knew it. Therefore, they continued to press their argument, embellishing it with stories of atrocities and laments and adding protestations of undying friendship for all whites. These actions, plus the treaty provision for protection and the four-hundred-thousand-dollar-removal money, might keep the survivors alive long enough to flee, if all else failed. The response of Marshall and Chilly McIntosh to General Gaines's solution to their problems, coupled with the by-now-standard complaint against Agent Crowell—"We believe him our worst enemy"—clearly showed a stiff and unanticipated resolve.[26]

Indeed, the response was so unexpected that Gaines did some

sleuthing and found that their original and presumably softer reply had been thrown out at 2:00 a.m., and that this hard-line response written by a local lawyer named McMartin, a strong supporter of Troup, had been substituted. This discovery, plus the character of the letter, which "evinces much of the tone and tenor of the *political* essays of a state political party," convinced the general that his efforts to bring calm to the Creek Nation were being deliberately sabotaged by the governor. That Troup sent three "commissioners" to represent the state in Gaines's councils with the Creeks, and that they met late into the night with Chilly McIntosh and his comrades, only deepened his certainty. The "commissioners" satisfied Gaines that they were troublemakers, meddlers, liars, and opportunists, and he incurred the boiling wrath of the governor by leashing and muzzling them at every opportunity.[27] But he could not get rid of them. Under orders from Troup the "commissioners" dogged Gaines's heels as he traveled into the Nation to meet the Council at Broken Arrow.

Gaines found when he reached Broken Arrow that as the crisis atmosphere had heightened in Georgia, it also spread west into the Creek Nation. More than half the people lived on ceded lands and did not know what to do. Worried by the planned survey, frightened by the near certainty that squatters would follow, and alarmed by the threat of a militia invasion, they were caught between the dangers of remaining and their reluctance to leave. In a state of near panic, they could only cling to the slim hope that the Council could somehow overturn the treaty.

Adding to the uncertainty, Big Warrior of Tuckabatchee, headman of the Upper Towns for nearly twenty years, died on 8 March 1825 while in Washington protesting the Treaty of Indian Springs.[28] His son, Tuskeneah, inherited his rank but not his talent. Into the vacuum of Upper Town and national leadership left by Big Warrior stepped his speaker, Opothle Yoholo. The speaker's vigor contrasted sharply with the age and infirmity of Little Prince, and even before the death of the latter in April 1828, Opothle Yoholo had become in fact, if not in name and rank, the political leader of the Nation.

Opothle Yoholo's leadership had its roots in the National Council. As its speaker he was the visible voice of the Nation, defining its policies, explaining its laws, justifying its acts. Among a people who cultivated and cherished eloquence, as if it were a rare and beautiful flower, Opothle Yoholo's voice and style identified him; his intellect put him foward. The death of Big Warrior, the execution of McIntosh, and the infirmity of Little Prince threatened to leave the Council leaderless in this calamitous time. The emergence of Opothle Yoholo perhaps reas sured the Creeks that the Council remained capable of governing.

Gaines's conference with the Nation's leaders at Broken Arrow opened on 28 June. Following a formal greeting by Yoholo Mico of Coweta, one of the oldest and most respected kings in the Council, the general delivered his address. The president sent his best wishes and invited a delegation from the Council to come to Washington in the winter for a visit. In the meantime he advised the Creeks to accept the money from the treaty—"it has been ratified, and *cannot be revoked.*" The president was very sorry if the treaty was a fraud, "but the laws must be obeyed. The treaty is a law, and no white man can break it." I "would rather lose my head," Gaines pledged dramatically, "than deceive you."[29] The president also regretted the "late extraordinary acts of violence" and wanted to know why they had occurred.

Opothle Yoholo replied with a detailed history of Creek law, the role of the Council, and the negotiations at Broken Arrow and Indian Springs the previous winter. "The Council made laws," he described, "and appointed persons to execute them. These laws have been confirmed in the Great Square, by a Council of all the Chiefs, to continue in effect under all future Chiefs." Despite the laws, McIntosh, who "was not a head chief," signed the treaty and sold the land. "The treaty was made by fraud, by thieves, by walkers in the night." When Crowell returned from Washington with the news that the treaty had been ratified and that the first installment of the purchase money was due, "we refused to receive it, for we did not consider our laws a joke." McIntosh refused to come before the Council to explain himself. "This refusal called for the execution of the law." As for current Council policy, Opothle Yoholo pledged, "If they take our land and knock us on the head, we can't help it. We will make no resistance, but, even then, extend the hand of friendship. Thus will our whole nation act, and let the world see and hear of it."

Opothle Yoholo's remarks as speaker for the Council were elaborated upon in an unusual statement by the aged Little Prince. "The white people have laws and execute them," he explained. "I am surprised at the interference of Georgia. It was an Indian law, and not a law of Georgia." By this refrain, to be repeated on several occasions, Little Prince expressed his frustration at the meddling of outsiders in the legal affairs of the Nation.[30]

Gaines continued to press. He presented the demands of the McIntosh people for compensation and described their fearful refusal to return to their homes. The Council belittled their fears. "They urge their claims at a distance," Opothle Yoholo sneered, "why do they not urge them here?" Anticipating disputes over the value of lost or destroyed possessions and unwilling to trust the fairness of the Council, Gaines wanted Agent Crowell to serve as arbiter. In the name of "justice" the Council agreed. The next day, however, Opothle Yoholo withdrew its consent. "The Muscogee nation has laws," he said, "and this would place them in the hands of strangers. The Agent knows that all disputes are decided in Council, and left to the chiefs. If the other party feel themselves aggrieved by the execution of the laws, let them submit their grievances to the Council." Gaines was dissatisfied—"an umpire is necessary," he lectured. If the agent did not suit, then some board of disinterested persons may be used, but "something of this nature *must* be adopted. . . . I require nothing but justice, and that you *must do.*" Opothle Yoholo was adamant. "We do not think it right to appoint persons to decide our laws. It will be like tying our hands." Gaines insisted, and by threatening the Council with the life-for-life demand of the McIntosh group, he won his point.[31]

The argument was over the forum for arbitrating the property claims of the McIntosh party. There was no disagreement over the fate of the people. "The Chiefs merely executed the law," Opothle Yoholo explained, "and McIntosh's friends have nothing to fear. They knew the law . . . [which] only extends to the heads of town . . . and . . . they had or have nothing to fear." Dissatisfied, Gaines demanded a formal statement from the Council that forgave all those who followed McIntosh, invited them to return home, promised to restore their property according to Gaines's program, and pronounced the death sentence on any Creek who killed one of the refugees in retribution for their agreement to the treaty. The Council pledged the peaceful reunion of the Nation and the end of the mistaken fears of the Georgians, but the headmen would go no further. Gaines could not crack their resolve and win a recognition of and compliance with the treaty.[32]

It is not clear what the general expected when he arrived at Broken Arrow. Before the talks, Major Andrews reported, "General Gaines had possessed himself, before his arrival at Milledgeville, of the most correct and general information, as to the state of affairs in this quarter." One suspects, however, that the full and detailed evidence he acquired at Broken Arrow came as something of a surprise. The numbers were perhaps most striking. He found that the gathering at the national square ground at Broken Arrow was not a harried and hysterical representation of one of two beleaguered Creek factions. Instead, Gaines met with the established government of the Nation. Seven hundred town chiefs, headmen, and Council kings and twelve hundred warriors gathered to see and hear the general and to explain what had happened. These representatives alone outnumbered by nearly four times the entire population of the McIntosh group. For the next several months Gaines tirelessly reported that "49/50" of the Creek people opposed the Treaty of Indian Springs and agreed with the decision of the Council to execute McIntosh. But Opothle Yoholo's quiet eloquence as he explained again and again the views of the Council was probably even more persuasive. The leaders of the Nation had signed no treaty and sold no land and would therefore accept no money. They would not remove nor would they resist removal with force. They would, instead, die where they lived. They had done nothing for which they were ashamed. They had faith in the president and in the justice of the United States, and they would rely on that fairness to protect them.[33]

Gaines was impressed. "They refuse to give any assent to the treaty," he reported to Secretary Barbour. They would

> readily lay down their lives upon the land in which the bones of their ancestors are desposited . . . and die without resistance; that the world shall know, that the Muscogee Nation so loved their country, they were willing to die rather than sell or leave it. They appeal thus to our magnanimity, and I cannot but say, I trust and hope their appeal will not be unavailing.[34]

As Gaines had dramatized his devotion to truth, by pledging to give up his head rather than tell a lie, so Opothle Yoholo had dramatized the Creeks' abhorrence of the treaty by promising to die quietly for the love of their country. Neither man's statement should be taken too literally. On the other hand, Gaines was an "excitable" and emotional patriot who, as a professional soldier, lived his life with the knowledge that he might have to die for his country. His career shows that he had made peace with the idea, and it would be hard to think of a federal officer more predisposed to be impressed by the speaker's pledge. Opothle Yoholo may have known Gaines well enough to have understood that. Certainly the Council's temporary secretary, John Ridge, a college-educated Cherokee, understood it. While the ideas in the written communications belonged to the headmen, many of the words were Ridge's and one can be confident that he translated the views of the Council with an eye to their maximum impact on the general. Between the two of them, Opothle Yoholo and John Ridge converted General Gaines from an impartial and dispassionate investigator into an ardent partisan and champion. Certain that the Creeks had been swindled by McIntosh, Campbell, and Meriwether, Gaines became increasingly outraged at Troup's efforts to magnify and exploit the sufferings of the Creeks and benefit politically from the fraud. Lieutenant Edward G. W. Butler, aide-de-camp to General Gaines, probably expressed the views of them both when he wrote in a letter to his fiancee, "Such a mass of corruption and bribery as has been elicited in the course of this investigation, and will be exposed at the next session of Congress, has never been presented to the world. The Indians have proven themselves superior to Americans, in virtue and magnanimity."[35]

Gaines made no effort to hide his opinions from Governor Troup. Judging from the volume of their correspondence, it would seem that the general took great pleasure in tormenting the governor. In mid-July Gaines held a private meeting with some McIntosh party leaders at Joseph Marshall's home on the Chattahoochee. The general informed them of the pledge of the National Council to welcome them home and restore their property, which they were glad to hear. In thanking Gaines for his efforts on their behalf, Marshall denounced the treaty they had signed as the work of fraud and corruption. The commissioners had deceived them, and the president and the Creeks had been sacrificed to Georgia's politics. Gaines also stumbled onto a piece of information that threw doubt on the entire legal argument Troup had assembled to justify his early survey of the Creek cession. Marshall swore under oath that McIntosh had not consulted with his supporters regarding Troup's request to mark off the cession. Therefore, whatever permission McIntosh may have given was invalid. Informally he asserted that he did not believe the dead chief had consented at all. In addition to informing the governor of his discovery, General Gaines saw to it that the letter was published in a Milledgeville newspaper along with the sworn testimony of Marshall and the corroboration of William Edwards, a white man who had been Troup's messenger. The general thus publicly confronted Troup with two possibilities. Either, as Gaines delicately phrased it, "Your excellency has been greatly deceived," or the governor of Georgia was exposed before the electorate as a liar. No matter which interpretation proved correct, the governor's reputation could not survive the discovery untarnished. His reaction was apoplectic, and the press war between Troup and Gaines began.[36]

While Gaines and Troup battled each other, President Adams and Secretary Barbour began to stiffen their opposition to the early survey. Gaines's reports describing the proportions of the pro-and anti-treaty Creek factions, the fraud of McIntosh and the commissioners, and Chilly's plots to exploit the known opposition of the Nation to the survey in order to provoke a war had persuaded them that Troup must be stopped.[37] Adams's skeletal summer cabinet worked two days on the wording of a momentous letter to the governor, and in their labors they made no effort to disguise the significance of the message. "I am directed by the president to state distinctly to your excellency," Barbour wrote for Adams, "that, for the present, he will not permit such entry or survey to be made." So there could be no misinterpretation of Adams's intent, the secretary included in the letter to Troup a copy of Gaines's new orders. "Should [the Governor] persevere in sending persons to survey the lands embraced within the treaty," it read,

> you are hereby authorized to employ the military to prevent their entrance in the Indian territory, or if they should succeed in entering the country, to cause them to be arrested, and turn them over to the judicial authority, to be dealt with as the law directs.

With these instructions the general had the power to prevent the survey and protect the Creeks from Governor Troup and his trigger-happy militia.[38]

Gaines was jubilant with Barbour's orders.[39] Bubbling with anticipation and confidence, he promised that the "just, enlightened, and moderate views and expectations of the President . . . ought and must be realized." The general also reminded the secretary of how neatly he had taken care of Aaron Burr—"a much more distinguished man than any one now opposed to me"—eighteen years earlier, and remarked that the present task could be accomplished with "little opposition, other than such as the *ideal tactics* and paper *squibs* of an electioneering campaign will be likely to produce." With contempt dripping from every word, Gaines cheerfully predicted that Troup was as good as his.[40]

The governor was too smart to be trapped so easily. Adams had decided to submit the controversy over the Treaty of Indian Springs to Congress for a final decision, and this action gave Troup the graceful escape he needed. He grandiloquently reported to the president that he would submit the controversy to the Georgia legislature; in the meantime, all preparations for the survey would cease. Both executives were looking for the same thing—some way to stall for time. The controversy had gotten out of hand, and both Adams and Troup found themselves headed for a confrontation that neither desired.[41] Troup had also discovered that he no longer needed to press for the survey in order to secure his election. General Gaines provided him with a better issue.

The Georgia press had served Troup well, but beginning in mid-July it outdid itself in becoming the ground upon which the indefatiguable governor could joust with a most willing enemy. The "Maj. Gen. Commanding," as Gaines styled himself, personified all the evils that Troup found profitable to attack. He represented the power of the central government in a state that was experiencing the development of a powerful states' rights sentiment; he was blocking Georgia's efforts to survey and settle a large tract of valuable territory; in his criticism of the Treaty of Indian Springs he dishonored two respected Georgians (Duncan Campbell was an influential member of the Georgia House of Representatives); he seemed to be taking the side of Indians to the detriment of whites; and he heaped upon the government of Georgia and the governor heavy doses of contemptuous and insulting language.

General Gaines clearly had talent as a pen-and-paper warrior. He unleashed his imagination in his published correspondence with Troup. Heaping insult upon vitriolic insult, the general pounded away at the governor, questioning his motives, denouncing his actions, impugning his honor, making innuendoes about his sanity, and sarcastically exposing him to scathing public ridicule. Governor Troup's battle plan was to publish letters of complaint to Washington. "With a corps of regulars at his heels," Troup roared, Gaines has been

> attempting to dragoon and overawe the constituted authorities of an independent state, and on the eve of a great election, amid the distractions of party, taking side with the one political party against the other, and addressing electioneering papers, almost weekly, to the chief magistrate, through the public prints, couched in language of contumely and insult, and for which, were I to send him to you in chains, I would transgress nothing of the public law.

Troup lacked the power to take his revenge himself, but if he could force the president publicly to disavow his special agent, he could turn the general's attack into tremendous political advantage. So he wrote that he expected the president's

> indignant reprobation of [Gaines'] conduct will be marked by the most exemplary punishment which the laws will enable you to inflict. I demand; therefore, as chief magistrate of Georgia, his immediate recall and his arrest, trial and punishment under the rules and articles of war.[42]

Adams reprimanded Gaines, but he did not fire him. Indeed, the reprimand was so half-hearted that Troup could have interpreted it as a personal vindication. Over the signature of Secretary Barbour, Adams informed Gaines that he saw "in the serious charges made against you by Gov. Troup, and the publicity given to them, and which the letter complained of were intended to repel, circumstances which go far, in his opinion, to palliate your conduct."[43]

The president's refusal to appease Troup by punishing Gaines shows the importance Washington assigned to the general's mission. He had come south with two duties—to preserve peace on the border and to persuade the Creeks to accept the Treaty of Indian Springs. The Indians were peaceful when he arrived and they remained so throughout his stay. But Gaines's presence, along with nine companies of infantry encamped in the Flint and Chattahoochee River valleys, were important in preventing either the McIntosh people or the Georgians from armed retalliation. He preserved the peace.[44]

Gaines totally failed to accomplish his second mission. No number of councils could persuade the Creek Nation to accept as valid the Treaty of Indian Springs. The arguments made at Broken Arrow and in private to General Gaines convinced him that the headmen were correct, so that after his first raising of the question of the treaty, he ceased pressing the matter. Indeed, by mid-July he was bombarding the War Department with requests that the testimony collected by himself and Major Andrews provide the basis for a complete review of the treaty and its negotiation. The Creeks had convinced the general that justice could be served best by the abrogation of the treaty. General Gaines's famous friend, Andrew Jackson, had concluded about the same thing. "Nobody did believe," he wrote to Lieutenant Butler, Gaines's aide-de-camp.

> that the Indians had any intention of commencing hostilities on the whites. The whole excitement was produced by designing white men, to draw the public attention from the means used in obtaining this fictitious treaty, signed by one or two chiefs, and the rest self-created for the purpose of multiplying signers to the instrument. I am sure that, with the evidence now before the nation, the Senate would not have ratified the treaty.[45]

During the summer of 1825, however, there was no reason for Gaines, Troup, or Jackson to expect that the Treaty of Indian Springs would be annulled. Even though Congress had the power, there was no precedent for declaring null and void a treaty that had been ratified by the Senate and proclaimed by the president. While Gaines urged such a course privately, publicly he took those preliminary steps necessary to execute the instrument. By 1 September 1826, he had to clear the Creek cession and distribute a two-hundred-thousand-dollar installment of the sum appropriated to defray the moving expenses of the emigrating Indians. To accomplish this, Gaines appointed an assistant agent as census taker to travel with an interpreter to every Creek town within Georgia's claimed boundaries recording the names and numbers in each family. The general expected this task to be completed by November, at which time he planned to hold a council on the Chattahoochee to pay the Creeks their money. Perhaps he could persuade the headmen at the time to accept the treaty, but in a revised form that would cost the Creeks only their Georgia holdings. "Beyond this," he urged, "no principle of justice or magnanimity can sanction—a demand on our part."[46]

Adams was interested. In agreement with the Georgians that the Creeks had to leave, the president saw no alternative but to keep up the pressure to force them out. Unlike Governor Troup, who had no scruples in the matter, Adams's sensitivities required that it be done legally, but there was no disagreement between them on the goal. In mid-September he ordered the general to try once more to persuade the Nation to accept the Indian Springs Treaty. If, as expected, that should continue to be impossible, Gaines had authority to negotiate a new treaty with the Creeks for the cession of their Georgia lands only. He could exchange acre for acre for a territory west of the Arkansas River and pay up to four hundred thousand dollars in cash. But whatever he worked out with the Indians would be contingent upon Senate ratification. The challenge to the Treaty of Indian Springs was unprecedented and there was no way to predict how the upper house of Congress would receive a new treaty.[47]

With the arrangements for the negotiations left to him, the general decided to ask for a meeting of the National Council at Broken Arrow late in October so that all the business could be completed before the distribution of money scheduled for November. He requested that if Agent Crowell had not already been informed of the details of the proposition to be discussed, he not be apprised of them. Gaines was shrewd enough to recognize the conflict of interest inherent in the agent's position, and he wanted to avoid the possibility of being forced into offering more than might be necessary. As the result of his efforts to prevent ratification of the Treaty of Indian Springs, Crowell had earned a reputation for advising the Creeks on the basis of their best interests and not always as the government wished. Gaines, a hard bargainer, wanted to be free to make his offers contingent upon the attitudes of the Creeks, not upon the recommendation of their overzealous agent. In an elaboration of the problem he wished to avoid, the general wrote a classic description of the nearly impossible position in which a conscientious Indian agent frequently found himself.

> The Agent should never be placed in a position so embarrassing as to possess information important to the interests of the Indians of his Agency, and at the time the most needed [by them] with hold it from them. Should he deceive them he loses their confidence, and with it the power of being useful to them, and to the Government who employs him:—for ex-

ample—if he is advised that I am permitted; in a certain event, to offer the Indians 400,000 dollars for that part of their country within the established boundary of the State of Georgia, with an equal quantity of land in the West;—and should he be consulted by them, as he probably may be, as to the propriety of their acceding to any previous proposition which I am authorised to make to them; he would at once feel the difficulty against which I wish to guard: he would be compelled either to deceive them, by withholding from them, as a public Agent in their confidence, the information all important to their interests, or, by communicating it, he would defeat the object, and disappoint the just expectations of his government; and thus force me to abandon all but the dernier proposition that I am authorised to make: for illiterate & ignorant as the Indians are supposed to be, they would not be likely to yield to a minor proposition, when advised of the existence of authority to place at their option one of greater value to them.[48]

During late October and early November 1825, General Gaines, denying the Creeks one of their most trusted sources of information, met with most of the National Council at Broken Arrow. Perhaps suspecting his purpose, Opothle Yoholo and several headmen left the Nation on the eve of Gaines's arrival and headed to Washington to meet the president. Little Prince was sick in bed, and Tuskeneah spoke for the Creeks. Gaines, repeating his stated preference for death before deceit, called on the Council to sell their lands in Georgia. The president, he explained, had sent the Treaty of Indian Springs to Congress, but in order to be sure that Congress would revoke it he wanted to submit a fair substitute.[49] If the Creeks would meet Georgia's demands by selling the land that state claimed, the United States would give them an equal amount west of the Mississippi plus three hundred thousand dollars. If they refused, the present corrupt treaty would probably stand and "your enemies will triumph." "The President and myself did not cause your distress; you must therefore aid us in our efforts to relieve you."

Tuskeneah remarked on the change in Gaines's position. In June the general had led the Creeks to believe he was there to settle their troubles and recover their land. Now he wanted half their property. Unwilling to argue about it, however, Tuskeneah said the headmen had already left for Washington and there was nothing the Council could do. Irritated, Gaines demanded to know the power of the delegation, to which Tuskeneah snappishly replied, "If you are going to Washington you can learn from them." The verbal sparring continued. Tuskeneah asked "if property sold by an unauthorized person can't be recovered by its owner?" Gaines responded evasively that it was "doubtful" what Congress might do. Therefore, Adams wanted to offer a substitute treaty "as unequivocal evidence of the friendly disposition of the *Creek Nation.*"

The direction of the talks turned at that point. Gaines's thinly veiled threat that the government would consider a refusal to "cooperate" as a sign of hostility brought Hopoi Hadjo, acting host for the Council, into the conversation. While Tuskeneah continued his belligerent tone, Hopoi Hadjo tried to soothe Gaines's rising anger. "We think the proposal a reasonable one, and that it should be agreed to," he said, "but, the delegation is appointed, and we cannot act." Gaines accused Hopoi Hadjo of lying, but failing to move the Council to treat on the spot, he offered to settle for a written statement authorizing Opothle Yoholo's delegation in Washington to sell the Georgia lands. Tuskeneah refused—"We don't like writing, as those who read cheat us." But in the face of Gaines's insistence, the Council finally agreed, contingent upon Little Prince's approval. The conference adjourned to the side of the old man's sickbed, and there a document was drawn and signed that empowered the delegation "to enter into any such treaty or arrangement" that settled "amicably all differences connected with the unauthorized and illegal proceedings at the Indian Springs in February last." Without specifying terms, the headmen pledged their willingness "to yield as much on our part as possible to effect so desirable an object" and agreed that "the last proposition of the President, made by General Gaines, to be reasonable, and as just as existing circumstances would authorize."

But the councillors believed that they were approving a compromise based on the Chattahoochee River as the boundary between themselves and Georgia. That was what Gaines, "influenced by the conviction that [any other] proposition . . . would not only have been rejected, but would have defeated the plan of obtaining a new Treaty," had finally suggested. They did not know that the president had not authorized such an offer. In his zeal Gaines overstepped his instructions and misled the Council and its delegation in Washington into thinking that the Adams government was prepared to accept a substitute treaty that would not require the cession of the entire tract claimed by Georgia. Opothle Yoholo and his colleagues were thus not prepared for the resistance they encountered in Washington.[50]

The negotiations in Washington, begun the end of November 1826, dragged on for five months.[51] "When we first started to see our Father," the delegates informed Barbour, "it was our determination to appeal to Congress for redress, and request of that civilized body the annulment of the treaty made by the United States' Commissioners and the traitor McIntosh." But in the meantime they had received the document wrung from the National Council by General Gaines and had talked to the president. Adams had made it clear that there was virtually no possibility that Congress would repudiate the treaty without a substitute satisfactory to Georgia. Learning this and hoping that "the tears of our grey-headed mothers may cease to flow, and that the Muscogee females may no longer suckle their babes in grief," Opothle Yoholo and his fellow delegates "consented not to run the risk of hazarding the whole in our appeal to the Representatives of a great nation." Fearful of an ungenerous congressional disposition, "We have yielded to policy, and contrary to our previous determination" are prepared to agree to a substitute treaty.

The delegates then submitted a draft containing ten acceptable articles. After declaring the Treaty of Indian Springs null and void, the delegates demanded the removal to the West, at United States expense, of every signer of the offensive document. Each would receive one square mile of land, paid for by the Nation. Based on the Council's authorization, the delegates agreed to cede the land east of the Chattahoochee, stipulating the high water mark on the east bank as the boundary. This left in Creek hands all islands and ferries, especially the busy one at the Federal Road crossing near Fort Mitchell and Coweta. The Nation also retained ownership of and jurisdiction over a tract one and one-half by three miles on the east bank at the Federal Road crossing for the relocated agency and two reserves of one square mile each on the east bank to be granted in fee simple to their Cherokee secretaries, John Ridge and David Vann. The United States was to pay those evicted from the cession for their improvements plus two hundred thousand dollars when the Senate ratified the instrument, one hundred thousand dollars in one year, and twenty thousand dollars per year "in perpetuity or forever."[52]

Annulment of the "late proceedings at the Mineral Springs" was the purpose of the negotiations; a cession east of the Chattahoochee was the price the Creeks were willing to pay. But they would not waver from the agreement made between the Council and Gaines. Willing to "surrender our claim and title to the lands East of the Chattahoochee river, for money," they would not part with any lands west of the river. The delegates were experienced neighbors of Georgia and therefore adamant in their insistence on a natural boundary. "A dry line will never do between us." Because they refused to consider removal west of the Mississippi, the subject of the boundary with Georgia was vitally important. "We may as well be annihilated at once, as to cede any portion of the land West of the river."[53]

Adams opposed the river boundary. Because Georgia demanded

possession of all the Indian lands within its claimed borders, "it would still leave the root of the controversy in the ground." The problem was that, though described in the Compact of 1802, those borders had never been surveyed. The exact limits of Georgia's claimed territory were unknown. Assuming correctly that Georgia would tolerate nothing less than everything, the president could see no purpose in negotiating a new treaty that did not fully and finally satisfy that grasping state. Indeed, he suggested that the negotiations cease and that the Creek delegation return home. Congress would refuse to annul the treaty, the Creeks would refuse to evacuate the cession, the government would have "no means to compel their compliance" without special congressional authorization, the treaty would become an unenforceable nullity, and the Adams administration would be off the hook. The president's cabinet wisely rejected that plan, however, as it would surely have caused bloodshed on the Creek-Georgia frontier.[54]

While Adams and Barbour insisted on a cession of all the Creeks' lands in Georgia, Opothle Yoholo cited the Council's agreement with Gaines on the Chattahoochee boundary. Gaines had not mentioned that detail in his report and, because Gaines had not been authorized to make such an arrangement, Adams resisted being bound by it. Barbour thought the Creeks' wishes were reasonable, however, and when he learned from Gaines that Opothle Yoholo's interpretation of his proposal was correct, the rest of the president's cabinet agreed to consider the Chattahoochee compromise if Georgia would tolerate it. Georgia Senator John Forsyth, anxious to prevent a general congressional debate on the Treaty of Indian Springs, believed a substitute treaty with a cession to the Chattahoochee would be acceptable. But Troup was outraged by the idea, and the Georgia congressional delegation joined in his demand for the immediate execution of the discredited document. Thus the issue remained unresolved throughout December and well into January 1826. Time was running out; Congress was approaching the final weeks of its session, and Opothle Yoholo, despondent over the stalemate, attempted suicide.[55]

In an effort to break the deadlock, the government recruited Lewis Cass, governor of Michigan Territory and a noted hard negotiator with stubborn Indians. When he proved unsuccessful, Thomas L. McKenney, head of the Indian Office, opened a private correspondence with John Ridge who, along with David Vann, attended the Creek delegation as secretaries. Writing unofficially as a private citizen and a "friend," McKenney urged Ridge to advise Opothle Yoholo to agree to a compromise suggested by Barbour that would mark the western boundary of the cession not with the Chattahoochee but with

Cedar Creek, a western branch of the larger river that flowed from the Creek-Cherokee border south into the Chattahoochee. This would preserve the natural boundary concept of the Creeks and increase the amount of land for Georgia. Describing the overwhelming disappointment of the Creek delegation over their failure to win a satisfactory treaty, Ridge replied that they were about to give up and return home. He followed McKenney's advice, however, and made the effort. It worked; Opothle Yoholo and his friends agreed. "As the Delegation is not in a condition to talk on a subject which excites their hearts to bleed," the Creeks turned over all final diplomatic responsibilities to the two Cherokees. "Mr. Vann and myself are authorized to agree with the Secretary on the articles of the treaty."[56]

A last-minute snag arose when McKenney, after further research on a better map of Georgia, found that there was no such stream as Cedar Creek. Instead he proposed that any creek "(should there be such a one,)" near the great bend of the Chattahoochee would suffice. Blandly ignoring the possibility that there might be no such stream, McKenney assured Ridge that "the basis, in point of fact, therefore, is the same." The Cherokees, anxious by this time to conclude the negotiations, agreed and "succeeded in convincing [the delegates] that the explanation you have given does not vary the principle." With that, Ridge announced, he and Vann would visit the War Department, examine the Georgia map, "and point out upon it the lines that will define the extent to which we can possibly go."[57]

Opothle Yoholo and the other delegates had reached the point of distraction. Adams, Barbour, Cass, and McKenney had been pounding away at them for two months. Agent Crowell had been so "assiduous in urging" them to surrender to the government's demands "that he has altogether lost his influence with them." William Hambly, the Creeks' trusted interpreter, suffered the same fate. Because there was no one in an official capacity to lend them sympathetic assistance, the Creek delegates increasingly depended on the Cherokees for advice. When they too urged surrender, the delegates' resolve crumbled, and in a fit of desperation they threw their fate into the hands of Ridge and Vann. The "Cedar Creek compromise" was a fake, and still the Creeks agreed. After two months of struggle, beaten down, isolated, threatened, and cajoled, they signed the Treaty of Washington, 24 January 1826. North of the Chattahoochee, the border was a surveyor's line estimated to conform to the unsurveyed Georgia-Alabama boundary.

While Secretary Barbour had struggled mightily to break the Creeks' attachment to the Chattahoochee boundary and thereby improve the chances of ratification by the Senate, he and his colleagues in the Adams cabinet had concluded that the Treaty of Indian Springs was already a dead letter. As Adams informed the Senate in his message covering the new treaty, "The question is not whether the treaty of the 12th of February last shall or shall not be executed." He had been "anxiously desirous" to carry out its provisions but, "like other treaties, its fulfillment depends upon the will not of one but of both parties to it." The refusal of the Creek Nation to be bound by the terms of the Treaty of Indian Springs had made the document unenforceable and "absolved [the United States] from all its engagements." There were two alternatives. The United States could "resort to measures of war to secure by force the advantages stipulated to them in the treaty or . . . attempt the adjustment of the interest by a new compact." "The nature of our institutions and . . . the sentiments of justice and humanity which the occasion requires for measures of peace" dictated recourse to the second option. The resulting treaty did not provide Georgia quite all the lands owned by the Creeks, Adams admitted, but it was all they would cede. He accepted their refusal to sell more in the "conviction that between it and a resort to the forcible expulsion of the Creeks from their habitations and lands within the State of Georgia there is no middle term." Considering his view that the Treaty of Indian Springs was already a nullity, Adams's message was a strong statement to Georgia that the Treaty of Washington was the best that could be done short of war and that state had better accept it quietly.[58]

The president's message was also a strong statement in recognition of the sovereignty of the Creek Nation. He expressed no doubt that the Council possessed a right equal to that of Congress to dissolve the Treaty of Indian Springs. Without acrimony or complaints of Indian perfidy and faithlessness, Adams simply accepted the fact.

The Georgia congressional delegation was dissatisfied, however, and in deference to their wishes, the Senate refused to ratify the treaty. Negotiations were reopened, during which the Creek envoys agreed to a revised estimate of the Georgia-Alabama border. Opothle Yoholo and his colleagues saw little reason to jeopardize the treaty for the sake of a small tract, the principle of a river boundary having already been surrendered. They therefore agreed to accept an additional thirty thousand dollars in return for the cession of a somewhat enlarged parcel northwest of the Chattahoochee. This final cession supposedly severed Creek title to all the lands claimed by Georgia, and with that understanding the Senate ratified the treaty, 22 April 1826.[59]

In its final form the Treaty of Washington varied substantially from the draft proposed in December by the Creek delegates. The southern two-thirds of the new border with Georgia was the Chattahoochee, but the line was marked at the middle of the river; there was no mention of the islands, and the loss of ownership of both banks forced the Creeks to share the ferry business with Georgians. The northern border extended northwest of the Chattahoochee along a line to be surveyed by Georgia under the supervision of three Creek commissioners, and it promised to be a continuing source of conflict. The Creeks also had to provide a tract of two square miles west of the river for the relocated agency. McIntosh's adherents, in the name of national unity, were well taken care of. Rather than expel them, the treaty stipulated that they "be admitted to all their privileges, as members of the Creek Nation." Assuming they would emigrate, however, the treaty contained several articles that authorized an exploratory party to locate a western home to be purchased by the United States, that promised removal at federal expense, subsistence for one year, one hundred thousand dollars as a "present," and that provided for the establishment of a fully equipped western agency. The Council also had to affirm its earlier agreement to pay damages to the McIntosh party for property losses sustained "contrary to the laws of the Creek Nation" when they fled to Georgia. A delegation of McIntosh people, also in Washington during the winter of 1825–26, as well as Barbour's sense of justice, demanded such generosity. Opothle Yoholo would not permit the McIntosh faction to participate in the negotiations, but on the day after the signing they signed a separate document agreeing to the provisions of the Washington treaty.[60]

In consideration for the cession, which had to be vacated by 1 January 1827, the United States agreed to pay $217,600 (plus $30,000 stipulated in the supplemental article), a $20,000 perpetual annuity, and compensation for the improvements abandoned by the refugees. Additionally, "the United States agree[d] to guarantee to the Creeks all the country, not herein ceded, to which they have a just claim, and to make good to them any losses they may incur in consequence of the illegal conduct of any citizen of the United States within the Creek country." This promise, coupled with the statement in Article 1 that "the Treaty concluded at the Indian Springs . . . is hereby declared to be null and void, to every intent and purpose whatsoever; and every right and claim arising from the same is hereby cancelled and surrendered," saved the land in Alabama and reaffirmed the obligation of the United States to defend the territorial integrity of the Nation and protect the Creek people from the crimes of U.S. citizens.[61]

In giving up the river boundary, the Creek representatives violated the instructions and repeated communications of the Council and, with good reason, feared the public response to their act when they returned home. There was an additional reason for them to be uneasy when they reported to the Council. The article in the new treaty that provided for an initial payment of $217,600 did not stipulate how the money should be distributed. Shortly after the treaty was signed, the Cherokee secretaries brought a paper to McKenney which listed several names and a sum of money to be paid to each. Ridge and Vann were marked for $15,000; Major Ridge, John's father, was to receive $10,000; Opothle Yoholo, Little Prince, Tuskeneah, Menawa, and several more headmen a like amount; and fourteen others were promised sums ranging from two hundred dollars to $6,000. When pressed to explain themselves, the Cherokees said it was the Creeks' business how the money was to be spent, and the War Department agreed that "it was their own affair." Thus, of the $217,600 purchase money, $159,700 went to twenty-four men, three of whom were Cherokees.[62]

It is difficult to interpret properly this arrangement. John Ridge and David Vann probably deserved whatever they received as payment for their services rendered in Washington. Ridge, particularly, rescued the negotiations at their point of collapse and engineered the compromise which won abrogation of the Treaty of Indian Springs and saved the Alabama cession. Most of the Creeks slated to receive funds were headmen who had various traditional obligations that were expensive. They were expected, for example, to help support indigent townsmen in times of need.[63] On the other hand, Opothle Yoholo, Little Prince, Tuskeneah, Charles Cornells, John Stedham, the three Cherokees, and others listed were acquisitive. All were owners of plantations, slaves, ferries, taverns, or similar properties that distinguished them as "wealthy." In later years, Opothle Yoholo was widely reputed to be the richest man in the Nation. The only apparent justification for the payment to Major Ridge, except that he was the father of John, was that he was the Cherokee ambassador to the Creek Nation and a respected member of the Council.[64]

Several irate senators, particularly those from "Indian states" who feared the precedent of abrogating an illegal treaty, bitterly denounced the payment schedule of the Treaty of Washington as a "work of great bribery" and a "fraud." With a show of moral outrage, and some hypocrisy, these defenders of the McIntosh document included in the appropriation bill enacted to fund the Washington treaty a provision which required that the money be distributed publicly before the National Council. Congress's effort to "balk the fraud of the corrupt distribution" failed, however, except that John Ridge and David Vann received only five thousand dollars of the sum promised.

With some murmuring, the Council paid the other grants.[65]

Though far from a clear and untarnished victory, the Creeks gained a great deal by the Treaty of Washington. Secretary of State Henry Clay, who agreed, thought the Creeks had made a better bargain than had Barbour. The new treaty, he announced, was "much more disadvantageous . . . to the United States than the former."[66] Official recognition of the right of the National Council to nullify the Treaty of Indian Springs was worth almost any price. No native nation had ever before persuaded the United States to tear up a ratified treaty, and none would ever succeed again. In addition, the Creeks won back their lands in Alabama, complete with renewed federal guarantees of protection from encroachment. The price had been high—the cession of the lands in Georgia—but Governor Troup and his fellow citizens had demonstrated quite forcibly how much higher the cost would have been if the Creeks had continued to defy Georgia's expansion. Adams told the Senate that the Treaty of Washington was the best deal he could get; Opothle Yoholo made the same report to the Council.

6
CREEK REMOVAL
FROM GEORGIA, 1826–27

THE TREATY OF WASHINGTON failed to end the trouble between the Creeks and Georgia. Nearly two hundred thousand acres of land remained in Creek hands within Georgia. While state forces, abetted by the Adams administration, demanded the surrender of this property, the Creeks continued the process begun during the previous few years of strengthening the National Council. With a renewed resolve to preserve their remaining territory intact, the headmen moved further down the road toward a centralized government, heaping added power on Opothle Yoholo and listening more intently to their Cherokee advisers. The adamance of Creek resistance, coupled with the intransigence of Georgia's governor George M. Troup, brought on a national civil crisis that one federal official called more "pregnant with threatened evil" than any "since the formation of our Government."[1]

During the negotiations in Washington, President John Quincy Adams's chief fears were of Georgia's response to a treaty that perhaps failed to acquire the last acre of Creek land in the state. In the hope of appeasing Troup, the administration considered offering him Crowell's head. Even though Major Andrews's elaborate investigation of Troup's charges had ended with an enthusiastic exoneration of the "innocent but . . . much injured" agent, Crowell remained a thorn in the governor's skin. Barbour explained the need for a "sacrifice" and promised that if Crowell resigned, he would write a letter "which should guard [his] fame." But Crowell refused to go quietly, and the administration dropped the scheme.[2]

When President Adams submitted the new treaty to the Senate

for ratification, he had good reason to expect trouble from the irascible governor. Troup's official line was that it was unconstitutional to abrogate a treaty. No new instrument could supersede one already ratified and proclaimed, he insisted, and the Treaty of Indian Springs must therefore stand as the "supreme law of the land." Underscoring this position, the Georgia legislature had directed him "to carry the Treaty into full effect according to its stipulations." As the state's chief executive, Troup claimed, he had no choice but to obey. Furthermore, the governor did not trust the new treaty. Because it described a bounded tract of land, it was uncertain if all the Creek country in Georgia had been acquired. That could not be known until the Georgia-Alabama line was surveyed. Troup suspected, however, that the new treaty would not prove as beneficial to Georgia. Outraged by the prospect that the treaty he had worked so hard to complete might be thrown out as a fraud, his fury at losing face and some land, no matter how little, was complete. "I have decided," he declared, "never to receive from the United States one square foot less than the entire country within the limits of Georgia."[3]

Troup was in a strong position from which to rail at the federal government and its executive leadership. The first popular election for governor of Georgia occurred in November 1825, and Troup won. The margin of victory was narrow, 20,545 votes to 19,862, but the triumph over the governor's archrival, John Clark, was still sweet. It was also a highly personal conquest—the Clark supporters carried the lower house of the legislature. The paramount issues of the campaign were Troup's handling of the Creek crisis and his policies toward Major Andrews, General Gaines, and the federal government. His victory at the polls seemed to vindicate those policies. With such a mandate, Troup was in no mood to be patient or conciliatory with his enemies.[4] Although the policy of both Adams and Troup was to remove the Creeks from Georgia as quickly as possible, the summer of 1826 began with all the elements in place for another collision between the United States and the state of Georgia.

During the summer of 1825, Troup had refused to abide by the provisions of the Treaty of Indian Springs and would not wait until September 1826 to survey the cession. Now, in the spring of 1826, declaring that the Treaty of Washington was invalid, he decided to insist upon the terms of the abrogated Treaty of Indian Springs and claim occupation of the cession on 1 September. The issue had passed beyond the stage of electoral necessity and had become, to the governor's satisfaction, a question of principle. States' rights and the integrity of the general assembly were at stake.[5]

In anticipation of the 1 September deadline, Troup issued a proclamation on 24 July ordering all "Sectional Surveyors" to meet in Milledgeville on 14 August to prepare for their task. As the time drew near, the Creeks still living on the cession became frightened. Already, "white people were . . . stealing their horses, hogs, and black cattle; turning Indian families out of their houses and taking possession before they can save their crops." With such encroachment occurring before the survey had begun, the Council greatly feared what would happen after the entry of the surveyors. At "that moment," Crowell predicted, "many of the citizens of Georgia, and frequently her worst citizens too, [will] feel themselves authorised, not only to explore the country, but to locate themselves, to the great annoyance of the Indians." The only peaceful redress open to the Creeks was to appeal, through the agent and any other person willing to write a letter, to the War Department. If those petitions were to go unanswered, Crowell warned, the peace of the country would be in jeopardy. The Creeks would not stand idly by and watch the suffering of their women and children, and Troup had mobilized the militia along the border to protect the surveyors. The danger was real, wrote one amanuensis, for "blood and carnage."[6] Troup responded to the problem by issuing a proclamation prohibiting intrusion into the "vacant territory" of the state and threatening legal action against those violating his order, but he would not admit to a connection between the encroachment of private citizens and the entry of surveyors under his orders. There would be no alteration of his timetable.[7]

Anxious to prevent open conflict on the Creek-Georgia frontier, the Adams administration began to put pressure on both sides. Writing to Troup, Secretary Barbour explained that the Treaty of Washington was a part of the "Supreme law of the land," the 1 January 1827 deadline for removing the Creeks was inviolable, thus the president "expected that Georgia will desist from any further prosecution of the proposed Survey." On the same day, expecting a negative reply from Troup, Barbour ordered Crowell to "reconcile the Indians to the wishes of Georgia." After all, he pointed out, there were only four months until they would have to remove anyway, so what purpose could be served by "insist[ing] on a literal execution—so as to keep up an unpleasant collision with Georgia. . . . Impress upon them," Barbour continued, "the President will be gratified in their acquiescence in this measure—by which they will have furnished a fresh claim to his kind protection which, in whatever is essential to their interests and rights he will with pleasure dispense to them."[8]

In the response to the uproar following McIntosh's execution, the

National Council had retrenched to a position of relative passivity. They had followed the guidance of the seemingly friendly Gaines and had exchanged the doomed land in Georgia for a reaffirmation of title to the Nation's holdings in Alabama. The Treaty of Washington promised federal protection in the act of removal, however, and in this, it seemed, the headmen were to be disappointed. From Crowell, Gaines, Barbour, and Adams, the Creeks learned in 1826 that they could expect little more than words to stand between them and the Georgians. With no choice but to surrender for the moment, the Council did as Barbour demanded and withdrew its objections to Troup's early survey.[9] At the same time, however, the Council continued its transformation, under the leadership primarily of Opothle Yoholo, to a revivified governing body for the Nation.

In this effort, and probably at the urging of Opothle Yoholo, the Council turned for advice to John Ridge. The Cherokee had to be present at the August 1826 Council in any case if he were to receive payment for his services in Washington. During the discussions over how the purchase money was to be divided, several of the headmen became angry at the size of the individual grants and, for a moment, considered dismissing Opothle Yoholo as speaker. Crowell reported that he saved him, but more likely it was Ridge. The agent's standing among the Creeks was low, but Ridge's reputation increased as he reported on the negotiation and the effort Crowell made to persuade the delegates to abandon the Chattahoochee line and cede the whole country in Georgia. This news, taken in conjunction with the recent evidence that Crowell could not (some thought would not) act effectively to protect their borders, further damaged the agent's image. By November the Upper Towns were "under the immediate guardianship of John Ridge," and Crowell had to confess, "I can't control them until his meddling can be checked."[10]

Crowell did not describe the situation accurately. The Upper Towns were not under Ridge's control. He and Opothle Yoholo were close friends. Ridge was glad to serve as an adviser, and because he was both an Indian and literate, he was highly useful to the Council in its dealings with representatives of the federal government. Furthermore, the Creeks and Cherokees had for several years enjoyed a friendly relationship. Since 1814 the two nations, surrounded by states, were isolated from contact with other Native people. And the Creeks had watched with increasing interest the changes occurring in the Cherokee Nation that were designed to strengthen its hold on its sovereignty and territory. Both nations faced the same problems of pressure from squatters and state and federal demands that they remove. The Cherokees had a tighter governmental organization and highly educated leaders; the Creeks had a large annuity income. Together, they were much stronger than they were alone.[11] But the Cherokees were a long way from having control over the Creeks. Crowell watched this harmony develop and either misunderstood or misstated what he saw. It was not a case of Ridge gaining control, but rather that the agent simply was losing his influence to a rejuvenated Creek national will.

Two things were happening in 1826 and 1827 that the Creeks resented. Surveyors and citizens from Georgia were ranging through their country, disrupting and often displacing the people, and agents of the government were trying to recruit people to move west. The Council found both these activities intolerable and, with the aid of periodic Cherokee advice and cooperation, moved to stop them.

With armed resistence essentially no longer an option (although isolated acts of violence did occur as Creek warriors eliminated particularly obnoxious squatters), the only apparent solution to the problem posed by surveyors and intruders was to improve contacts with Washington. To that end the Council demanded the removal of Agent Crowell, whom they considered incompetent. He "will not do any thing for us, we want [an Agent] sent to us that will take care of us, and not suffer us intruded on as we have been by this one." John Ridge became involved in this decision when the Council asked his help in sending the letter to Secretary Barbour, but there is no evidence to support the suspicion of the War Department that the Cherokee engineered the request.[12]

Until the War Department could act, however, Crowell was the only source of federal protection available, and the Creeks needed him. West of the eastern boundary of the Creek Nation established by the Treaty of Washington lay 192,000 acres still in Georgia. Arguing that the intent of the treaty was to acquire all the Creek land in the state, just as the Treaty of Indian Springs had done, Troup decided that this tiny tract would have been included in the cession if the negotiators had known of it and therefore it rightly belonged to Georgia. The fact that it had not been purchased from the Creeks was irrelevant, and acting on this logic, the governor sent his surveyors in to mark it off.[13] Enraged, the Council demanded from Crowell a letter ordering the surveyors to "desist from stretching a chain over any of our lands, not ceded by the . . . Treaty." "Eight or ten lusty fellows" carried the warning, signed by Little Prince, into the various surveyors' camps and succeeded in persuading the men to stop their work and withdraw across the boundary. The surveyors reported to Troup, who recognized Crowell's handwriting on Little Prince's order and concluded, as was his wont, that the agent was the "prime mover and instigator" of the incident. The governor fumed over the "indignities and insults" heaped upon the officers of Georgia by the "subaltern Agent" and demanded that he be punished.[14]

While Troup spluttered, the Council turned its attention to the government program to recruit migrants to the West. David Brearley received federal appointment as recruiter 13 May 1826, but at that time the assumption was that he would carry off just the McIntosh people. Because Alabama was also interested in Creek removal, however, his duties were expanded to include efforts designed to move as many Creeks as possible from the Nation. The most likely candidates for removal were those who had to move from the cession in Georgia, but no one was exempt from his blandishments. The Cherokees had faced this problem before, as groups of their people had moved west during the previous twenty years. This piecemeal migration had elicited a claim from the United States for a cession in the East equal in size to the region granted the emigrants, and in 1817 the Cherokees had been forced, on the basis of this argument, to cede two large tracts of their eastern country. Learning from the Cherokees' experience, and no doubt also realizing that their strength depended on their large numbers, the Creek headmen, both unofficially and with the force of Council action, tried to discourage emigration. Law menders threw obstructions in Brearley's way, threatened people thought to be considering enrolling for removal, beat up those who had enrolled, and generally terrorized those Creeks who looked with favor on the idea of fleeing the East. Brearley responded with a corps of hired agitators and increased the level of his activity, but it was never enough to persuade many Creeks to move west. Indeed, there is a self-serving quality to Brearley's complaints, which suggests that the most potent factor obstructing his success may have been not so much the terrorism of the law menders and as the general unwillingness of many Creeks to leave.[15]

As the Council worked to define its policies of response to these new pressures, it became increasingly clear that both in structure and personnel the government of the Nation required an overhaul. While the Council was not prepared to embrace the Cherokee form of centralization, it did realize that some tightening and strengthening would be necessary if the Nation were to survive its time of crisis. The first step was to depose Tuskeneah. For reasons not entirely clear (he was "appointed by the influence of a few and not in the order known to the Nation"), the Council had chosen him to fill the position vacated by the death of Big Warrior, his father, and it had been a mistake. Tuskeneah, charged the headmen, was "incompetent to sustain the responsible duties of his office. . . . His conduct has been distinguished for selfish ignorance, boyish caprice and Jealousy, void of prudence and capacity to fulfill the duties of his station." More likely, however, he stood in the way of Opothle Yoholo. In his place the Council chose two headmen, Nehathlucco Hopoie and Coosa Tustunuggee, who were to divide the responsibilities of leading the Upper Towns. They were charged to

> love the children of other families as their own, . . . be as father to all & equally love them & not exalt a few to exercise power & rule & hold secret consultations among themselves. Business hereafter must be done openly & justly in full Council or by persons lawfully appointed by the assembled Chiefs in Council.

Whereas this is a good description of the responsibilities of Creek headmen, neither man had been prominent in Creek public affairs, and one suspects that their chief qualification was their deference to the powerful speaker. Opothle Yoholo, appointed "prime minister or Chief Councillor of the Nation," received Talsee Fixico and Tusconah Coochee as aides. This was an important modification of the Council, but it should be understood within its context. The only act which was unprecedented was the replacement of Tuskeneah by two kings. By itself, the deposition of a leader was by no means unusual. Appointing Opothle Yoholo as prime minister was no more unique—only the title was strange. As a recognition of a man who had risen above his station, Opothle Yoholo's designation as prime minister is reminiscent of Alexander McGillivray's position as Great Beloved Man.

The headmen also recognized John Ridge as an adviser and member of the Council. Government officials, learning to fear and hate Ridge as an uncontrollable Indian patriot, pointed to this as proof of his domination of the Creeks. But his father, as representative from the Cherokees, had sat on the Creek Council for years, and William McIntosh, until he betrayed his trust, had occupied a similar position on the Cherokee Council.[16]

There was no evil genius at work in this reorganization—rather, it was one further step in the adaptation of Creek political form to meet new and unexplored conditions. By placing increasing reliance upon Opothle Yoholo, the Council was, if anything, returning to the centralist movement begun forty years before by McGillivray. But any action that suggested an increase in the ability of the Creeks to chart their own course and resist the dominance of their public affairs by the United States was bound to meet concerted federal opposition. In this case, the reorganization that had taken place came to be defined in Washington as a conspiracy by John Ridge and his Creek dupes, primarily Opothle Yoholo, to gain control of the Council, steal the annuity income, destroy the influence of Agent Crowell, and prevent Governor Troup from acquiring the remaining sliver of Creek land in Georgia.[17]

Maintaining a momentary silence on the reorganization of the Creek government, however, the Adams cabinet united behind the president's determination to defend the territorial rights of the Creeks. Barbour informed Troup that his illegal entry and attempted survey of the unceded tract was a "disturbance of the public tranquility. . . . Charged by the constitution with the execution of the laws," the secretary warned, "the President will feel himself compelled to employ if necessary all the means under his control" to protect the Creeks from Troup's illegal survey. This veiled threat of military action received strong support from Secretary of State Henry Clay, who "urged the necessity of protecting the rights of the Indians by force." But Adams hoped "The civil process will be adequate to the purpose." To that end Barbour ordered the United States attorney and marshal of Georgia to arrest and prosecute under the 1802 Trade and Intercourse Act all surveyors found in the Creek Nation. Lieutenant John R. Vinton, aide-de-camp to the commanding general of the army, carried the letters to Milledgeville and Savannah. Troup interpreted Adams's warning, carried by an army officer, as a "military . . . menace" and mobilized two divisions of the state militia. At the same time, he ordered the state attorney and solicitor general to release any surveyors arrested by federal authorities. The United States had rarely been so close to constitutional disaster.[18]

Few appreciated the severity of the crisis more fully than President Adams. On 5 February 1827 he sent a message to Congress ("the most momentous . . . I ever sent") describing his actions and the reasons for so acting and asked the legislators for their collective view. He was authorized by previous legislation, he pointed out, to use troops to oust the surveyors and to order their arrest and trial. He decided not to use troops because the surveyors were officials of Georgia and the legislature of that state had ordered them into Creek country. It was also clear that federal forces would be greeted by militia, and Adams was anxious to avoid civil war. Still, the president hastened to add, the governor and the assembly of Georgia were acting in violation of federal law, the president's oath of office required him to enforce that law, and if the Georgians persisted in their illegal acts, "the arm of military force will be resorted to." This prospect was unprecedented, Adams reminded the legislators, and much to be deplored, but unless the laws were changed he would do his duty.[19]

The president had one further course of action that could avert civil bloodshed in Georgia. For the past two years he had desired to remove the Creeks from Georgia, and he had hoped that the Treaty of Washington had provided for that removal. One more cession from the harried Indians could accomplish that goal and at the same time erase all the difficulties with Governor Troup. Thus, when Lieutenant Vinton set off for Georgia, he also carried orders to Agent Crowell

> to adopt such mode, as may seem in your discretion to be best, to obtain their consent to relinquish their hold upon those pine barrens which can be of no value to them; and thus secure that state of quiet which it is so much the desire of the Executive to realize.[20]

The agent could hardly have received these instructions at a worse time. Confused by the Council changes and intimidated by Ridge, he was also distrusted and unwelcome in the Nation, and at no time in his career was his influence with the Creeks lower. Indeed, Barbour changed Vinton's orders to include an investigation of the Council's charges against the agent and a report on his effectiveness. Expecting the worst, Barbour also ordered the young lieutenant to open separate talks with the headmen regarding a cession. In his conversations with Little Prince and other Council kings, Vinton was told that the trouble with Georgia over the surveyors was too critical and they preferred to wait for a quieter time to change agents. The headmen, for the time being, withdrew their demand that he be dismissed. They also refused to consider selling more land for Georgia.[21]

Although "it's a subject . . . upon which they are verry sensative," Crowell did his best to persuade the headmen to sell the last parcel of land in Georgia. He talked for two days at the meeting of the Council in March 1827, and succeeded in winning a grudging promise to send a delegation to the tract in question to look it over. Crowell was lucky to get that concession. The headmen had interrupted his harangue at its beginning to make "a positive refusal" to sell anything.[22]

On the eve of the proposed excursion, and perhaps anticipating a negative result, Crowell hatched a scheme to intimidate the Creeks into parting with the sliver of land. Not only had Georgia surveyed the tract, he told the headmen, she had also occupied it, and "the President would not take up arms against his own people, to protect the Indians in a matter of so little importance to them." Since they had already lost the country, they owed it to their Great Father to give up their claims to it. If they refused, he would not protect them again. Crowell asked Barbour to send an official document corroborating the threat, and the War Department sent two. The documents did not clearly state that the government would refuse to help the Creeks defend their territory, as Crowell had hoped, but President Adams did point out that if the United States "should . . . find it necessary to interfere for the protection of the Indians in their possession of [the tract], they must inevitably be the sufferers in the end." Barbour contented himself with a recounting of all the good things the president had already done for the Creeks and concluded with the expectation that, in return, they would "cheerfully agree to a cession of this small and worthless strip of land, and thus evince their respect for his wishes, and give a new proof of their claims upon him for the exercise of his future kindness."[23]

The absence of a hard-hitting threat from Washington probably made no difference because the inspection tour became a fiasco when the Upper Town party declined at the last minute to make the trip. Crowell thought the excursion had persuaded the Lower Town leaders to sell, however, and he called a meeting of the National Council while they might still be amenable. After a lengthy speech in which the agent "used all possible arguments to induce them to give up the land," Little Prince replied, uncharacteristically, by letter. "You know that we have no land to spare," he reminded the agent indignantly. "You know that we have been selling our land to our father the president until we have but little left. . . . You know that we are very thickly settled. . . . We cannot comply with the talk of our father because we have no land to Spare." Refusing to accept the Council's answer, the frustrated Crowell continued his harangue until the headmen were compelled to adjourn the session "in a disorderly manner" to escape him, "expressing very angry feelings towards" their agent as they stalked from the square ground.[24]

The headmen did not break up the Council without renewing their demand for Crowell's dismissal. Lieutenant Vinton, they claimed, had received a biased report on Crowell from the agent's official interpreter and close friend who "did not give a right construction to our words." Not only was their agent incompetent, the headmen charged, he was also dishonestly and illegally involved in his brother's store and tavern at the Fort Mitchell agency. And he should be replaced by a man who came from a state north of Virginia. The headmen wanted no more southerners meddling in their affairs.[25]

Although Crowell was willing to admit that the Creeks were disgusted by his persistent demands for a cession, he preferred to lay the blame for his failures on John Ridge and David Vann. Ridge had been in Tuckabatchee when the Upper Town leaders decided to forego the jaunt into Georgia, and that was enough to convince the agent that Ridge's "advice and interfearance" had kept them away. More significantly, Vann had written Little Prince's letter of refusal to sell. "Sanguine of success" at the outset, "the views of the government" were defeated by the Cherokees, Crowell was convinced. "Unless the Government should feel disposed by some means to destroy their interfearance, it will be difficult if not impossible to obtain the cession." Adding insult to injury, the agent also charged the two with "very indecorous and Impudent remarks and conduct in relation to yourself [which has] lessened that habitual respect and veneration which the Nation have always heretofore entertained for the high functionaries of the U. States Government." Having raised the ire of Secretary Barbour with that rumor, Crowell suggested a way, using another rumor, by which the two young men might be brought down. "Some of the Chiefs of the Cherokee Nation have said . . . that the conduct of Ridge and Vann in relation to Creek affairs, did not meet the approbation of their own Nation and that their main object among the Creeks was self agrandisment." Barbour soon learned of the falsity of the latter story when the Cherokee National Council ignored his threat that the "tranquility and happiness" of the Cherokees would be "seriously affect[ed]" if they did not stifle Ridge and Vann immediately.[26]

More threats followed in quick succession. Barbour wrote to Little Prince that if the Creeks refused to sell the parcel, there would be more trouble with Georgia, and this time the United States would do them no "favors." Crowell, preferring the more direct approach, asked (unsuccessfully) for two companies of troops. Citing as a reason his fear that trouble would erupt over the unwillingness of the Council to pay the McIntosh people twenty thousand dollars in damages for losses suffered at the time of the execution, he also added that soldiers would "enable me more effectually to carry into effect the views of the Government, in relation to Creek affairs."[27]

Unwilling to give up, Crowell tried again in July, and again he believed he had the Lower Town headmen convinced when in marched John Ridge with the Upper Town councillors. "I dispared of success," the agent moaned, "and my apprehentions were well founded." The Council drafted a letter to Secretary Barbour not only again refusing to sell but demanding that he not ask another time. This "insolent" document, Crowell reported, was in Ridge's hand. He must "be disposed of."[28]

Throughout the summer of 1827, the National Council successfully frustrated the wishes of Georgia and the United States. An absolutely determined and strengthened Creek government fully exercised the right implied by the treaty system to refuse to treat, and in so doing presented the United States with an unexpected problem. Removal—the Adams administration policy—was supposed to progress smoothly and easily. Since the execution of McIntosh the Creeks had shown their refusal to be cheated, but the abrogation of the Treaty of Indian Springs, the president thought, had renewed their faith in him and his wishes. Such stubborn resistance for a small piece of "worthless" land could only mean conspiracy, and Crowell encouraged that view with every report from the agency. By ignoring the decision of the headmen to recognize Ridge as a fully authorized participant and member of the Council, the agent helped to perpetuate the belief in the War Department that it was the evil genius of the "meddling" young Cherokee behind Creek inflexibility.

Ridge's old friend, Thomas L. McKenney, head of the Indian Office, ended a six-month swing through Indian country in the Creek Nation. Kept informed along the way of the Council's every act, McKenney carried orders to buy "the disputed tract." He arrived in the Nation in late October 1827 and found what he called "a contest for power" between the Upper and Lower Towns. Little Prince and the Lower Creeks were reputedly angry at the deposition of Tuskeneah by the Upper Creeks. The Lower Town headmen were also "unanimous" in their willingness to sell the small tract, whereas their Upper Town counterparts, though generally opposed, appeared to be divided.

McKenney met informally with most of the Creek leaders, including Opothle Yoholo, and all agreed to sell. They could not act, however, without a formal convening of the Council. Opothle Yoholo called the Council to meet at Tuckabatchee, and fifteen hundred people came, but not Opothle Yoholo, the presiding officer. Several days later, Opothle Yoholo finally arrived with Ridge and Vann in tow. McKenney was disgusted by the delay in the negotiations. He claimed that the Creeks had agreed in Washington to give up all their land in Georgia and had received money for the cession. It was only an accident that the small tract of "pine barren" was left, and Troup's claim to that land was technically correct. The president was so generous, however, that he was willing to pay again just so the Creeks would know that they had not been cheated. It was a specious argument, and not true in its essential fact, but McKenney hoped to play on the Creeks' sense of justice and make them feel guilty for having tried so hard to protect their territory. If they accepted his interpretation, they would more likely resist Ridge's advice to stand firm. McKenney knew the Council decision had to be unanimous, and with Ridge present he feared the worst.[29]

McKenney's fears were realized.

> The two educated Cherokees . . . were much esteemed by [Opothle Yoholo], who probably expected through them . . . to protect himself from any artifice that might be practiced in the phraseology of the treaty . . . while

they used their advantage . . . to thwart the design of government, and keep alive the existing agitation.

Even before the Council met formally the word was out that it would refuse McKenney's demands. In order to save the day, McKenney decided he had to destroy Ridge's influence—something Crowell had been demanding for months. He remembered that eighteen months before, during the negotiation of the Treaty of Washington, Opothle Yoholo had sent him a letter written by Ridge asking if the Creeks

> have . . . the power as a Nation to control all monies due us and paid over to us, from the United States, and if so, have we the right to appoint a board and a Treasurer to receive the money . . . and appropriate it in such a manner as we in our Legislative Capacity think will be best adapted to promote the general good of our people?

It was a gamble, McKenney later admitted, but guessing that Opothle Yoholo and Ridge were still planning to erect a treasury department, he accused them of conspiring to organize the Creek Nation into a constitutional republic like that of the Cherokees with Ridge as secretary of the treasury. Although McKenney's accusation had been a stab in the dark, Opothle Yoholo's reaction convinced McKenney that he had guessed right. In a tirade against Ridge, McKenney charged that he, a foreigner, planned to use Creek money for his own or for Cherokee purposes. Opothle Yoholo said to his interpreter, "Tell him he talks too much," but McKenney continued. "The effect was electrical," he recalled, and Opothle Yoholo "saw that his life hung upon a thread." Having dropped his bombshell, McKenney stalked out of the square ground before Ridge or Opothle Yoholo could respond, saying he was off to tell Little Prince the story.[30]

Little Prince responded even more favorably than McKenney had hoped. He ordered Ridge and Vann expelled from the Nation and announced he would kill them if they returned. The headmen also agreed to sign McKenney's treaty.[31] Drawn at the agency 15 November 1827, the Treaty of Fort Mitchell severed the Creeks' claim to "all the remaining lands" in Georgia. They received $27,491 plus $15,000 in goods, school tuition money, and improvements.[32]

The action of Little Prince was quite extraordinary. In agreeing to the treaty, he defied the will, stated repeatedly, of the National Council. The document was not to be considered binding until ratified by the Council, thereby protecting the lives of Little Prince and the five headmen who signed it, but it was nevertheless an act of daring. It is not clear what his reasons were. Opothle Yoholo's rise to power, probably over the objections of the deposed Tuskeneah, may have alarmed the aged headman. Little Prince had opposed Alexander McGillivray in the 1780s and '90s, and he may have seen in Opothle Yoholo's political schemes the same kinds of tampering with traditional form that had turned him against the Great Beloved Man. Little Prince may also have believed that Ridge and Vann were becoming too influential and that Creek national interest was being submerged to serve some unaccountable Cherokee purpose. Reportedly senile, he may simply have been irrational.

Little Prince's support of the treaty did not make its approval by the Council automatic. Opothle Yoholo boycotted the ratification session and tried to prevent others from attending. "Enough of those that were competent to make treaties did attend," Crowell assured Barbour, but it took the whole of Little Prince's considerable influence, "presents," five thousand dollars more purchase money, and a rewriting of the table of expenditures (to exclude horse mills) before enough headmen ratified Little Prince's fait accompli to make it legitimate. Opothle Yoholo never did concur.[33]

The Treaty of Fort Mitchell cut the last tie that bound the Creeks to Georgia. Governor Troup had fulfilled his ambition to expel them from his state. And President Adams, although he would have done it differently, agreed with Georgia that the removal of the Creeks was just and proper and in the best interests of all concerned. The expulsion from Georgia was a milestone in the history of the continuing Creek experience of retrenchment and retreat. In less than a century after the arrival of General Oglethorpe and the first Savannah settlers, the balance of power had been reversed, absolutely and catastrophically, and no part of Georgia remained Creek. But even in crisis the Council grew as a dynamic institution. Experimenting with new forms and concepts of government, the headmen struggled to gather together and concentrate in their hands what remained of the Nation's power. Taking a chance on centralization and the vigorous leadership of Opothle Yoholo, its "Prime Minister," the Council prepared for the fight to survive in Alabama.

UPPER CREEK LANDS
IN ALABAMA

N

COOSA R.

CHATTAHOOCHEE R.

St. Clair Co.

Shelby Co.

Abihka

TALLAPOOSA R.

Abortive Cession 1825

Autauga Co.

Broken Arrow

Columbus

Coweta

Tuckabatchee

Cusseta

Montgomery

Fort Mitchel

Montgomery Co.

COOSA R.

Pike Co.

Clayton

Eufaula (Irwinton)

0   20   40 miles

ADAPTED FROM ROYCE, INDIAN LAND CESSIONS IN THE U.S.

7
ALABAMA INTERLUDE,
1827–36

AT THE END of 1827, the Creek Nation had been reduced to a five-million-acre tract within boundaries claimed by the state of Alabama. The ancient seat of the Upper Creeks, the region became a place of refuge for the people of the Lower Towns uprooted from their homes in Georgia. As they relocated across the Chattahoochee onto Upper Creek lands, many Lower Creeks found solace, if not comfort, in the reality of nationhood. Beyond the ties of their clans, their identities had been linked to their towns, which were autonomous within the Confederacy. For most, the concept of nation had been too ambiguous to have much meaning. They now discovered, however, that they had the right, as Creeks, to a new home in the lands of people they knew only within a national context. Not even bound by a shared language, the only thing tangible they had in common was the National Council, where their headmen met. It now fell to the Council to protect them.

Under the terms of the treaties of Washington and Fort Mitchell, all Creek association with the region claimed by Georgia legally ended. The Washington document required the abandonment of most of the Georgia cession on or before 1 January 1827; the Fort Mitchell instrument presumed an immediate surrender of the remaining tract. Ancient ties of sentiment and economic dependence could not be so easily broken, however, and for the remaining years of the 1820s there was a continuous movement of Native people back and forth across the Chattahoochee. Some were tardy emigrants, others waited to collect compensation for the improvements they had made to their homes and fields. More were hungry refugees who returned to familiar hunting and fishing sites, food caches, or the farms and stores of recent settlers and looked for food or plunder that could be traded for food.

Exacerbating the problem, the Alabama portion of the Nation, containing two-thirds of the twenty thousand Creeks, could not readily absorb the seven thousand refugees who came in 1827. Fields could not be prepared quickly enough to feed the influx of people, many of whom arrived "in the most miserable and wretched condition it is possible to conceive. Many of them Skeletons and their bones almost worn through the skin."[1]

In their bitterness, some sought the blood of Georgians to avenge the suffering of their people. There were many on the Georgia side of the river who richly deserved whatever injury the Creeks caused. Unprincipled men opened stores and saloons from which they dispensed shoddy and worthless goods and whiskey at outrageous prices. In conjunction with Solomon Betton, a Georgian appointed by the president to appraise the home improvements left behind by the displaced persons, at least one hastily organized firm began nefarious speculation in compensation claims, which cheated hundreds of Creeks of several thousand dollars.[2] And this speculation scheme was only one small scene on the large canvas of dishonesty and corruption.

Conditions did not improve and conflicts continued. "A large group of Creeks, armed, are in Lee County," complained Georgia governor John Forsyth, Troup's successor, in late 1827. Crowell could not prevent the Indians from crossing the Chattahoochee, the National Council was not equipped to control the movements of its people, and persons lost their lives, both Georgians and Creeks. Forsyth demanded federal protection, and the Creeks sought food. The Council and the agent were unable to satisfy either. In March 1828, Crowell received permission to buy provisions on credit against the anticipated congressional appropriation to fund the Treaty of Fort Mitchell, but even that was a stopgap measure, and the Nation paid the bill. At the end of 1828 the Georgia legislature enacted a law prohibiting Creeks from crossing the Chattahoochee without a permit issued by the agent; so supplied they could remain no longer than ten days. But Governor Forsyth did not believe such legislation was the proper answer to Georgia's problem of having Creeks for neighbors. He really wanted soldiers stationed at the Fort Mitchell agency to patrol the border. For a variety of reasons, including a desire to mollify Forsyth and stop Creek expeditions into Georgia, the War Department agreed and drew orders for a company of infantry to be transferred there.[3]

Few disagreed, however, that the final solution was removal to the

West. The interest of the Adams administration in removal, inherited from its predecessors, reached a peak during the winter of 1827–28. The crescendo of emigrationist enthusiasm visible in the War Department during those months was largely the result of the western tour of Thomas L. McKenney. That excursion influenced enormously the thinking of those in Washington responsible for making and administering Indian policy, primarily because it produced, in the highest levels of government, someone who had actually been among the Indians. McKenney returned tremendously impressed with "the ignorance and weakness of the Creeks," their "poverty and distress . . . and . . . habitual drunkenness," and their inability to recover from their "long train of miseries, *whilst they retain their present relation to the States*. Humanity and justice unite," he cried, "in calling loudly upon the Government, as a parent, promptly to interfere and save them." This meant finding the Creeks a "last home, . . . providing suitable means and support for their transportation; and taking them kindly, but *firmly,* by the hand, and telling them *they must go and enjoy it."* There were, he went on, those within the Nation who opposed such a plan. These individuals, both Creeks and their foreign advisers, must be made to realize that the policy of the government is "intended wholly to better their condition, its determination is final; and that no persons will be permitted, with impunity, to interfere in it." To make certain there was no misunderstanding, "a few troops only would be required."[4]

McKenney included every Anglo-American misconception about Indians in this document— Native depravity and incapacity, conspiratorial oppositon to humane federal policy, the government's right to determine the best interests of Indian people, and the necessity of the United States to save the "children" from themselves. He had held these views before, but having been among the Creeks, and other nations, McKenney spoke with enhanced authority. "I have seen, for myself, and therefore know," he announced. As a result, the removal concept took on a new air of respectability and, because of the actions of Georgia and Alabama, removal of the Creeks assumed a new urgency. "This policy applies in its fullest extent to the Creeks," McKenney wrote.[5] As the people and government of the state of Alabama seemed anxious to demonstrate, the Creeks were in the worst possible situation.

There was a large Native population within the boundaries claimed by Alabama, but until the mid–1820's her impatience for their removal did not equal that of Georgia. Alabama's non-Indian inhabitants, whose numbers were many fewer than Georgia's, did not press as vigorously against the tribal boundaries. Alabama's political life did not seem to require the flamboyant expansionism that George M. Troup pursued in Georgia. By the Treaty of Fort Jackson, Alabamians had acquired the vast central section of their state from the Creeks. And Alabama was a public-land state. Unlike Georgia, which as an old colony had a charter claim to her lands, Alabama was the creation of the federal government, and title to all Indian lands within her boundaries belonged to the United States. Therefore, while interested in Indian removal as an ultimate goal, Alabamians did not initially pursue it with the single-minded lust of the Georgians.

Still, Alabamians considered the emigration of their Indian neighbors a prerequisite to the future development of their state. The four major southeastern nations—Creeks and Cherokees on the east, Chickasaws and Choctaws on the west—owned perhaps as much as half the state. Of these nations, the Creeks held by far the largest tract—a rough semicircle in east-central Alabama totaling 5,128,000 acres.[6] The abortive Treaty of Indian Springs, by which the Creeks allegedly ceded their Georgia holdings, had also severed the Creeks' claim to roughly the northern two-thirds of their Alabama land. Alabamians welcomed the acquisition, but Governor Israel Pickens refused to cooperate with George Troup in Georgia's frantic effort to survey the cession before the date established for the withdrawal of the Indians. And when informed by General Gaines that the treaty was a fraud, Pickens asserted that his people "would not desire [the cession] on terms that would leave a stain on the national honour." Expressing continued interest in the removal of the Creeks from Alabama, Governor Pickens hoped "another effort may be made for negotiation for the whole of the Creek territory."[7]

During the winter of 1825-26, while the Creek delegation was in Washington negotiating a replacement for the fraudulent treaty, the Alabama legislature discussed the possible impact the revocation of the Treaty of Indian Springs might have on their state. Newly elected governor John Murphy addressed the legislators with a moderate, almost diffident, message on Indian affairs. He expressed no opinion about the honesty of the treaty but confined himself to a commmentary on the value to Alabama of the cession, if properly acquired. The bulk of the address was a plea for a federal policy of Indian removal based on honor and justice for both the states and the Indians. Murphy was painfully aware of the brewing crisis in Georgia and was anxious to avoid the development of a Troup-like spirit in his own government.

Murphy's speech was an interjection into a running debate on Alabama's relations with the Native people within her claimed limits.

Beginning in November 1824, the legislators had argued the question of extending the limits of neighboring counties into contiguous Indian country for the purpose of enforcing Alabama law upon Indian people. It was a lackadaisical debate that generally failed to proceed beyond a reading of the state constitution, which stipulated that land "only to which the Indian title shall have been extinguished" may be incorporated into a county.[8]

When the Alabama legislature met in November 1826, however, the Treaty of Indian Springs had been abrogated and the Treaty of Washington ratified. In the process, Alabama watched some three million acres of Creek land, ceded by the first treaty but guaranteed to the Creeks in the second, slip from her grasp. Governor Murphy, in announcing his chagrin at the loss, called attention to Alabama's "interests, as a third party, which have not been regularly set aside." Instead, without consultation, the United States and the Creek Indians took from Alabama the land they had previously given her. That, it seemed to Murphy, was not proper. "If any thing has been done irregularly; if our rights as a State have been informally passed upon, we owe to ourselves, as well as the Union, to take a temperate notice of it."[9]

The mood of the Alabama senate had gone beyond the point where "a temperate notice" would suffice. With one dissenting vote, that body passed a strong states' rights resolution which, among other things, announced that "the abrogation of the treaty of the Indian Springs . . . without the consent of the governments of Georgia and Alabama, parties in interest, was a high-handed exercise of federal power, and an infringement of the sovereign rights of said states."[10]

In this frame of mind, the Alabama legislators returned yet a third time in as many years to the question of extending the power of the state into the domain of the resident Native nations. The attitude of the legislature was that "no power known to the constitution could divest the state of the use and enjoyment of [the Creek cession] without the consent of its state Legislature, the proper organ of its State Sovereignty." Therefore, title to the three million acres in question had passed to Alabama, satisfying the obstructing provision of the state constitution, and the legislators possessed the power to assume control of the region. The proper method for taking such control was "to extend the civil and criminal jurisdiction of the state over the country acquired within its chartered limits by the treaty of the Indian Springs." The lawmakers did so by passing a bill extending the limits of Autauga County to embrace the erstwhile cession and activating the county's court system within the region. The law carried the proviso that no Indian would enjoy "any political or civil rights, other than those of protection under the laws of this state; and that the performance of no public duties, and the payment of no taxes, be required of the same."[11]

On 11 January 1827, Governor John Murphy signed into law two ominous pieces of legislation. One was the extension bill; the other forbade any Creek Indian from hunting, trapping, or fishing "within the settled limits of this State, or upon any lands in this State, to which the Indian title has been extinguished." Considering the language of the extension law, the second bill was obviously designed to apply in the Creek territory just attached to Autauga County. If enforced, this law would have worked tremendous adversity on the harried Creeks. Approximately seven thousand of them were moving from Georgia into Alabama, and as only some two million acres remained outside the jurisdiction of Alabama law, twenty thousand Creeks would be forced to subsist on a country capable of bearing a fraction of their number. The combined effects of those two laws could have been nothing less than catastrophic. Doomed to hardship, if not starvation, the Creeks would also have to contend with "many of the citizens of that State, [who] will feel themselves authorized by the [extension] law to occupy the lands within the limits prescribed by that act."[12]

The extension law of 1827 was only the beginning of a program of legislative persecution of the Creeks that continued throughout the next several years. In January 1828 the lawmakers extended the civil and criminal jurisdiction of St. Clair and Shelby counties into the area supposedly ceded by the Creeks in the Treaty of Indian Springs. This action was designed to ease the judicial burden imposed on the courts of Autauga County by the 1827 law. In January 1829 the legislators completed their work by extending the jurisdiction of Pike and Montgomery counties into the remaining Creek territory. This final step, no longer rationalized by appealing to the cession of the defunct Treaty of Indian Springs, made the entire Creek population in Alabama subject to the legislative whim of the state.

Dixon Hall Lewis, the house delegate from Montgomery County, wrote the report for the committee on the State of the Republic which recommended this bold step. He was a leader of the growing coterie of public men in Alabama who proclaimed the doctrine of nullification, and his report reflectd an extreme states' rights philosophy. Lewis asserted

locality is the proper measure of jurisdiction, and that its exercise depends more upon the place where than the subject upon which it is exercised. . . . All sovereign states have a right of jurisdiction over their entire chartered limits, and . . . this right does not depend on the class of subjects upon which it operates.

Developing an argument that was becoming increasingly persuasive in the South, Lewis asked:

> If Congress can invade the jurisdiction of a State, and in any way extend or abridge the rights of individuals, what is to prevent its interference with the slave population of the southern states? If it can say to the state of Alabama, that Indians cannot be citizens, it can by a similar exercise of municipal power within its limits, say that Negroes shall not be slaves.

The point was not, however, to incorporate Indians into Alabama's body politic.

> The great object of the proposed measure must be to bring about their removal. It is believed that when they shall discover that the state of Alabama is determined upon her sovereign rights, and when they see and feel some palpable act of legislation under the authority of the state, that their veneration for their own law and customs will induce them speedily to remove to that region of country west of the Mississippi, which the munificence of Congress has procured as more congenial with their pursuits, and affording more facilities to that extensive system of beneficence which the objects of humanity imperiously require.

Thus assured, the legislators approved the scheme.[13]

In January 1832, the lawmakers drafted and approved a bill with even broader provisions that brought the Cherokees as well as the Creeks under the authority of Alabama law. The bill exempted Indians from militia and jury duty, taxation, and road work. Within their counties of residence, they were to enjoy the privileges of white people in recording official documents, but their testimony in court was admissible only in suits involving other Indians. These exemptions and benefits were slight compensation for the serious inroads the Alabama legislators had made into the culture, national integrity, and political institutions of the Native people. The 1832 extension bill prohibited "all laws, usages, and customs" of the Creeks and Cherokees that violated "the constitution and laws of this state." The lawmakers also forbade "any Indian or Indians [to] meet in any council, assembly, or convention, and there make any law for said tribe, contrary to the laws and constitution of the state." While attempting to emasculate the Creek and Cherokee governments, the legislators kept open all possible avenues for further cessions of land. They provided that "it shall, at all times, be lawful for the chiefs and head-men, or any portion of any of the Indian tribes within this state, to meet any agent or commissioner of the United States, or this state, for any purpose whatever."[14]

Greatly alarmed, Agent Crowell sent Secretary Barbour copies of the laws of January 1827. The agent had called a meeting of the Creek headmen to explain the legislation, and he expected "serious difficulties" if Alabama attempted to enforce them. President Adams, on the other hand, seemed strangely unperturbed by the action of the Alabama legislature. He permitted a month to pass before his administration responded, and he acted then only when Georgia Senator Thomas Cobb demanded to know why the president had failed to denounce Alabama with the vigor he used against Georgia. The reason, Adams reported, was that the 1802 Trade and Intercourse Act prosecuted the deeds of "citizen[s] or other person[s]" and not the actions of the legislatures of the states. At Adams's request, Secretary Barbour wrote Governor John Murphy to assure him that the Adams administration had not the "slightest intention to interfere in any manner with the Legislative enactments" of his state. On the other hand, he hoped Alabama would not permit the execution of the acts in question "to conflict, in any manner with the laws of the Union which relate to Indian Affairs."[15]

While making no further statement on the extension of civil jurisdiction by Alabama over the Indians, the Adams government indicated by its actions that it had no interest in challenging that state's desire to continue on its course of legislative harassment. During 1827, the president was deeply involved with Troup and Georgia, and he no doubt wanted to avoid getting caught in an additional crisis with another state over the Indians. Therefore, the Adams administration simply intensified its efforts to secure the removal of the Creeks. McKenney's conviction, so passionately expressed in November, that their emigration was their only salvation, merely covered the government's political needs with a cloak of humanitarianism. This was the context in which the War Department's decision was made in the summer of 1828 to send troops to Fort Mitchell. Events demonstrated almost immediately upon their arrival that their purpose was not so much patrolling the Chattahoochee boundary as encouraging emigration.

Persuading the unwilling Creeks that it was in their interest to remove to the West was an almost impossible task. During 1827 recruiter David Brearley and Crowell's subagent, Thomas Triplett, worked incessantly to assemble a party of emigrants. When they left in November, the group numbered only 707 of the total 20,690 Creeks, and they were followers of William McIntosh who had been preparing to move for two years. Crowell did not take active part in the recruitment, "other duties having prevented my personal attendance," but it is unlikely that his participation would have increased the number.[16] The pains of living in Alabama had not yet become severe enough to drive the Creeks away.

But uncertainty and confusion reigned. Balanced against the natural reluctance of many Creeks to abandon their familiar surroundings and embark on a long and uncertain trip to a strange place was the view of others that "if we are to go we had better go soon."[17] And there were plenty of people, in and around the Nation, who were actively encouraging both attitudes.

Brearley, Triplett, and William Walker, son-in-law of Big Warrior and a former subagent under Crowell, were all paid to recruit, organize, and lead expeditions of emigrants west. There was money to be made in such an enterprise (salaries, supply and transport contracts), and there were people anxious to get a share by encouraging removal. Profits were available to others, however, if the Creeks did not move. With an annuity of $34,500,[18] the Council controlled one of the largest pools of cash in Alabama, and traders, whiskey sellers, speculators of various sorts, and contractors for agency supplies all had reasons to encourage the Creeks to remain where they were. Outside the range of these parasites sat the settlers of Alabama and Georgia, like vultures on a fence rail, waiting hungrily for the Nation to crumble so they could swoop down and claim the remains—the eastern extremity of the Alabama Black Belt.

The Cherokees also had an interest in Creek affairs. Linked together by geography and common enemies, the two nations seemed destined to survive or succumb in tandem. A weakening of the Creeks made the Cherokees more vulnerable to the demands that they, too, remove. In the name of self-defense, therefore, the Cherokees worked to keep the ties bound tightly. John Ridge, able to enter the Nation after Little Prince's death on 14 April 1828, continued to consult with Opothle Yoholo about stiffening the resolve of the Council. Opothle Yoholo welcomed the support.

But removal was the order of the government. Armed with legislative authorizations, money, arguments, and threats, a host of officials of all ranks and stations bribed, cajoled, bullied, and begged the Creeks to leave the East and move west. The general failure of those officers demanded explanation. Unwilling to accept as rational the decision of many Creeks to remain on their land, the government, once again found a charge of conspiracy a convenient excuse for failure. There was a better explanation.

In the Creek Confederacy, where the principle of town autonomy prevailed, the Council represented the towns. Headmen became councillors through recognition earned in their towns; they carried their sense of town identity to the Council sessions; they determined and administered national policies with an eye on town interests; and they depended on town support to enforce their decisions. The Council authorized the law menders, but they were appointed by and served within their towns. A national police force violated the concept of town autonomy, and the law menders were rarely used outside their towns. At moments of crisis, however, the Council claimed the power to intervene directly in local affairs. As Opothle Yoholo explained to General Gaines at Broken Arrow in late June 1825, the law that William McIntosh violated had a special provision stating, "If People of a particular town would not put the law in force, then other men of other towns should be appointed to do so."[19] None of the law menders who participated in the execution of McIntosh came from his town of Coweta. The execution, like the broken law it mended, was truly a national phenomenon, and it was that, as much as the uniqueness of the execution itself, which demonstrated the staggering signficance of the execution in Creek political history. That special provision in the law showed the readiness of the Council to act in the national interest as it defined it, even if it meant defying the principle of town autonomy.

The Council was an unlikely source of political innovation. Made up of the established political elite, it was more usually a bastion of conservatism. The last institution to seek change, the Council had long been one of the first to confront the pressures imposed from the outside to alter its philosophy of governing and adapt to Anglo-American principles. As the Council resisted those forces, it became increasingly reflective of a social system that was eroding and a population which was shrinking. In a very real sense the Council was in danger of losing its relevance to a growing number of people.

The root of the problem lay in the continuing cultural transformation of the Nation and the effect of that upon town organization. The assimilationist pressures, which were transforming the Lower Creeks more rapidly than the Upper Creeks, had several visible effects, one of which was the relative disintegration of town life among the Lower Creeks. People had drifted away from the tightly knit communities to establish farms, ranches, and plantations and to participate in the frontier market economy. Once scattered, these Lower Creeks lost some of the social cohesion that living closely together had provided, and they became more vulnerable to the undermining qualities of Anglo-American culture. It was a cyclical process, by no means complete, which was producing by the late 1820s a distinctive, almost hybrid, society. It was a society which, like many of its leaders, was genetically and culturally mixed. Town life among the Upper Creeks had not undergone so much of this structural breakdown. Relatively insulated from assimilationist pressures, the Upper Creeks had not been so drawn from their communities, and as their towns survived, the institutional defenses which shielded their people survived as well. As assimilation bred assimilation in the Lower Towns, traditionalism bred traditionalism in the Upper Towns.

Because the Council relied upon and drew its strength from the towns rather than directly from the people, its constituency shrank as the towns disintegrated. And because the Lower Towns were breaking apart more rapidly than the Upper Towns, the center of political power in the Nation became increasingly identified with the more conservative Upper Creeks. As this process continued, the Council became increasingly conservative, which widened the gap between its values and those of the less conservative Lower Creeks. A small but articulate group of missionized Upper Creeks augmented the number of assimilating Lower Creeks, and together they constituted a growing body of people who, with no way significantly to influence Council decisions, went their own way. Some were willing, even anxious, to emigrate. "We have been under difficulties in this nation for several years," explained John Davis, a young, full-blooded Tuckabatchee educated by the Reverend Lee Compere at the Baptists' Withington Mission.

> We see the whole nation is sinking gradually into destruction every day. Because the chiefs do not listen to the voice of the government and they try to walk in the old way—though they know we have no laws to prevent white people—when they are determined to enjure us.[20]

Many believed the Council could not protect the people. Exposed and vulnerable to the oppression of whites, some sought safety through escape. But every person who left weakened the Nation and encouraged its white enemies, both national and state, to try harder to remove them all. In the interests of national preservation the Council found itself experimenting with centralist innovations, and Council leaders turned to the Cherokees for inspiration and procedural advice. As it pursued its efforts to reunite the Nation, the Council ceased being merely irrelevant to the growing numbers of assimilating Creeks and instead became oppressive. For these people, escaping the Council became as important as escaping from Alabama, and removal under federal auspices with assurances that United States laws would govern them in the West became an increasingly attractive alternative. "There never was a time when the Indians apart from their chiefs were as willing as they now are to remove provided they could do so under proper security that the laws by which they would be governed would be in the hands of the U.S.," wrote Reverend Compere, an astute observer.

> But as I intimated to you those laws should be drawn up, fully and farely explained to them and the Indians should be most solemnly assured that the U.S. would see them put into execution. Such a course as this would meet with the most determined opposition from some of the present rulers, but notwithstanding all their opposition, the Indians generally being disgusted with their present system, if another and better were fairly recommended to them, it could not fail of drawing the Indians after it. You may carry the chiefs with your money, but the Indians you may take with your laws.[21]

Compere distorted the situation with his suggestion that this was a division between the headmen and the "Indians." Many, perhaps most Indians supported the Council position. It was not a class struggle between the rulers and the governed, but rather more a conflict between assimilating and traditional Creeks, or between those with and those without strong town ties. Before 1827, the breaking of those ties was primarily a Lower Creek phenomenon. The transformation of Lower Creeks into refugees in 1827 intensified the process as large numbers of individuals scattered throughout the Upper Creek country seeking new homes. The vastly accelerated disintegration of the Lower Creeks towns that accompanied the removal from Georgia continued during the unstable period of temporary residence in Alabama. Many Lower Towns simply never reorganized themselves during those years. Instead, Lower Creeks faced the pressures to go west alone or in small groups, and many decided to go on rather than dally. It was this decision which the National Council, under the influence of the Upper Creeks, resisted so bitterly.

The indecisive and "restless," caught between the pressures of both sides, might respond to the traditional mechanisms for producing conformity. For this purpose, there was nothing more powerful than the clans. Kinship ties cut across town boundaries and influenced personal behavior throughout the Nation. To organize and apply this power, "the Kings directed that the heads of the different families [clans] should meet and bind the families up against the emigration. The Tiger, the Wind, and the Potato families met" and "but 1 of the 25 or 30" people Walker had enrolled to remove "will now go."[22] The most assimilated, on the other hand, had substituted individualism for kinship obligations. The headmen tried other measures to persuade them.

> Every exertion is used by the chiefs and those under their influence to

prevent the people from emigrating. Chiefs had visited the camp and ap-
plyed every argument in their power to get them to return and not to go
—and have resorted to the creation of the most foul falshoods about the
country on the Arkensaw.[23]

And non-Creeks in the Nation known for their support of removal
were intimidated as well.

A host of complaints—beatings, stolen horses, burned houses, verbal harassment, rumors of a Council decision to kill all those who enrolled to remove, threats against "Indian countrymen" who worked for
Walker—all had their effect. Walker corresponded with members of
Alabama's congressional delegation, thus involving those with important political interests in the matter, and they put heavy pressure on
McKenney to send troops to the Nation. Crowell seconded their call.
"The chiefs of the upper Towns have, within the last twelve months,
been guilty of many disorderly acts, and, manifested a strong disposition to put at defiance the authorities of the Government, and it will
be impossible for me to control them, without the aid of a small military force."[24]

As the charges filled the air, the War Department, already predisposed to believe them all, responded with interest to the request for
troops. Governor Forsyth, demanding a patrol on his western border,
provided the perfect justification. But there was a second purpose for
sending troops to Fort Mitchell. In addition to guarding the Georgia
frontier, the soldiers would "produce an effect upon those who have
been active in their opposition to emigration" and, thereby, encourage
those of faint heart who were anxious to move west but afraid of the
Council. Troops might intimidate the officials of the Creek government into changing their policy on removal or, short of that, encourage
Creek individuals to defy the government of their Nation with promises of protection from Council efforts to enforce the law.[25]

Brearley objected to the location of troops at Fort Mitchell. The
"same secret influence" of the headmen had kept "many hundreds"
from the fall 1828 emigration party, he charged. Worse, the Council
"basely" announced that the soldiers were sent to protect the Creeks
from the Georgians. To break the opposition and show the Nation the
true role of the army, the troops should be stationed among the people.
There was no resistance to removal on the Chattahoochee. "It is from
the Upper Towns that we have been openly outraged and have the
greatest reason to expect insolence." Put them in Tuckabatchee,
Brearley urged Congressman Owen, where they could do the most
good.[26] President Adams approved the idea, the War Department assured Governor Forsyth that the soldiers would return if needed, and
the troops went to Tuckabatchee. Their commanding officer's orders

directed him "to refer to Col. D. Brearley agent for the emigrating Creeks as to the object in view, and to afford him every aid and facility within his control in carrying it into effect."[27]

Adams's decision to send the soldiers to Tuckabatchee reveals, perhaps more clearly than any other step taken by his administration, the extent of his commitment to removal. If the incursions of Indians into Georgia and the intrustion of squatters and herders into the Creek country was the real purpose for the troops, then Fort Mitchell was the logical place to station them. Situated on the Chattahoochee, Fort Mitchell was perfectly located to enable the army to patrol the border and prevent trouble between the Creeks and Georgia. But special agent Brearley reported that many headmen were terrorizing those Creeks willing to emigrate. Alabama congressmen repeated the accusation, and Adams sent the troops to Tuckabatchee.[28] It seems clear that the major reason to dispatch troops to Fort Mitchell was not to keep peace on the border but to intimidate the Creeks into emigrating. When the president discovered they would serve this purpose more effectively at Tuckabatchee, he immediately transferred them there.

Neither the War Department nor the president fully appreciated the gravity of the decision. Troops could, "with propriety," be stationed at Fort Mitchell because it was on the agency preserve and owned by the United States. In addition to its strategic location at the crossing of the Chattahoochee River, it was the only place in Creek country that belonged to the United States. On the other hand, ordering the troops to Tuckabatchee required that they must "march over, and occupy" Creek lands. Even more serious, Tuckabatchee was "the seat of their Councils, and in the midst of their people." In peacetime, ordering the occupation of an Indian capital was unprecedented. As McKenney dramatically stated:

> It has been; always, the policy of the Government, and its invariable practice, not even to enter the Indian Country with a compass and chains, much less with guns, . . . without first, getting the assent of the Indians. . . .It has . . . been a point always well guarded not to be, in a government capacity, the first aggressors on Indian lands, in *any form*— but above all not to irritate them by marching among them a military force, except in war.

Whether or not the Creeks would tolerate such an invasion, McKenney declined to speculate, but he raised important questions about the future relations between them and the United States. There were treaty provisions in force that were supposed to protect the Creeks from the occupation of their country by troops, and "how far they may consider the Treaties with them as binding after this act" was something the War Department now needed to consider. The tone of McKenney's letter is decidedly pessimistic. The Adams administration, in its anxiety to achieve removal and perhaps win votes from southern frontiersmen in the impending presidential election, had clearly taken a drastic step. This decision not only violated various treaty provisions, it set a dangerous precedent for using the threat of force in time of peace to win concessions from Indian nations. And it showed how little the United States respected the Creek right to self-government.[29]

The National Council met for ten days in October 1828 while the troops occupied Tuckabatchee. Tuskeneah, Opothle Yoholo (reputedly home sick with "billious fever"), and the invited Cherokee representatives did not attend. Brearley pressed charges of destruction and harassment against some of the headmen, but those accused satisfied Captain Philip Wager, commander of the soldiers, with their explanations, and he refused to arrest them. Thus cleared, the rump Council took care of a variety of housekeeping tasks, including the establishment of five blacksmith shops among the Upper Towns. The headmen also paid all the claims brought against them by whites, no matter how false, believing that whites would use any unsettled claims to justify driving them away. These various actions convinced the removal agents that "the emigration is over with the exception of a few more halfbreeds."[30]

Such news was ill-received in Washington where, in the early spring of 1829, the federal government intensified its efforts to remove the Creeks and the other southeastern Native people to the West. Andrew Jackson's electoral victory in November 1828 has generally been interpreted as, among other things, a southern mandate for Indian removal. John Eaton, an old friend from Franklin, Tennessee, was appointed Jackson's secretary of war. Together, Jackson and Eaton picked up where the Adams administration had left off, continuing the efforts to encourage emigration and win passage in Congress of a law to authorize and fund wholesale removal. Jackson had his own ideas, however, for hastening the process. Unlike Adams, who had bristled at Troup's interference with the administration of federal Indian policy in Georgia, Jackson defended and even encouraged states' efforts to drive their native residents away.

Alabama's technique of including the Indian territory and its people within state legal jurisdiction received Jackson's public blessing. In his first annual message, submitted to Congress 8 December 1829, President Jackson pointed out that several states had extended their laws covering the Indians. He argued that they had the constitutional right to do so and that the only option open to those Indians who did not want to live under the laws of those states was to move. Removal, he noted, had long been the policy of the United States, and as a means of hastening the process, Jackson urged upon Congress the efficacy of setting aside "an ample district west of the Mississippi" to receive the emigrants. The alternative had been, and would continue to be, tragedy.

> Surrounded by the whites with their arts of civilization, which by destroying the resources of the savage doom him to weakness and decay, the fate of the Mohegan, the Narragansett, and the Delaware is fast overtaking the Choctaw, the Cherokee, and the Creek. That this fate surely awaits them if they remain within the limits of the States does not admit of a doubt. Humanity and national honor demand that every effort should be made to avert so great a calamity.

It was too late, he argued, to worry about the injustice of past acts. The crisis was now, and it required a solution.[31]

President Jackson outlined what later became the reknowned Removal Bill, but for the several months before its passage in May 1830, he and his secretary of war were busily seeking removal under the system established by his predecessors. Within three weeks of his inauguration, Jackson outlined his policy in a letter to the Creeks. "My white children in Alabama have extended their law over your country," he wrote. "If you remain in it, you must be subject to that law." They could escape Alabama law, however, by moving beyond the Mississippi. There they would be free from troublesome whites to live as they pleased, under their own laws, and in the "care of your father, the President;" and the land would belong to the Creeks "as long as the grass grows or the water runs, in peace and plenty." These were the only alternatives he offered, however. Jackson would not protect the Creeks from Alabama.[32]

Alabama law as it was enforced in the Creek Nation was not an abstract problem. Almost immediately after the passage of the January 1829 extension act, Opothle Yoholo and Jim Boy, a prominent Upper Creek, received summons to appear before the Montgomery County Circuit Court to answer charges of "trespass (with force and arms)" and the destruction of property valued at $10,000. Jim Boy received another writ in relation to an alleged bad debt of $64.14½ owed Polley Brinton, and Opothle Yoholo was called to court on a debt of $2,325 claimed by David R. Mitchell. The two headmen argued, through their attorney, that the court lacked jurisdiction because the warrants were served in the Creek Nation, and the cases should be dismissed. The judge ruled the objections were made too late to be admitted, however, and heard the case. The outcome was a mistrial. The trespass case arose from a public whipping given James B. Reed, a white man. The judge refused to consider the question of jurisdiction and ordered the jury to decide only on the facts of the case. With no attempt made to deny the whipping, the court awarded Reed $4,500 in damages.[33]

Such judicial harassment of one of its most influential members strengthened the resolve of the National Council to accept neither of the president's alternatives. Instead, it demanded the third, "impossible," option. "Our country has and is still annoyed by the appearance of whitemen under the garb and character of agents, sub agents etc., persuading bribing and by all the arts of deception endeavor to get our people to go to that unhospitable clime, near the borders of the Rocky mountains." By the Treaty of Washington, the headmen reminded the president, "the Government of the United States *guaranteed* to the Creek Nation *forever* all the lands we now hold. . . . All we want we expect and all we desired is the *complete fulfilment* of that Treaty." The harassment they suffered, they argued, "is inconsistent, and contrary to the Treaty made at Washington and contrary to many promises made us by the officers of the Government of the United States, and contrary to the principles of free government which the United States so much boast of." Surely, the headmen protested, a treaty signed and ratified by both nations deserved to be honored and could not "be broken by the whim or caprice of any State Legislature." But that was exactly what had happened to the Treaty of Washington.

> The white People in the State of Alabama [are] so inimical and un-friendly to ourselves our interest and our future prosperity [that] they wish to drive us from our Land and our Houses by inacting laws extending the Jurisdiction of said State over the Creek Nation. To this *Measure we do most solemnly protest against* it, and we humbly call upon Your Excellency as the President of the United States, to interfere in our behalf, to put a stop to such unlawful measure.[34]

The letters written by Jackson and by the Creeks crossed in the mails. Despite their previous experience with the United States, the headmen were shocked to hear that the president would not help them resist Alabama's judicial encroachment. In their amazement they concluded that the message from Jackson was a forgery concocted by Crowell to make easier his continuing efforts to remove them. Once having accepted this premise, it was a natural step to believe that Alabama did not want the Creeks' land, that the extension of state jurisdiction was a trick, and that the United States would never permit the state to execute its laws in violation of the treaties. Certain Alabama swindlers who wished the Creeks to remain until they had lost their last dollar encouraged the Council in these beliefs. In response to Crowell's statements and explanations to the contrary, the Council enacted a law prescribing a public whipping for any Creek who expressed the intention to emigrate or advised another to do so and also renewed its demand that the War Department fire the agent.[35]

Throughout the summer of 1829, despite the stiffened resistance of the Council, Crowell continued the struggle to remove the Creeks. The small but persistent group of people who were willing to go encouraged his optimism, and he believed that with more troops to protect the volunteers from the headmen, the bulk of the Nation could be transported within a few years. Indeed, according to the agent, his most serious problem in attempting to remove the Creeks was his shortage of money. In April, he predicted that with one hundred thousand dollars he could lead four thousand to five thousand tribesmen west that fall. In May, Crowell believed he could "progress pretty well" with fifty thousand dollars. In June, the agent dispatched a party of some fourteen hundred emigrants, led by his brother Thomas, at a cost of twenty thousand dollars, and if he had had more funds, he claimed, the party would have been doubled. In October, Crowell announced that he had the names of two thousand more willing emigrants, given in secret to avoid punishment by the headmen, and if he could just have enough money he could lead out of Alabama over the next three years 80 percent of the remainder. The agent's glowing predictions seem optimistic and highly unlikely to be realized. He was completely serious, however, and self-confident enough to risk sarcasm in his reply to Secretary Eaton's failure to send the money. "On the subject of funds," Crowell complained, "I regret your having deferred acting upon it. I am required to keep you constantly advised of the progress I am making; in reply I have to remark that no progress can be made without funds." Crowell received the twenty thousand dollars spent by his brother to convey the fourteen hundred, but the massive sums he requested in the spring were simply unavailable and remained so until the passage in May 1830 of the Removal Bill.[36]

There remained a substantial number of people willing to emigrate. These were mostly Lower Creeks, and they enrolled despite the efforts of the Upper Creek–dominated National Council to stop them. And there was a danger that Upper Creeks might join them if conditions in the Nation did not improve. Fearful they could not "prevent their people from emigrating, unless the Government [took] measures to prevent the laws of Alabama from being executed in their country," the headmen agreed in Council on a course of action designed to make

Alabama's laws inoperative.[37] The provisions of the treaties between the Creek Nation and the United States seemed to provide adequate protections if they could be brought to bear. Unable to act alone, the Council decided to send a delegation to Washington to make a personal appeal to the president. If that failed, the delegates would petition Congress. The Cherokees were making similar arrangements, and the councils of the two nations hoped that through joint action they could appeal to the conscience of the government and gain relief.

The plan was a "secret." Crowell learned of it indirectly, only after the delegates had left for the Cherokee Nation. John Coffee, close friend of Jackson and a spy sent to encourage emigration, wrote that many of the Lower Creek leaders were also unaware of the scheme. He also reported the intent of the delegates to invite John Ridge to accompany them and be their adviser. This, Coffee announced, was proof that the Upper Creeks were "being influenced by the Cherokees," something "they had always before denied."[38]

McKenney, who thought he "broke" Ridge in 1827, was incensed by the "impudence" of the Creeks. The visit to Washington was unauthorized, the delegates were pledged to object to removal, not agree to it, and Ridge's presence reconfirmed in the War Department his reputation as a troublemaker and as the evil genius behind Indian resistance to federal policy. Adding to the government's inconvenience, the visitors came to Washington during the heated congressional debate on the removal bill. Articulate native opponents of the administration's measure would not improve its chances of passage. These reasons were enough to make the Jackson government reluctant to receive the delegates. If they could be forced to agree to a cession of the Alabama country and remove, Eaton should recognize them as legitimate, McKenney advised. On the other hand, if they came only to demand their rights, which seemed most probable, the War Department should withhold recognition, challenge their credibility, and create the public impression that they were only a handful of unrepresentative troublemakers. Either way, McKenney advised his inexperienced superior, the effect of the Creek delegation could be controlled.[39]

The delegates reached Washington in January 1830. Finding no justice in the Jackson administration, they submitted a formal petition to Congress. Dated 9 February 1830, it was a detailed recounting of the treaty relations between the Creek Nation and the United States, liberally quoting those provisions which guaranteed the protection of the unceded lands and unsurrendered rights of the Creeks and describing the "unprecedented attack upon [the] liberties [of the] nation, . . . in gross violation" of the treaties "by our neighbor, the State of Alabama." Alabama could claim no intent to protect the "life and property" of the Creek people. Rather, she was

> determined to grind down the hopes and subdue the spirits of the Indians, in the unequal government to which they are not accustomed, and to which they have not even devoted a thought, unless it was to anticipate the rigors of its plunder, or to drag our people to distant tribunals, to answer complaints, not before a jury of peers and vicinage, but before a jury of strangers, who speak a language as strange.

Despite such harassment, the Creeks pledged never to give

> Alabama an opportunity to excuse herself to the world, by any concession on their part, to the schemes she has adopted to expell us from our lands. Her grasping rapacity and tyranny must stand, as a monument to future generations, of wanton violation of laws respected by civil and barbarous nations!

In conclusion, the Creek delegates responded to Jackson's recent message on removal.

> The doctrine, that Indians are an erratic people, who have only run over lands of extensive bounds in pursuit of the chase, [and] are not therefore, justly entitled to the same, is inapplicable to our people, who have settled habitations in villages and towns. . . . We beg permission to be left, where your treaties have left us, in the enjoyment of rights as a separate people, and to be treated as unoffending, peaceable inhabitants of our own, and not a borrowed country.[40]

The Jackson government could hardly tolerate such a spirited and articulate attack on its policies. Turning to McKenney, it followed his lead in its counterattack. And McKenney, a loyal Calhoun supporter whom Jackson heartily mistrusted, served the president enthusiastically. As soon as the War Department realized it had no hope of controlling Opothle Yoholo and his comrades, it set out with care and deliberation to destroy their credibility.

The key to McKenney's scheme lay in the assertion of both Crowell and Coffee that the Lower Creek headmen had not known about the Council's plan and had no hand in drafting the delegates' instructions. This, to McKenney's satisfaction, made the delegation a "self created party." With evidence from the Nation, especially from the more cooperative Lower Creeks, that the delegates did not express their wishes, he could undercut their position and render them harmless.[41]

The Creek delegates carried several documents to Washington, all signed by the headmen of the Nation, including some of the Lower Creeks. In addition to containing demands for protection from Alabama law and intruders, the documents charged Agent Crowell with defrauding the Nation of several thousand dollars and urged his dismissal.[42] McKenney called this charge a "special evil" and produced a document signed by Crowell's foster son and interpreter, Paddy Carr, denying Creek opposition to the agent and charging that the bill of complaint against him was a forgery.[43] A second such disclaimer reached the War Department at the end of January with a packet of documents acquired by Brigadier General George M. Brooke, commanding officer at Fort Mitchell, and signed in his presence by Eneah Mico, Tuskeneah of Cusseta, and other Lower Creek headmen. They also claimed that their signatures on the letter of accusation were forged.[44] Then, on 1 February 1830, some Lower Creek headmen drafted a carefully worded and tightly reasoned rebuttal to the anti-Crowell petition of the delegates. Their defense of Crowell was half-hearted, but their opposition to Opothle Yoholo's alternative, Captain William Triplett, was sharp. They did not know him at all, but "we are well acquainted with his brother [Thomas Triplett, former subagent and emigration officer], and if that is any criterion by which to judge him, Lord forbid us from wishing his acquaintance."[45]

Such differences of opinion and alleged tampering with documents raised questions about the legitimacy of the other papers. Coffee relayed the rumor that on the document describing their powers the councillors had listed the delegates and signed their names but had left the middle of the page blank, to be filled by the Cherokees. If this were true, McKenney could prove his charge that the Council had not drawn the instructions and that the delegates did not represent the Creek Nation. Closer examination of that document showed, to McKenney's satisfaction, that the instructions were written in Ridge's hand. Discounting the possibility that he had written what the headmen had dictated, McKenney charged Ridge with inventing the whole affair to serve his own diabolical purposes. The proof lay in the absence of the signature of any "responsible name" as witness.[46]

McKenney recruited Crowell to help discredit the delegates. Opothle Yoholo and the others argued that they were in Washington by order of their government on official business. Crowell, who certainly knew better, reported that they had no government. "Civil government is unknown among [the Creeks]; they have what they call laws, and these are mostly executed in a summary and cruel manner."[47] With this testimony the administration could not only belittle the pretensions of the Creek delegates, it could denounce as "savage tyranny" the laws of the Council designed to stop the emigration of individual Creeks.

The conference between Eneah Mico, Tuskeneah of Cusseta, and other Lower Creek headmen and General Brooke produced several countervailing documents of significance. In addition to their pledge of friendship for Crowell, they drafted a second body of instructions to the delegates in Washington. Claiming to be the "head Chiefs of the Creek Nation in Council," they stripped Opothle Yoholo and two other delegates of their power to represent the Nation and denied the Cherokee advisers the right to speak for them. The Lower Creek headmen also restricted the delegates to a discussion of Alabama laws, which they agreed were offensive.[48]

Arguing that the Lower Creek headmen were superior to their Upper Creek counterparts, perhaps an honest error because Little Prince had outranked Big Warrior, McKenney grasped this document as final proof that the delegates were imposters. "The leading Chiefs, with the principal at their head," he crowed, had scuttled the troublemakers, reduced Opothle Yoholo to the role of observer, and silenced John Ridge. Despite the fact that these Lower Town headmen did not represent the council that sent the delegation to Washington, McKenney took positive pleasure in returning letters which carried the signatures of the two recalcitrants.[49]

The Creek delegation remained in Washington into the spring, waiting until the end of March for an official response from the executive office. It distressed the president, Eaton finally wrote, to see "his Muskhogue children separated from each other." They should be together in the West, "a united and happy people." In Alabama "it is impossible you can be happy."

> Look to your true condition. While you were in Georgia constant troubles and difficulties hung around you. The Indian knew not his home, for he could not tell how soon the white man would come to interrupt, and force him further back into the wilderness. . . . The same difficulty still exists, even to a greater extent than before, because the laws of the State are now extended over you, and your Great Father, has not the power to prevent it.

Things could only get worse, Eaton warned, and before long the president expected to see "the soil you occupy stained and fattened with the blood of his children." When that evil day occurs, "Will you appeal to your Great Father to afford protection? He will answer he cannot, because he has not the power! Will you unbury the tomahawk and go to battle? You are too weak and cannot do it." There was hope only in removal. "The President . . . feels that he is consulting your interest and happiness—nay more, your safety." In the West "the soil will be yours. . . . No white men will be there . . . to disturb the repose of your wigwams." The Jackson government left the Creeks no choice. "It is idle to console yourselves with the hope that Congress will interpose in your behalf," Eaton warned. "Congress has no power over the subject. Your Great Father has none. It belongs to the State in which your lands are situated, to regulate and to direct all affairs within her limits, and nothing can prevent it."

After this long and labored description of the desperate and hopeless position of the Creeks in Alabama, Eaton concluded with an attack on Creek national unity, disguised as a lesson in the civics of Jacksonian Democracy. Thinking of the "common Indians" groaning under the oppression of Council tyranny, the secretary demanded that the headmen repeal the law "you never should have made" that forbade individuals to sell Creek lands. "Leave the sentiments and opinions of every man, free to be directed as his judgment may suggest," Eaton lectured. "Your Great Father will not consent that any of his red children shall be maltreated, for exercising the freedom of speech which should belong to all men." In reducing the question of Creek national survival to a First-Amendment issue, Secretary Eaton betrayed a staggering insensitivity to the rightful aspirations of the Creeks. He revealed that he had no conception of the Creek Nation as a legitimate political entity or as a complex social unit. Discounting the federal obligations and responsibilities accumulated in many treaties and underscored by the Trade and Intercourse Acts, President Jackson's mouthpiece hid behind an antiquated definition of states' rights to harry the people from their homes. Compounding the insult, Eaton ended his letter with the offer of a cheap bribe. Send back to Washington delegates prepared to sign a removal treaty, he wrote, and they "will be received and treated with kindness—their expenses . . . paid, and everything of liberality extended." And to those who hoped to be rid of Crowell, Eaton offered the emigrating Nation the agent of their choice.[50]

The headmen received Eaton's letter in Council, heard it, and appointed a committee to reply. Undaunted by the secretary's words, they agreed that their will was unchanged. "Some of our people have gone," they answered, "but we do not wish to go but wish to be protected by our Great Father on our land. . . . We say to him as we said before that we do not wish to leave our Country." The same Council gave Crowell a strong vote of confidence, explaining that a few headmen opposed him, only because he urged removal, and they were encouraged by "a few designing . . . White men" who wanted his job. Most had perfect confidence in Crowell and hoped he would be retained.[51]

While Opothle Yoholo and the others were in Washington, a crisis occurred at home. On 6 February 1830 Tuskeneah stopped the mail stage as it traveled the Federal Road through the Nation from Fort Mitchell to Montgomery. He held the driver and passengers at knife point, harangued them for crossing his land, and after thoroughly terrifying them, permitted them to continue on their way. The sheriff of Montgomery County, accompanied by two troops of Alabama cavalry, marched into the Nation to arrest Tuskeneah but failed to find him. Secretary Eaton then ordered the troops at Fort Mitchell to capture him and turn him over, along with any accomplices, to the United States marshal in Alabama. John Elliot, United States attorney for the Southern District of Alabama, prepared the indictment, charging Tuskeneah with a felony count of attempting to rob the United States mails and with two misdemeanor charges of obstructing the passage through the Creek Nation of the driver, Arnett S. Peters, and the mail. A "Counsel of professional respectability" defended Tuskeneah, who was found innocent of robbery, guilty of obstructing passage, and fined one hundred dollars. According to District Attorney Elliot, "The outrage . . . was greatly magnified and imbellished in the prevailing rumors which preceded his trial and conviction." On the other hand, "the prompt energetic and efficient" prosecution of the case had a sobering effect on the Creeks. They learned, Elliot reported, "that no office, dignity or station can or will shield such of them as may daringly violate the laws from summary and condign punishment." Had Tuskeneah's crime been ignored, his followers "would be disposed . . . to go and offend likewise."[52]

Elliot's interpretation of the effect of Tuskeneah's prosecution was somewhat self-serving. The Council had already found him an embarrassment. Before his trial, the headmen demoted Tuskeneah a second time and put in his place Eneahthlocco Hopoie (Little Doctor) of Tuckabatchee. The Upper Towns had wanted him to be their head chief for a long time, the Council informed President Jackson, and they now appointed him. There was no reference to the mail-stage incident.[53]

The strange career of Tuskeneah as head chief of the Upper Creeks is an important indicator of the extent of the confusion in Creek government during the late 1820s and early 1830s. While headmen rose and fell in the estimation of the Council, they rarely did so with such amazing speed. Tuskeneah's father, Big Warrior, had ruled the Upper Creeks for nearly two decades. Big Warrior's death in 1825 had left a leadership vacuum among the Upper Creeks which became fully apparent only in succeeding years. Opothle Yoholo's rise to prominence had depended on his relationship to Big Warrior. His death had catapulted the speaker into a more decisive role than his position warranted, and it took time for it all to become workable. That the problems of leadership occurred simultaneously with the unprecedented crisis of national survival only denied the Creeks the luxury of being able to afford a time for floundering. Had the National Council, increasingly dominated by the more conservative Upper Creeks, been spared the ongoing uncertainties of leadership, it might have succeeded better in reconciling the divisions within the Nation. And, in partnership with the Cherokees, the Creeks might have mounted a more united defense against the intrusions of Alabama.[54]

Eaton was correct, however, when he reminded the Creeks that they could no longer protect their country with the "tomahawk." Their only defense from the swindlers, peddlers, squatters, and adventurers who haunted their towns and staked out their lands was federal enforcement of their treaty guarantees. Alabama law and intruders were two halves of the same problem, and it was impossible to deal with one without attacking the other. Alabama jurisdiction meant county organization, officials, and taxpayers, and there was no way to permit all that and at the same time keep out intruders. If Alabama jurisdiction was legal, there was no such thing as intruders. But Eaton and others in Washington believed many whites in the Nation acted to obstruct Creek emigration. Rather than discriminate between those and "peaceful" squatters, the Jackson government acted contrary to the logic of its policy and tried to sweep the country clean of intruders.

Eaton responded to renewed Council demands for protection with the assurance that "your white brothers are not to molest, or interrupt, or intrude upon you. It is in the power of your Great Father thus far to maintain the laws, and to keep them away." Indeed, two months before, Eaton had ordered the troops at Fort Mitchell to evict all whites in the Creek Nation without either a permit or an Indian wife. Major Philip Wager, commanding officer of Fort Mitchell, issued a public proclamation giving those subject to ouster fifteen days to leave voluntarily. The "said proclamation," announced the Pike County grand jury, "has created [much] fear and confusion among the white settlers in that part of the County of Pike, once known as a part of the Creek Indian nation." Arguing that Pike's jurisdiction was legal under the 1829 Alabama extension law, the grand jurors declared that Wager's proclamation and the federal policy it represented were "against the laws, the peace and dignity of the State of Alabama."[55] With some justification, Pike County officials were a bit confused by this recent turn in federal policy.

Throughout 1830, Pike County remained a source of trouble for the Creeks. Desiring a link to the Chattahoochee and Georgia, the citizens of Pike sought and received permission from the Alabama legislature to cut a road to the river. Contracts were let, and construction began during the late summer. The Creeks were alarmed by the arrival of the crew "cutting and spoiling [our] lands by making a large Road." A delegation from the National Council appeared at Fort Mitchell while Major Wager was with most of his troops in the Cherokee Nation. Suspecting that any activity authorized by the state did not qualify as intrusion as defined by Secretary Eaton, acting commander Lieutenant F. D. Newcomb refused their request to remove the road builders. Unable to obtain satisfaction from the army, the Creeks sent a force of some four hundred warriors to the construction camp and chased the workers out of the Nation. The legislature considered mobilizing the militia to guard the roadmen but dropped the idea. Eaton commended Lieutenant Newcomb for his inaction, asserting that as the road was "within the limits of Alabama and authorized by an act of the Legislature of the State, there is no authority in the General Government to interfere."[56]

There can be no doubt that the Jackson administration was using the hardships imposed upon the Creeks by the intruders and the operation of Alabama law to force them into accepting removal to the West. In June 1830, thinking that enough time had elapsed to persuade the Indians to emigrate, the president and Secretary Eaton decided to meet delegations of the four major southern nations at Eaton's home in Franklin, Tennessee, and negotiate their removal. Notices went to the four agents, informing them of the plan and ordering them to promise their Indians very generous terms if they would agree to sell all their present holdings and emigrate. The Creeks refused to attend, and Jackson was furious. Eaton wrote Crowell, to be passed on to the Creeks,

> our Red brothers must now be contented to live under the laws of Alabama, & complain no more—they have made their election [by refusing to remove] and the President earnestly hopes that they may make good citizens & strictly conform to those ordinances of Government; which they have now voluntarily shown a disposition to live under.

To drive the point home, the secretary warned Crowell that Jackson was considering closing the Creek agency at the end of the year. He argued that its reason for existence ceased when the Creeks decided to become Alabama citizens.[57]

"Alabama citizenship," such as it was, brought the Creeks little but trouble. This, plus additional administrative torment, influenced the Lower Creeks to send a delegation to Washington. The major complaint remained intruders and Alabama law, confused by the unclear federal definition of which intruders merited eviction, but there were other problems demanding answers as well. In June 1830, for example, the Jackson government ordered that henceforth all annuities must be divided per capita rather than be paid in a lump sum to the headmen. The policy was designed to reduce the power of Native leaders and to prevent the establishment of tribal treasuries by such nations as the Cherokees, then preparing the Supreme Court case of *Cherokee Nation* v. *Georgia*. Creek headmen, in their role as dispensers of national aid to the sick and hungry, had incurred debts in their names to be paid from the annuity money. A change in the payment procedure would make them personally responsible for the costs. This danger was particularly threatening to the Lower Creek headmen, whose refugee people had required a great deal of help. Thus they sent Tuckabatchee Hadjo and Octeahchee Emathla to see the president, with instructions to petition Congress if the executive was unresponsive.[58]

The two Creek delegates addressed five written appeals to administration officials but could get no reply. Eaton was, he claimed, too busy to respond. S. S. Hamilton, a War Department clerk and McKenney's temporary successor in the Indian Office, charged that they had come to lend Creek support to the Cherokees in the Supreme Court and refused to meet with them. And Congress, holding a short session, had a full calendar and would not entertain their petition. The Upper Creek headmen heard a rumor that Tuckabatchee Hadjo and Octeahchee Emathla were instructed to sell the Nation. In a panic, they sent off another delegation to counter this effort and affirmed the death sentence for any who agreed to a cession. In Washington the Upper Creeks learned the truth about the Lower Creek delegation, and the two united in their frustration of the government's refusal to respond to their letters and petitions.[59]

After the delegates returned home, the Council continued to bombard Washington with requests for a response to their complaints. "Our aged Fathers and Mothers beseach us to remain upon the land that gave us birth, . . . [it] is health and plentifully rich for us to make a plenty." The western country, though reportedly fertile, had a bad reputation. Those who had already moved "cannot refrain from writing us [of] the unhealthiness of the country [and] the many deaths that have taken place amongst them. . . . From all that we have received, it is a graveyard." The Council was equally concerned about the number of deaths that had occurred in the East. "Murders already have taken place, both by the red, and the whites," and if the government did not stop the intruders soon, more would occur. There were Creeks who would defend themselves.[60]

Finally one of the oldest and most highly respected headmen appealed for help. "I have been a Chief for fifty five years," wrote Tuskeneah of Cusseta, and

> I have witnessed all the Treaties of my Nation with your Government since the Old British War. I have ever been the friend of the white man [and] I have never seen the necessity of complaining until now. [But] your white sons and daughters are moving into my country in a band, and are spoiling my lands and taking possession of the Red peoples improvements that they have made with their own labour. Contrary to the consent of the Nation. Your soldiers have refused to prevent it. This makes me sorry and have caused me to give you the talk Believing at the same time that you will not give a deaf ear to it. . . . These are the kind of characters that settle among us. They steal our property they swear to lies they make false accounts against us they sue us in your State courts for what we know nothing of the Laws that we are immeaneable to are in words that we have no possible means to understanding. . . . This fills my old head with trouble. . . . Such of your White citizens that intrude upon us are of your bad children, they have run away from your law they cant live with honest white people. And I dont want them among my Red children. . . . The Uchees a small part of our Tribe have in small parties crossed into the settlements of Georgia where game they believed more plenty. It is likely such of them, as did cross the line may have killed white people stock. The Whites have collected themselves in bodies and hunted up such as did cross into Georgia and shot them as if though they were deer. From the best information I can learn in the course of the three last months there has been seventeen Red people killed by the whites and nothing thought of more than if they had been so many wild hogs. . . . But yet such conduct is in your white sons. they drive there stock into our country they spoil our Range. they kill our hogs & cattle they kill your white children stock running in my country and lay it to my red children to have to bear the blame. . . . I shall endeavor to prevent the Red people from doing any thing that will offend you or my white neighbours. All I want is peace and be protected in what belongs to the Red people, and have been solemly guaranteed to them by your Government.[61]

Tuskeneah's pleas failed to rid his country of the plague of intruders. The National Council hired a white man, William Moor, to survey the extent of intrusion. He submitted a report in December 1831, after a "disagreeable tour of 25–30 days," that included the name, occupation, and place of settlement of 185 families. Moor estimated eight members per family, totalling 1,480 intruders. His list, however, was incomplete. He had been unable to cover the Creek territory thoroughly, and he had not enumerated

> another class much more numerous, who have only marked out situations they design occupying, by blazing and cutting initials on trees around tract. . . . If present Congress, or General Government, doesn't interfere in your behalf, your country will be entirely overrun, and all land fit for cultivation immediately occupied by this group.[62]

The year 1831 was one of special hardship. The torments caused by Alabama law shrank before the onslaught of starvation and smallpox. Hungry Creeks invaded Georgia begging for food. Crowell bought what he could get on credit, but frantic appeals to Washington were rebuffed. "Let a practice obtain for them," Eaton theorized, "that whenever hungry the Government will interpose, and then resting upon that expectation, they will make no exertions for their own relief." The United States had repeatedly offered to remove and provide for the Creeks in the West. They refused and had no just reason to complain if life was hard for them in the East. The president, Eaton pointed out, had given the Creeks every chance. The government, however, did more to fight smallpox. The post surgeon from Fort Mitchell spent from July to December vaccinating over seven thousand people, but many others died.[63]

Reeling from these special afflictions and continuing to suffer the harassment of unchecked intrusion into the Nation, the Council decided in December 1831 to send yet another delegation to Washington. Headed by Opothle Yoholo, the representatives trod a well-worn path as they tried, for the third consecutive year, to shake the Jackson government, gain enforcement of their treaty rights, and cleanse their country of the growing hordes of illegal aliens.

Secretary Lewis Cass, Eaton's replacement in the War Department gave them no satisfaction. They presented their memorial to Congress, and late in January they prepared to return to Alabama. The delegates had been deluged by demands to emigrate. Upon hearing Cass's adamant refusal to protect them and seeing Congress's unsympathetic response to their petition, they were disheartened. They had no authority from the National Council to treat for a full cession of their lands, but they had become convinced that the Creeks could no longer avoid it. John Brodnax, their "conductor," and one delegate planned to remain in Washington, the balance would return to consult with the Council. "Should they consider it best to do that which we feel unauthorized to do, our friend will be informed; and, through him, the particulars will be made known to [the Secretary]." Cass interpreted their decision as a breakthrough and ordered Crowell to confer with the saddened travellers the moment they returned. If they and the National Council recommended a negotiation, the agent was to hasten to Washington with three or four principal leaders to begin the talks.[64]

Crowell had anticipated the order and had broken the resistance of the lately reinstated Tuskeneah and Eneah Mico. They agreed to present to the Council a plan for selling the land in Alabama. The two kings resisted removal, however, and argued instead for reservations of land for each head of family in fee-simple title. "After six days' exertions and management," the Council agreed to send a second delegation to Washington "with ample instructions to enter into some arrangement with the government relative to their present situation."[65]

The enlarged delegation, in the company of Crowell, arrived in Washington by mid-March 1832. Immediately upon their arrival, the headmen submitted to Cass a detailed statement of the terms they would accept in a treaty. They demanded: the continuation of the agency under John Crowell; reservations of five sections to each head chief, two sections to each headman, one section to each head of family and to individuals without families, four reservations of two sections each for town houses, reservations for white men with Creek wives, the two-section agency preserve for Crowell, and one section on the Tallapoosa to include the mills built by Barrent Dubois; speedy survey of the cession so the reservations could be quickly located; protection for those who wished to sell their reservations; equal legal rights for Creeks in Alabama; compensation for damage done by intruders; the guaranteed right to continue "our old customs and laws in relation to our local and internal affairs;" compensation for the loss of ferries and causeways; tuition for educating Creek children; payment for blacksmiths; annuities paid to headmen; payment of all public and private debts; payment of several old claims for damages done by whites; pensions for a few select old headmen; compensation for the loss of the use of boundary rivers; and a general sum of money to be paid at ratification.[66]

This was a carefully thought out and detailed list of specifications designed to preserve the Nation essentially intact under increasingly impossible circumstances. Although it included Council recognition of the principle of severalty, the expectation that the reserves would be located in blocks would keep the towns intact, and with the provision for the maintenance of traditional local ways, things might change relatively little. The guarantee of legal equality would protect Creeks from the harassment of whites, and the generous financial arrangements would wipe away all debts and provide a useful income to the Nation. Most importantly, however, this design kept alive the political machinery of local Creek self-government for those who wished it. Flexibility, the tradition of Creek society, was built into the plan. Those highly assimilated individuals could pursue their interests on their reserves while traditional people could preserve their community values intact.

Cass would not accept the proposition. Primarily, the reserves were too large and too numerous. He and the delegates agreed to a compromise, however, and on 24 March 1832, the treaty was signed. Ninety headmen received reserves of one section, heads of families one-half sections. Locations were to include improvements if possible, if not they would be clustered in town blocks. Twenty sections were set aside for orphans. Grantees could not sell their reserves for five years without federal supervision and approval; after that time they were to receive fee-simple patents. The government agreed to expel intruders, but those who had not stolen the improvements of Creeks could delay their departure until after harvest. For compensation the United States stipulated to pay annuities totalling two hundred ten thousand dollars over twenty years, one hundred thousand dollars in cash at the time of ratification, and compensation for various lost improvements and properties and pensions for stipulated individuals. This was not a removal treaty, but the government stated its hope that the Creeks would sell their reserves and emigrate to the West. To encourage that decision the United States agreed to pay removal costs, subsistence for one year in the West, plus other material benefits. The government also "solemnly guaranteed to the Creek Indians" the Creek country west of the Mississippi, "nor shall any State or Territory ever have a right to pass laws for the government of such Indians, but they shall be allowed to govern themselves, so far as may be compatible with the general jurisdiction which Congress may think proper to exercise over them." In addition, the United States promised to "cause a patent or grant to be executed to the Creek tribe" for their western country.[67]

The Treaty of 1832 is one of the most important landmarks in the history of the Creek people. The last instrument signed while the Creeks were in Alabama, it marks the end of the recognized existence of the Nation in the East. To ensure that fact, the Jackson government closed the Fort Mitchell agency at the end of the year, leaving only a temporary caretaker subagent to conclude local affairs. Henceforth, most United States relations with the Creeks were conducted in Indian Territory.[68]

Most of the Creek people, however, remained in Alabama. Preparing to meet an uncertain future, they had to learn what the Council's solution meant for them. If all went according to plan, conditions could have improved substantially. The design submitted to Secretary Cass by Opothle Yoholo was sharply altered, but flexibility remained the characteristic. Emigration at government expense was one option, remaining as assimilated citizens another, continuing semi-traditional town life was a third. No totally traditional style was possible, however, because under the treaty terms the Nation sold its hunting country. Town-dwelling Creeks would have to embrace market agriculture if they remained in the East. This would threaten the customary social order somewhat, but the necessary adjustments could have been controlled and developed within the context of adaptation that had characterized Creek society during previous generations. The provision for paying future annuities as the Creeks had dictated meant that the money would continue to go to the headmen. There was no guarantee more important than this for securing the domestic role of the Council. Control of the national income kept the headmen in the center of local affairs and ensured that they would continue in their ancient duty of supervising the distribution of community assets. Once hunting and agricultural lands, these assets were now money and the goods it could buy, but the responsibilities of apportioning them remained, along with their political implications, the same.

The flaws in the document related to the legal protections the Creeks wanted for defense against Alabama. The United States agreed to protect the property rights of reservees until they received patents for their tracts, but there was no guarantee of legal equality in Alabama. The rights of Creeks in court, particularly as witnesses against whites, would depend on the Alabama legislature, and the extension law of 1832 denied Indians that right. Without it they remained vulnerable to fraudulent suits brought by unprincipled whites in the state and county courts. The treaty also failed to guarantee the right of the Creeks to local government according to "our old customs and laws." This shortcoming, coupled with the provision of the 1832 extension law which forbade "all laws, usages, and customs [of the Creeks] contrary to the constitution and laws" of Alabama, put much of Creek affairs under potential legal proscription and partially nullified the effect control of the annuity had on maintaining the Council. The full intent of the Alabama legislature is evident in the further provision in the 1832 act which forbade the Creeks to meet in Council to "make any law . . . contrary to the laws and constitution of this state." Such imprecision of definition left to the Alabama courts the final right to decide what actions of the Creeks were legal.[69]

There were many hazards in the treaty of 1832, but most were potential. If the United States had honestly fulfilled its obligations incurred by the treaty and properly defended the Creeks in situations where they could not protect themselves, the people might have had the opportunity to make a well-informed choice to remain or remove.

The Creeks put their faith in the treaty and in the willingness of the United States to enforce it. Considering their previous experience in such matters, one wonders why. The only apparent explanation is that the alternative to believing the unbelievable was to give up all hope of retaining their homes and emigrate. This continued to be an acceptable option for some, but for most Creeks it was intolerable— "they view a removal as the worst evil that can befall them."[70] With no independent power to prevent their ejection from Alabama, they had to depend on the United States and hope their faith would not be betrayed.

8
REMOVAL FROM ALABAMA

OF THE MANY GUARANTEES written into the Treaty of 1832, the promise most immediately important to most Creeks was contained in Article 5, wherein the United States agreed to expel intruders from the ceded tract. If the Creeks were free from the harassment of whites, they could quietly locate their reserves, sort out their lives, and decide how best to deal with their new status as individual landowners and citizens of Alabama. The failure of the United States to fulfill this provision set the stage for "the Creek frauds," the so-called Creek War of 1836, and removal.

Article 5 read, in part:

> All intruders upon the country hereby ceded shall be removed therefrom in the same manner as intruders may be removed by law from the public land until the country is surveyed, and the selections made; excepting however from this provision those white persons who have made their own improvements, and not expelled the Creeks from theirs. Such persons may remain 'till their crops are gathered.

The United States kept squatters off public land under the authority of an act passed 3 March 1807. Federal marshals executed the law with the aid of troops, if necessary.[1]

On 5 April 1832, the day after President Andrew Jackson proclaimed the Creek treaty, Secretary of War Lewis Cass directed Robert S. Crawford, United States marshal for the Southern District of Alabama, to enforce the stipulation of Article 5. That same day, Major General Alexander Macomb ordered Major Philip Wager, commanding officer at Fort Mitchell, to be ready to help Crawford expel intruders from the cession. Crawford immediately published a notice in three Alabama newspapers that warned all whites who had forcibly occupied Creek improvements to withdraw by 15 July and announced that those who had prepared their own fields would have to leave as soon as their crops were harvested. Failure to comply would result in eviction by the troops.[2]

It was clear, well before the middle of July, that there would be trouble with the illegal settlers, for it was difficult to define precisely just who was illegally settled. Crawford found a number of Alabamians living close to the boundary who had appropriated Creek fields for their own use but who did not actually live on site. Cass ordered the marshal to leave these people alone. They did not live in the cession and were thus "without the jurisdiction of the General Government."[3]

There were many others, however, who were unquestionably within Marshal Crawford's authority. And it was rapidly becoming important for the credibility of the United States that, regardless of his legal obligation, the marshal act with dispatch against those intruders. Other federal officials, busily trying to persuade the Creeks to sell their rights to allotted tracts and hasten west, were meeting a stone wall of mistrust and skepticism. "Nothing we can say will be believed," complained John Brodnax in July 1832. The Creeks

> can [not] be induced to believe but that they would, notwithstanding their exile from their ancient home, no matter to what realm they might be banished, or in what region settled, again be reduced to subservience to the (to them) odious trammels of the laws, and government of the white men. They can no longer be persuaded to repose confidence in our promises, nor to entertain a hope of the realization of the prospects we would hold out to them. A melancholy experience of the *past* has instilled into them the gloom of despair for the *future*. Neither effort nor pains have been spared . . . to remove from their minds such illusions; but we believe that time only and a continuation of conciliatory measures, can ultimately dispel them.[4]

Not even the spectacular destruction of Irwinton persuaded the Creeks that the promises in the treaty were not empty and that the assurances of self-determination in the West could be believed.

Within days of the expiration of the 15 July deadline the marshal and a company of soldiers from Fort Mitchell burned the town of Irwinton. Incorporated by the Alabama general assembly in 1830, Irwinton had been laid out on the Chattahoochee to compete for the commerce of the fertile Creek cession with Columbus, Georgia, situated further up the river. Steamboats plied the river, the population was growing rapidly, and the future seemed bright for the ambitious little town. Among other things, the troops burned a large, uncompleted cotton warehouse.

Irwinton had been built illegally on the site of the Lower Creek town of Eufala. Creeks had been forcibly evicted from their homes, their gardens and fields had been platted as the new commercial district, and roughnecks and hooligans had terrorized the people, stolen their possessions, and driven the Indians into the woods. Blatant violators of the terms of Article 5, the squatters at Irwinton were "some of the most lawless and uncouth men I have ever seen; some of them are refugees from the State of Georgia, and for whom rewards are offered." In reporting on the destruction of their unlawful town, Marshal Crawford explained, "Rough men require rough treatment." Secretary Cass agreed. "The Department receives the explanation of your proceedings as perfectly satisfactory," he assured Crawford, "and approves of the manner in which you have fulfilled the instructions of April 5th." It appeared, by the end of July, that the Jackson government meant business.[5]

As their buildings lay smoldering, the enraged residents of Irwinton turned for help to the authorities of Pike County. The grand jury issued a civil warrant and ordered the sheriff to serve it on Captain John Page, the commanding officer of the troops involved. The precedent for such action was well established in Alabama. Squatters frequently called on sympathetic grand juries and sheriffs in the counties created by the state in the Creek cession. County officers issued bundles of writs of trespass against Creeks who tried to reclaim their possessions after intruders were ousted, and they made several efforts to serve writs and processes against Marshal Crawford and the various military personnel stationed at Fort Mitchell who cooperated with him. According to Article 5, until the cession was surveyed and the Creeks had located their allotment, virtually every white person in the area was an intruder, including all the county officials so frantically issuing and serving writs. That designation also covered anyone who might sit on a jury if any of the charges came to trial. The chances of a fair trial were remote, and the marshal and the troops were understandably reluctant to be served. A private allegedly bayoneted the Pike County sheriff when he tried to arrest Captain Page after the burning of Irwinton.[6]

The town of Irwinton was reconstructed again almost as soon as Crawford turned his back. Wherever he and his squad of soldiers went, the result was the same. The old intruders returned or others came to take their place. In November 1832, Jeremiah Austill, Crawford's deputy, wrote, "It would require a volume to repeat the acts of cruelty and impositions imposed upon the Indians" by the "outlaws" who lived at Irwinton. "Fifty men would be sufficient to drive them all out, but it would take Five Hundred to keep them off." Troops in such numbers were not available. Crawford's bold stroke against Irwinton had proved ineffectual.[7]

Fear of intruders forced the National Council to convene in September 1832 at Witumpka, a Lower Creek town built at the falls of Yuchi Creek. This was not a normal meeting place for the Council, but Witumpka's location near Fort Mitchell and the military protection it afforded made it an increasingly popular site. There was a deluge of federal officials there—census takers, commissioners to oversee the selection of allotted reserves, commissioners to adjudicate claims against individual Creeks, and emigration agents. All of them, and Agent John Crowell as well, belabored the headmen with descriptions of the evils of life in Alabama, of the need for allottees to sell their rights to their reserves and remove, and of the benefits of life in the West free from the harrassments of whites. The Creek leaders were unimpressed. "We cannot help feeling somewhat surprised in receiving such a talk," the Council kings replied. "We are at a loss to know who could have given [the president] such information concerning our wish to sell out our land, and move west of the Mississippi State. . . . We are surrounded by speculators and enemies who are craving our lands," they acknowledged.

> Our country is crowded with the white people; we are oppressed by the laws of Alabama; we are prevented from building new houses; our lives are threatened by such as have moved among us, should we make selection of their improvements. [But] there is not a dissenting voice among us who wish either to sell or move west of the Mississippi. . . . If, upon experience, we ascertain we cannot live in peace, we will communicate to our father, the President, accordingly. Therefore, it will be useless for the Government to make any further propositions short of such a communication.

The Council stood by the treaty, declared its satisfaction with the provisions contained therein, and simply and stubbornly demanded its enforcement.[8]

There was little the Council could do to ease the burden of its people. Denied the essential attribute of independent self-government— the ability to protect its people—the Council was limited to complaining. "Our only alternative is protection from the United States," cried the headmen. The list of grievances was long. During the treaty negotiations in Washington, for example, Secretary Cass had promised that if the Creeks would permit intruders who made their own improvements to remain in the cession until their crops were harvested, the Indian allottees could then claim those improved lands as their reserves and enjoy the increased value of the property. That "was the inducement that caused [the delegates] to consent for such white people . . . to remain and gather their crops." But the intruders resented breaking and fencing fields only to hand them over to the Indians. "We are daily threatened for fear we should make choice of their improvement." Furthermore, the locating agents connived with the intruders by refusing to permit Creeks to claim them. "Instead of our situation being relieved [by the treaty] as anticipated, we are distressed in a ten fold manner."[9]

In addition, the cession was crawling with traders and whiskey peddlers who sold their wares at high prices on credit. For security, they induced their Creek customers to sign mortgages on their property. Enoch Parsons, one of the census takers, believed that the number of such Creek debtors was so large that

> whenever a party of Indians shall be ready to emigrate, bail writs, under the laws of Alabama, will be served upon almost every head of a family who may be of such a party, and the jails of Alabama will be full of Indians, or the Indians will have to surrender their reservations . . . and any other [property] they may possess which is of any value, to release themselves from custody; when perhaps the main or only consideration of such a claim . . . was whiskey.

"In the end," Parsons predicted, "the Government will be compelled to remove them, protected by an armed force, or to pay those unjust claims."[10]

As 1832 wore on to a close, conditions in the Creek cession only grew worse. The number of intruders steadily increased and their "treatment . . . to us you would hardly believe." As complaint followed complaint, promise piled upon promise. Officials in Washington paid lip service to Council demands and pretended to agree with the Council's interpretations of treaty provisions as well as the delegates' recollections of Cass's verbal assurances. In a steady stream of memoranda designed to placate the headmen, the War Department made a show of deference to the Council. Believing that pretense should suffice, exasperated bureaucrats then complained that "the multiplication and repetition of enquiries, which have been already so numerous and minute, [has made] the supervision of the execution of this treaty exceedingly difficult and troublesome." "Nothing improper will be intentionally done," Cass's clerk lectured Crowell, and the Council should believe that and "abstain from pressing complaints and enquiries upon the Department." But nothing changed in the cession. With no force of troops available that was large enough to keep intrusion in check, the number of illegal settlers rose daily.[11]

Secretary Cass had no other intention. While the Creek headmen deluged the War Department with complaints of mistreatment at the hands of the intruders, the intruders and their poliltical representatives bombarded the department with complaints of mistreatment at the hands of Marshal Crawford. And while Cass made promises to the Creeks that he had no plan to fulfill, he also made promises to Alabama politicians. "As little injury, as possible, should be inflicted upon our citizens," he assured Alabama senator Gabriel Moore. "No measures will be taken to remove the peaceable occupants" from the cession.[12]

At the same time, Secretary Cass complicated the political relations between the United States and the Creeks and reduced the effectiveness of their complaints by dismissing Agent Crowell and closing the agency at Fort Mitchell. This was a contingency authorized by the 1830 Removal Act, and the intent of Congress was to transfer agencies from the East to the West as the tribes emigrated. In this case, the Jackson administration made remaining in Alabama more inconvenient for the Creeks and added a further inducement for their removal. Unable to overlook their continued presence in the state, however, Cass appointed to the office of part-time Creek subagent Leonard Tarrant, an elderly Alabama politician who, as a member of the House Committee on Indian Affairs, had helped draft the various bills which extended Alabama law into Indian country. Clearly, no one in Washington expected Tarrant to represent the Creeks as vigorously or as capably as had John Crowell, an eleven-year veteran in the agency.[13]

Though hampered by Washington's duplicity and the absence of a proper force, Marshal Crawford and his deputy tried to respond to the most blatant outrages against the Creeks committed by illegal settlers. Hardeman Owens was one of the worst criminals. Recently appointed county commissioner of Roads and Revenue, Owens settled in Russell, one of the counties created by the Alabama legislature in the Creek cession. He forcibly occupied the farm of an Indian and busied himself at a variety of unsavory tasks. In addition to driving the owner from his house, Owens reportedly

> dispossessed . . . a young girl of another farm of 100 acres of valuable land, and broke her arm for complaining; and with others (among them a dentist), robbed the Indian graves—the dentist for the teeth, and Owens, for the silver ornaments and beads, which are always buried with the Indian dead, and these he afterwards sold in his shop.

Deputy Marshal Austill described him as "the most daring man I have ever met with, and one of the most dangerous." Responding to numerous complaints, the deputy ordered Owens from the cession, but he refused to leave. Austill left on other business but was brought back by several Creek men who said Owens had threatened them with a knife for having lodged a complaint against him. After arrest, Owens begged to be released, promising to leave the cession peacefully. Deputy Austill agreed and went on but was again stopped by Indians who said Owens had attacked them. This time, Austill returned with troops. Owens politely invited him into the house, but the Indians warned him that it was mined, and while the deputy stood in the front yard, the house blew up. Meanwhile, the infantry arrived and chased Owens into the outlying fields. The fugitive evaded his pursuers and returned to the remains of the house, vowing to kill Austill on sight. The deputy then sent another detachment after him. Caught and surrounded, Owens tried to shoot his way free but was himself killed by one of the privates.[14]

Hardeman Owens's death caused an outburst of fear and anxiety in the region. Worried that they might be next, angry squatters gathered together for armed defense, drafted resolutions to the governor and general assembly denouncing the murder, and appealed to the county court for help. That body issued warrants for the arrest of Deputy Austill, the commanding officer at Fort Mitchell, the officer commanding the detachment that shot Owens, and every soldier present.[15]

Owens's murder symbolized the developing conflict between Alabama and the United States over jurisdiction in the cession as well as over opposing interpretations of the law, the treaty, and the rights of Creeks and white Alabamians. Which intruders were peaceful and deserved to remain and which were not; what constituted a Creek improvement and how should it be protected; what standards of evidence should apply; what role should the Alabama court system play, if any, in determining Creek rights relative to whites; what authority did the marshals have; could soldiers of the United States Army legally be used to enforce the terms of the treaty? These and other questions of detail all flowed from the overriding issue of jurisdictions. In the era of George Troup, John C. Calhoun, and nullification, Alabama soon found itself the newest issue in the hottest national political debate of the antebellum period.[16]

While the debate raged overhead, the position of the Creeks continued to deteriorate. Alabamians, encouraged by the news that "peaceful" intrusion was acceptable to the Jackson administration and emboldened by the knowledge that there were not enough soldiers to make the expulsion of "illegal" squatters stick, became ever more insolent. Surveying the Creek cession took much longer than expected, unanticipated problems delayed the census, and the large number of questionable claims pressed by whites held up their settlement. One harvest season turned into two and December 1832, the presumed date when Creek allottees would claim their reserves, came and went. The most optimistic projection for the completion of the allotment became January 1834.[17]

For both the United States and Alabama, the route of escape from the immediate controversy lay in the removal of the Creeks to the West. Cass had always considered the removal articles the most important provisions of the treaty. Allotments, in his view, were little more than elaborate bribes to the headmen and families of the Nation. He expected the Creeks, once they had claimed the allotments, to sell to whites, pocket the money, and leave. No one expected the Creeks to remain in Alabama as independent landowning citizens of the state. Certainly Alabama had no plan to incorporate over fifteen thousand Creeks into its society.[18]

Most Creeks probably had no interest in becoming participating citizens of Alabama, but neither did they wish to leave. The Council's proposition for the 1832 treaty indicates a desire to retain traditional forms of town organization and government and probably de facto communal use of allotments grouped together. Some Natives, however, continued to prefer removal. Benjamin Marshall, a Coweta headman and close associate of William McIntosh, informed Secretary Cass, "A great majority of the Nation are disposed to take their reserves of land under the late treaty, and immediately to sell to private persons, and then without further delay to emigrate." If the government would send someone to organize the trek, a large party was ready to go, and as soon as the reserves were allotted and sold, "there will be more candidates for emigration than the Government can possibly carry at any one time." The "few of our chiefs and people who are opposed to emigrating" could not stop them. Indeed, "such will be the peculiar and embarrassed condition of the few who will remain, that in a short time, they too will follow their friends and countrymen."[19]

Cass was skeptical. The United States had spent a substantial amount of time and money trying to organize removal parties, but so few had been recruited that the effort had been abandoned. There was no advantage in removing small groups if the majority of Creeks remained behind. The cost was high and the problem of Indians resident in the states remained. Cass's advice was to be patient. If, after the reserves were allotted, the large numbers Marshall predicted really clamored to emigrate, then the government would arrange their removal. In the meantime, Cass would wait and see.[20]

In fact, Cass had a different plan. Not willing to remain passively waiting, his policy was to conclude yet another treaty with the Creeks. Commissioners began talking to the headmen about negotiating the sale of all the reserves and removing to the West as early as July 1832, but it was not until the summer of 1833 that Colonel J. J. Abert and Enoch Parsons made a concerted effort to win an agreement. They recited the usual litany of sufferings in Alabama and the blessings of the West, but the headmen refused to be swayed. "We are perfectly satisfied with the present treaty," they repeated, "if it had been carried into effect. We are not disposed to enter into any further treaty with the United States, and sincerely request the treaty already made [be] complied with." Abert and Parsons blamed the evil influence of speculators for their failure, and to a degree they were correct. Whites anxious to buy choice reserves at low prices admitted working to prevent the successful conclusion of a new treaty.[21]

But the self-interest of speculators was not the only or the most important reason for the failure of the talks. Something far more fundamental had happened to doom Cass's effort to negotiate a smooth and speedy removal of the Creeks from their Alabama reserves. The dramatic changes in Creek life which had begun before the removal from Georgia and had been accelerated by that event had proceeded with increased speed after the Treaty of 1832 and the allotment of the Nation. Enoch Parsons, one of the locators, described the most obvious aspect of this change. "They have no more land to sell as a Nation," he wrote in February 1833, "the whole of their land is now individual property."[22] Abert and Parsons were asking the Council, stripped of its ability to govern, to agree to the collective sale of several thousand privately owned tracts at an estimated average price. No government claimed such power, certainly not the Creek National Council. That the U.S. Government expected the Council to assume that authority reflects better the frantic anxiety of the United States to oust the Creeks rather than any intelligent assessment of the Council's past functions or its current impotence. Ironically, federal policy was thwarted by its own success. The people remained, but the Nation was gone. All that was left was "individual property" in the hands of people whose traditions, values, and cultural and economic heritage had not prepared them to conceive of such a thing. Most had not acquired enough of the cultural baggage of white America to enable them to deal with the concept of individual reserves intelligently. None had the political rights in Alabama to protect their property. Still, they understood that it was theirs and no one had the right to take it away.[23]

During the summer of 1833 the Creeks remained at home more or less, and the United States and Alabama geared up for the acrimonious constitutional debate that had been touched off by the killing of Hardeman Owens. The oppressions of Creeks by whites in the ceded region continued, but their effect was vastly more terrifying than it had been before because each individual faced them alone. Intruders drove people from their homes and terrorized them from their fields. Homeless and hungry, many simply scattered into the woods to subsist on whatever they could find. Few of the institutions of Creek society worked. Towns were disintegrating, and the National Council had deteriorated into a gathering of disillusioned men who occasionally met but who, as though paralyzed by some outrageous foreign disease, could do little. Helpless to fulfill their historic functions, some headmen fell to bickering over the disposition of the ninety sections earmarked for chiefs. Factionalism became irrelevant as individuals sold their reserves for a few dollars and melted into the forest. Speculators had a field day. Swindlers concocted fraudulent notes of indebtedness and won judgments in the newly created county courts that stripped hundreds of Creeks of their remaining possessions. Others, tortured and terrorized, simply dropped everything and fled.[24]

Scattered killings occurred throughout 1834 and 1835. Settlers killed isolated Creeks, Creeks killed isolated settlers. Most of the trouble occurred in the Chattahoochee valley and in western Georgia, and most of the Creeks involved were refugees from the Lower Towns. Their special grudge against Georgians was intensified during those years. Georgians dominated the land companies most deeply involved in the "Creek frauds," and the first allottees they swindled had lived on the Georgia border. As the initial victims, these Lower Creeks felt the humiliation of fraud and the sting of starvation long before the thieves made their way further west into the Upper towns.

At Tuckabatchee, Opothle Yoholo watched the swindlers approach his door. When a scheme hatched by a group of Montgomery speculators to send two hundred Creek families to Texas collapsed, Opothle Yoholo and the headmen of a half dozen related Upper Towns decided it was time to leave.

> Our people yet abhor the idea of leaving all that is dear to them—the graves of their relatives; but circumstances have changed their opinions; they have become convinced of their true situation; that they cannot live in the same field with the white man. Our people have done that which

we did not believe they would have done at the time we made the treaty; they have sold their reservations—it is done and cannot now be helped; the white man has taken possession, and has every advantage over us; it is impossible for the red and white man to live together.

The group set 15 October 1835 as their departure date and vowed to go if their reserves were sold.[25]

When the time came, Opothle Yoholo and his friends did not go. There was too much unfinished business, they said, but it is likely that they never intended to migrate. Instead, it seems that with his promise Opothle Yoholo tricked Cass into launching an investigation of the speculation in reserves. For months the headmen had lodged complaints against the federal agents responsible for locating reserves and approving their sale. The headmen charged that those officers issued choice allotments to pliant Creeks and "floated off" the proper recipients to distant barren or swampy tracts. They approved the sale of reserves to speculators by Creeks who impersonated the rightful owners. They connived with swindlers to recognize invalid signatures on forged receipts, and they closed their eyes to acts of violence against intransigent allottees. These and similar deeds kept the Creeks in a turmoil, and the lethargic federal response to their charges impeded the emigration of even those who wanted to go. No one cared to abandon his reserve or give up his efforts to recover the property stolen or tricked away by the hordes of Georgia and Alabama swindlers. But now that Opothle Yoholo and many of the most influential Upper Creek people seemed ready to leave, Secretary Cass authorized a more vigorous investigation of the frauds. During the winter of 1835–36, for the first time, an apparently energetic federal enquiry was under way.[26]

The "Creek War of 1836" brought the proceedings to a halt. Begun in the Chattahoochee valley, the war involved primarily the Lower Creek towns of Hitchiti, Yuchi, Chiaha, and Georgia. Sporadic conflict escalated during the spring and exploded in May with a collision between Creek warriors and the Georgia milita. Within a few days, parties from the "hostile towns" burned several houses and outbuildings, a tavern on the Federal Road, a mail stage, the toll bridge over the Chattahoochee between Columbus, Georgia, and Gerard, Alabama, and two steamboats. Both states responded with hastily recruited companies of militia. To keep him under control, Opothle Yoholo was arrested and briefly held for nonpayment of "a debt, for which he is as much responsible as he is for the national debt of Great Britain." Cass suspended all inquiries into the charges of fraud so quickly that several contemporary observers concluded that the war was a "humbug . . . devised by interested men" to halt the exposure of their unlawful deeds. Homeless and starving, most Creeks had reasons of their own to hate the Georgia and Alabama speculators and squatters.[27]

Whether starvation or conspiracy precipitated the war, removal ended it. Cass sent Brevet Major General Thomas S. Jesup to Alabama to command the combined force of regulars and militia gathered "for the suppression of hostilities in the Creek country." "Your efforts will be directed to the unconditional submission of the Indians," Cass ordered. "As fast as this is effected, and as any portion of them can be collected, they must be disarmed, and sent immediately to their country west of the Mississippi." There may be some Creeks who are not at war, Cass opined, but they will probably become hostile "unless prevented by a timely removal." All Creeks must be transported west. "The friendly disposed part of them" should be treated "with the kindest attention," but Jesup was "to send them off as speedily as practicable [and] by a military force if necessary." Any investigation of fraudulent practices in the location and sale of their reserves could be concluded after the Creeks were gone.[28]

In five groups, 14,609 Creeks left Alabama during 1836 for the western Creek Nation. Of that number the War Department classified 2,495 as "hostile." The next year the army transported about five thousand more, mostly Creek volunteers discharged from service in the Seminole War and their families. A few others remained in Alabama; some never left.[29]

The army accomplished in a few months what politicians and treaty talks had failed for fifteen years to achieve. For generations Creek security had rested on the unquestioned military power of the Confederacy, and the Nation's foreign policy had been predicated on the might of its warriors. When the Creek War of 1813–14 ended that power, the Nation's leaders were forced to devise new techniques to protect their people from their enemies. The reforms of Alexander McGillivray and Benjamin Hawkins had demonstrated that the way lay in political organization, strong national government, and unity. But the Creeks had no such advisers or political scientists in their midst during the 1820s and 1830s. Imperfectly recalling the 1780s and 1790s, Big Warrior, William McIntosh, Opothle Yoholo, and others had little more than a vague sense of what might be done. Dedicated to preserving the territorial status quo, their politics lacked a positive direction. The Council's most imaginative governmental decisions—the death sentence for unauthorized land sales and the execution of McIntosh—were designed to prevent change. Creek leaders in the late 1820s and early 1830s, reeling from the whirlwind of external reaction to those decisions and forced into retreat onto their Alabama lands, faced crisis after crisis in a state of confusion. Thousands of refugees needed care and attention; escalating political interference by Alabama demanded continual response; aggressive squatters from Georgia and Alabama threatened the lives and property of growing numbers of people. Every new emergency demanded a new idea from the National Council, but as the Lower Towns disintegrated and the composition of the Council changed, it became increasingly more conservative and more committed to the status quo. Its fresh ideas were limited to new ways to force a small but growing minority of Creeks to hold fast in the face of the problems it could not solve.

The Council's formula for the Treaty of 1832 was its last hurrah. Bending to the inexorable pressures to sell the last of the Nation's territory, Opothle Yoholo and the other headmen devised a scheme for allotting the land to individual Creeks which, along with provisions to guarantee the preservation of local self-government and social and religious customs, would maintain a truncated but intact version of the status quo. Although this seemed an imaginative solution to the problem it should have required no imagination on the part of the Creeks to realize that it would never work. There was no will in the governments of either the United States or Alabama to respect the wish of the Creeks to remain, and there was an overwhelming popular demand to be rid of them once and for all. Because of the lack of any institutions able to protect their rights, many Creeks tried to protect themselves. Some fled, others struck out, most sank into a confused malaise and waited for something decisive to happen. Along with the Nation, Creek society in the East simply deteriorated. And because of that disorganized condition, it was easy for the army to gather up and remove the people.

During the next quarter century the Council and its leaders picked up the pieces and reestablished the political integrity of the Creek Nation. The traumatic memory of removal receded, Indian Territory proved hospitable, people put down new roots. Neither the society nor the government of the Nation remained unchanged, but for a time the crises were past.

NOTES

Abbreviations Used in the Notes

ASP:IA	*American State Papers: Indian Affairs*
CA	Creek Agency
CE	Creek Agency, Emigration
DRT	Documents Relating to the Negotiation of Ratified and Unratified Treaties with Various Indian Tribes, 1801–1869
HD	House Document
HED	House Executive Document
HR	House Report
LR	Letters Received, 1824–1881
LRIA	Letters Received Relating to Indian Affairs, 1800–1823
LS	Letters Sent, 1824–1882
LSIA	Letters Sent Relating to Indian Affairs, 1800–1824
LSMA	Letters Sent Relating to Military Affairs, 1800–1889
LSP	Letters Sent to the President
OIA	Office of Indian Affairs
RG	Record Group, National Archives
SD	Senate Document
SW	Secretary of War

Chapter 1

1. Useful general descriptions of the southeastern country and the relationship between Native people and geography are: John Bakeless, *The Eyes*

of Discovery (New York: Dover Publications, 1961), chap. 1; Charles Hudson, *The Southeastern Indians* (Knoxville: University of Tennessee Press, 1976), pp. 14–22 and passim; Carl O. Sauer, *Sixteenth Century North America* (Berkeley: University of California Press, 1971); William Bartram, *Travels of William Bartram,* ed. Mark Van Doren (New York: Dover Publications, 1955). The map that most clearly delineates the southeastern physical geography is Erwin Raisz, "Landforms of the United States," 6th ed. rev. (Cambridge, Mass.: Erwin Raisz, 1957).

2. Benjamin Hawkins, *A Sketch of the Creek Country in the Years 1798 and 1799,* Georgia Historical Society *Collections,* Vol. 3 (1848), pt. 1; Raisz, "Landforms." See also John R. Swanton, *Early History of the Creek Indians and Their Neighbors,* Bureau of American Ethnology Bulletin No. 73 (Washington, D.C.: Government Printing Office, 1922), pl. 1, "Indian Tribes of the Southeastern United States."

3. Verner W. Crane, "The Origins of the Name of the Creek Indians," *Journal of American History* 5 (December 1918): 339–42.

4. Hawkins, *Sketch.*

5. Hudson, *Southeastern Indians,* pp. 291–99.

6. James Adair, *The History of the American Indians,* ed. Samuel Cole Williams (Johnson City, Tenn.: Watauga Press, 1930), pp. 433–34; Hudson, *Southeastern Indians,* pp. 272–89.

7. John R. Swanton, "The Social Significance of the Creek Confederacy," International Congress of Americanists *Proceedings* 19 (1917): 327; Swanton, *Early History,* pp. 434–37. William Bartram, "Observations on the Creek and Cherokee Indians," American Ethnological Society *Transactions* 3 (1853): 55, contains a map of a "typical" Creek town, drawn about 1789.

8. Albert S. Gatschet, *A Migration Legend of the Creek Indians* (Philadelphia: Daniel G. Brinton, 1884), pp. 59–61.

9. See John Phillip Reid, *A Law of Blood: The Primitive Law of the Cherokee Nation* (New York: New York University Press, 1970), especially chap. 5, for an interpretation of clans and how they functioned. A recent anthropological description is in Hudson, *Southeastern Indians,* pp. 184–202.

10. This is an ideal description of Creek matrilineal institutions. William S. Willis, "Patrilineal Institutions in Southeastern North America," *Ethnohistory* 10 (Summer 1963): 250–69, shows that in practice there were important father-son relationships that defied the matrilineal ideal.

11. John R. Swanton, "Social Organization and Social Usages of the Indians of the Creek Confederacy," Bureau of American Ethnology *Annual Report* 42 (Washington, D.C.: Government Printing Office, 1928), pp. 363–65; Alexander Spoehr, "Changing Kinship Systems: A Study in the Acculturation of the Creeks, Cherokees, and Choctaw," Field Museum of Natural History *Anthropological Series,* 33 (1947), p. 200; J. N. B. Hewitt, "Notes on the Creek Indians, " Bureau of American Ethnology *Bulletin* no. 123 (Washington, D.C.: Government Printing Office, 1939), pp. 145–46.

12. Reid, *Law of Blood,* chap. 5, pp. 8–11; Hewitt, "Notes on the Creek

Indians," pp. 147–49. Hudson, *Southeastern Indians,* pp. 229–30, describes this clan function as retaliation rather than compensation.

13. Reid, *Law of Blood,* chap. 5; Ross Hassig, "International Conflict in the Creek War of 1813–1814," *Ethnohistory* 21 (Summer 1974): 255; Keith F. Otterbein, "Internal War: A Cross-Cultural Study," *American Anthropologist* 70 (1968): 277–89.

14. Swanton, "Social Significance of the Creek Confederacy," pp. 329–30. Spoehr, "Changing Kinship Systems," pp. 199–200, is impressed by the elaborate social organization of the Creeks. Their highly developed institutions, he argues, enabled them to resist social change imposed by whites more effectively and for a longer period than either the Cherokees or Choctaws.

15. Hawkins, *Sketch,* p. 32; Swanton, *Early History,* p. 254; Gatschet, "Towns and Villages of the Creek Confederacy in the XVIII and XIX Centuries," Alabama Historical Society *Miscellaneous Collections* 1 (1901): 398; Swanton, "Social Organization and Social Usages," pp. 249–53; Adair, *History of the Indians,* p. 166.

16. There is much talk in the eighteenth-century literature about the need for a young man to take a scalp before he could pass into adulthood. Following the impeccable logic of Francis Jennings, I have reduced that deed from a requirement to an option. See his *The Invasion of America: Indians, Colonialism, and the Cant of Conquest* (Chapel Hill: University of North Carolina Press, 1975), pp. 150–51.

17. Caleb Swan, "Position and State of Manners and Arts in the Creek, or Muscogee Nation in 1791," in Henry Rowe Schoolcraft, *Historical and Statistical Information Respecting the History, Condition, and Prospects of the Indian Tribes of the United States,* 6 vols. (Philadelphia: Lippincott, Grambo and Company, 1851–57). 5:280; Swanton, "Social Organization and Social Usages," pp. 297, 366. A description of the naming ceremony is in Frank G. Speck, "The Creek Indians of Taskigi Town," American Anthropological Association *Memoirs* 2, pt. 2 (1907): 116–17.

18. Swanton, "Social Organization and Social Usages," pp. 363, 437;Gatschet, *Migration Legend,* p. 165.

19. Swanton, "Social Organization and Social Usages," p. 297.

20. Ibid., pp. 196–97, 240. Contemporaries, if not scholars, have usually translated miko as king.

21. Bartram, "Observations on the Creek and Cherokee Indians," pp. 23–24; Swanton, "Social Significance of the Creek Confederacy," p. 331; Swanton, "Social Organization and Social Usages," p. 280.

22. Swanton, "Social Organization and Social Usages," pp. 295–97.

23. Gatschet, *Migration Legend,* p. 157; Swanton, "Social Organization and Social Usages," pp. 192, 293–94; Swanton, "Social Significance of the Creek Confederacy," p. 331.

24. Swanton, "Social Organization and Social Usages," pp. 302–5.

25. Ibid., pp. 251–52; Swanton, "Social Significance of the Creek Confederacy," p. 330; Mary R. Haas, "Creek Inter-town Relations," *American An*

thropologist 42 (July–September 1940): 479.

26. Swanton, "Social Organization and Social Usages," pp. 165, 254, says that in recent times the purpose of the moiety system has degenerated to "determining what towns were to play with and against each other in the ball games." I believe that originally, at any rate, the reverse was more nearly true —the most important purpose of the ball game was to keep alive the moiety rivalry. See also Swanton, "Social Significance of the Creek Confederacy." pp. 330, 332.

27. Haas, "Creek Inter-town Relations," especially p. 483; Swanton, "Social Significance of the Creek Confederacy," p. 332; Hudson, *Southeastern Indians,* pp. 235–37. The ball game was sometimes used to settle intertribal disputes. Henry S. Halbert and T. H. Ball, *The Creek War of 1813 and 1814* (Chicago: Donohue and Henneberry, 1895), p. 36, describe how the Creeks and Choctaws settled a boundary dispute with two ball games.

28. Haas, "Creek Inter-town Relations," pp. 481–89. The match game was an extraordinarily boisterous contest which could involve teams of two hundred players or more. Each player carried two sticks, much like lacrosse sticks, with which he caught and threw a ball made commonly of deerhide. The game was played on a field often two hundred yards or more in length; the object was to throw the ball between two upright poles planted three feet apart at either end. The first team to make twenty scores won. Contemporary descriptions abound, but see Hudson, *Southeastern Indians,* pp. 409–11, for a convenient, recent description.

29. John H. Goff, "The Path to Oakfuskee, Upper Trading Route in Georgia to the Creek Indians," *Georgia Historical Quarterly* 39 (March 1955): 1–3.

30. Swanton, "Social Organization and Social Usages," pp. 314–15; Swanton, "Social Significance of the Creek Confederacy," pp. 327–34.

31. Chekilli said that the Appalachicolas introduced the four allies to black drink. Ritualized consumption of black drink became an integral part of Creek life, serving as a rite of purification preceding discussions, councils, ceremonies, and other male gatherings. Charles M. Hudson, ed., *Black Drink: A Native American Tea* (Athens: University of Georgia Press, 1979). See especially Charles H. Fairbanks, "The Function of Black Drink among the Creeks," pp. 120–49, in ibid.

32. An unedited copy of Chekilli's legend is published as "Some Ancient Georgia Indian Lore," *Georgia Historical Quarterly* 15 (June 1931): 192–98. Gatschet, *Migration Legend,* provides a detailed analysis of Chekilli's legend and a rich mass of additional Creek history. Many more versions of the Creek origin traditions, both previously published and unpublished, are in Swanton, "Social Organization and Social Usages," pp. 33–75. He provides additional analysis of them in ibid., pp. 259–67.

33. Swanton, "Social Organization and Social Usages," pp. 248–49; Swanton, "Social Significance of the Creek Confederacy," p. 332; Swanton, *Early History,* passim.

34. George Stiggins, "A Historical Narrative of the Genealogy traditions

and downfall of the Ispocaga or Creek tribe of Indians, written by one of the tribe," in Theron A. Nunez, Jr., "Creek Nativism and the Creek War of 1813-1814," *Ethnohistory* 5 (Winter 1958): 36; Swanton, "Social Organization and Social Usages," pp. 266-67; Haas, "Creek Inter-town Relations, pp. 479-89.

35. John R. Swanton, "Religious Beliefs and Medical Practices of the Creek Indians," Bureau of American Ethnology *Annual Report* 42 (Washington, D.C.: Government Printing Office, 1928), p. 546. There are many descriptions of the Busk. The best early eyewitness accounts include George Stiggins, "Historical Narrative," pp. 40-41, 131-32, and John Howard Payne, "The Green Corn Dance," ed. John R. Swanton, *Chronicles of Oklahoma* 10 (1932): 170-95. Swanton has gathered together much additional material in "Social Organization and Social Usages," and in "Religious Beliefs and Medical Practices."

36. See Vine Deloria, Jr., *God Is Red* (New York: Dell Publishing Co., 1973), for an instructive explanation of the interdependence between a people's religion and their homeland.

Chapter 2

1. Nancy O. Lurie argues that "the material differences between the Indians and the European colonists, who lived before the full development of the industrial revolution, were equalled if not outweighed by the similarities of culture. . . . There was actually little in the Europeans' imported bag of tricks which the Indians could not syncretize with their own experience." She is interpreting Powhatan-English contact at Jamestown in the early seventeenth century, but it seems that her point can be applied to the first contacts of southeastern Native Americans with the Spanish sixty years before. See her "Indian Cultural Adjustment to European Civilization," in *Seventeenth-Century America: Essays in Colonial History,* ed. James Morton Smith (Chapel Hill: University of North Carolina Press, 1959), pp. 33-60. The quote is on p. 38.

2. See Sauer, *Sixteenth Century North America,* for early Spanish-Native contacts in the Southeast. The descriptions of DeSoto's expedition by the Gentleman of Elvas and Luys Hernandez de Biedma are conveniently gathered in Buckingham Smith, trans., *Narratives of De Soto in the Conquest of Florida* (Gainesville, Fla.: Palmetto Press, 1968). The quote from the Gentleman of Elvas is on page 63. A recent analysis of DeSoto's invasion that is sensitive to Native victims is in Sauer, *Sixteenth Century North America,* chap. 9. On European disease and the decimation of Native Americans, see Alfred W. Crosby, Jr., *The Columbian Exchange: Biological and Cultural Consequences of 1492* (Westport, Conn.: Greenwood Press, 1972); Wilbur R. Jacobs, "The Tip of the Iceberg: Pre-Columbian Indian Demography and Some Implications for Revisionism," *William and Mary Quarterly,* 3rd series 31 (January 1974): 123-32; Henry F. Dobyns, *Native American Historical Demography: A*

Critical Bibliography (Bloomington: Indiana University Press, 1976). A Spanish census of 1738 (Swanton, *Early History of the Creek Indians,* pp. 434–37) listed 2,063 Creek men. If multiplied by 4.5, the common figure to convert numbers of "gunmen" to total population, the 1738 Creek population approximated 9,284 people. Dobyns, "Estimating Aboriginal American Population: An Appraisal of Techniques with a New Hemispheric Estimate," *Current Anthropology* 7 (October 1966): 414, suggests a depopulation ratio of 20:1 or 25:1, producing a precontact Creek population ranging from 185,680 to 232,100. Such estimating of Creek population trends over several centuries is exceptionally conducive to error, however, because tribes and groups of people were continually entering and leaving the Confederacy. There was never a consistent base from which to compare changes.

3. J. Leitch Wright, Jr., *The Only Land They Knew: The Tragic Story of the American Indians in the Old South* (New York: Free Press, 1981), pp. 22–26; Henry F. Dobyns, "Major Dynamics of the Historic Demography of Indoamericans," paper delivered at the Organization of American Historians Annual Meeting, Atlanta, 1977, p. 8 n. 21, n. 25; Alexander Cameron to Augustine Prevost, 15 October 1779, K. G. Davies, ed., *Documents of the American Revolution, 1770–1783 (Colonial Office Series),* 20 vols. (Shannon: Irish University Press, 1972–79), 17:233; Prevost to Henry Clinton, 2 March 1780, Historical Manuscripts Commission, *Report on American Manuscripts in the Royal Institution of Great Britain* 4 vols. (Dublin: His Majesty's Stationery Office, 1906), 2:96; Account of Dr. W. L. Wharton, 5 December 1831, OIA, LR, CA, RG 75, reel 222:537–38.

4. See Verner W. Crane, *The Southern Frontier, 1670–1732* (Ann Arbor: University of Michigan Press, 1956), on early trade relations between Europeans and the Creeks. For a perceptive analysis of the growing dependence of Native people upon European merchandise, consult Jennings, *Invasion of America,* chap. 6.

5. Hudson, *Southeastern Indians,* pp. 275–76, 435–36; Crane, *Southern Frontier,* p. 112. See Theda Perdue, *Slavery and the Evolution of Cherokee Society, 1540–1866* (Knoxville: University of Tennessee Press, 1979), especially chap. 2, for the impact of slave raiding on the society and culture of the Creeks' northern neighbors. Mark F. Boyd, Hale G. Smith, and John W. Griffin, *Here They Once Stood: The Tragic End of the Apalachee Missions* (Gainesville: University of Florida Press, 1951), pp. 1–106, describes the destruction of the mission towns in western Florida in 1704 by Charlestown and Creek slave raiders. Carol I. Mason, "Eighteenth Century Culture Change among the Lower Creeks," *Florida Anthropologist* 16 (September 1963): 65–80, shows, through an analysis of artifacts excavated at Ocmulgee Old Fields, that the male role was altered more decisively than that of the female in Creek society. For evidence of early commercial agriculture, see Crane, *Southern Frontier,* p. 258 n. 10.

6. Adair, *History of the American Indians,* p. 456.

7. Angie Debo, *The Road to Disappearance* (Norman: University of Oklahoma Press, 1941), pp. 33–34; Crane, *Southern Frontier,* passim.

8. Theda Perdue's *Slavery and the Evolution of Cherokee Society* has influenced my thinking here and elsewhere in this book. Comparable documentation for early Creek history does not exist, but similarity of experience and outcome has emboldened me to borrow heavily from her work. I gratefully acknowledge her willingness to permit it.

9. Crane, *Southern Frontier,* is the best analysis of early European trading relations with the Creeks. See especially Chaps. 7 and 11. Further elaboration may be found in David H. Corkran, *The Creek Frontier, 1540–1783* (Norman: University of Oklahoma Press, 1967), chap. 2, and Swanton, *Early History of the Creek Indians.*

10. See Wilbur R. Jacobs, *Diplomacy and Indian Gifts: Anglo-French Rivalry along the Ohio and Northwest Frontiers, 1748–1763* (Stanford: Stanford University Press, 1950); reprinted as *The Northern Colonial Frontier, 1748–1763: Wilderness Politics and Indian Gifts.* (Lincoln: University of Nebraska Press, 1966), for an explanation of European competitive diplomacy among the Native nations.

11. Adair, *History of the American Indians,* p. 277; Corkran, *Creek Frontier,* p. 61.

12. Crane, *Southern Frontier,* pp. 254–58, 264–66.

13. Quoted in Swanton, *Early History,* pp. 225–26.

14. Brims and the policy of Creek neutrality are described in Crane, *Southern Frontier,* pp. 258–60 and Corkran, *Creek Frontier,* chap. 3.

15. "Oglethorpe's Treaty with the Lower Creek Indians," *Georgia Historical Quarterly* 4 (March 1920): 12–15; "Journal of the Trustees of Georgia," 11 September 1734, in Allen D. Candler, ed, *The Colonial Records of the State of Georgia* 29 vols. to date (Atlanta: Franklin Printing and Publishing Co., 1904), 1:184–85; "An Act for maintaining the Peace with the Indians of the Province of Georgia," 9 January 1735, ibid., 1:31–42. Useful interpretations of Oglethorpe in Georgia and Georgia's relations with the Creeks are Phinizy Spalding, *Oglethorpe in America* (Chicago: University of Chicago Press, 1977), especially chaps. 4 and 6, and Leslie F. Church, *Oglethorpe: A Study of Philanthropy in England and Georgia* (London: Epworth Press, 1932), chap. 9.

16. The most elaborate analysis of the Georgia trade act and the resulting conflict with South Carolina is John Pitts Corry, *Indian Affairs in Georgia, 1732–1756* (Philadelphia: George S. Ferguson, 1936), chaps. 2–3.

17. "A Ranger's Report of Travels with General Oglethorpe, 1739–42," in Newton D. Mereness, ed., *Travels in The American Colonies* (New York: Macmillan, 1916), pp. 215–22; Spalding, *Oglethorpe,* pp. 88–91; Corkran, *Creek Frontier,* pp. 99–105. John Duffy, *Epidemics in Colonial America* (Baton Rouge: Louisiana State University Press, 1953), pp. 83, 83 n. 25, says smallpox ravaged the southern Natives, especially the Cherokees, in 1737–39, and the Indians blamed the outbreak on the English. Oglethorpe, Duffy writes, "managed to allay their suspicions of the English" in the fall of 1739 in extended talks with them. The implications are that the disease had occurred among the Creeks as well, and that the outbreak of the disease was also a topic of conversation at Coweta.

18. "Oglethorpe's Treaty with the Lower Creeks," pp. 6–8.

19. Spalding, *Oglethorpe*, p. 92; Benjamin Hawkins, *Letters of Benjamin Hawkins, 1796–1806*, Georgia Historical Society *Collections* 9 (1916), p. 250. Louis DeVorsey, Jr., *The Indian Boundary in the Southern Colonies, 1763–1775* (Chapel Hill: University of North Carolina Press, 1961), pp. 139–43, suggests the physical limits of the Georgia colony may have been informally established before the 1739 Treaty of Coweta.

20. Candler, *Colonial Records of Georgia,* 6:147–48. Roger Williams used the same argument, in virtually the same words, one hundred years before. See Ruth Barnes Moynihan, "The Patent and the Indians: The Problem of Jurisdiction in Seventeenth-Century New England," *American Indian Culture and Research Journal* 2 (1977): 13.

21. E. Merton Coulter, "Mary Musgrove, 'Queen of the Creeks': A Chapter of Early Georgia Troubles," *Georgia Historical Quarterly* 11 (March 1927): 1–30, sheds much light on the first twenty years of Georgia-Creek relations and the influential role of Mary Musgrove-Matthews-Bosomworth therein. John Pitts Corry, "Some New Light on the Bosomworth Claims," ibid., 25 (September 1941): 195–224, doubts Coulter's conclusion that Mary was a wholly disruptive force and suggests that Georgia dealt unfairly with her, particularly in light of her important contributions to Georgia-Creek relations. Although she was clearly his inspiration, the central figure in Dee Brown's recent *Creek Mary's Blood* (New York: Holt, Rinehart and Winston, 1980) bears no resemblance to Mrs. Bosomworth.

22. Corkran, *Creek Frontier,* pp. 229–35; Kenneth Coleman, *Colonial Georgia, A History* (New York: Scribners, 1976), p. 195; Trevor Richard Reese, *Colonial Georgia: A Study in British Imperial Policy in the Eighteenth Century* (Athens: University of Georgia Press, 1963), p. 115; John Richard Alden, *John Stuart and the Southern Colonial Frontier: A Study of Indian Relations, War, Trade, and Land Problems in the Southern Wilderness* (Ann Arbor: University of Michigan Press, 1944), pp. 89–95, 179. For a perceptive account of the relative strengths and weaknesses of the British and French competitive positions regarding southern Indians, see Wilbur Jacobs, ed, *Indians of the Southern Colonial Frontier: The Edmund Atkin Report and Plan of 1755* (Columbia: University of South Carolina Press, 1954); reprinted as *The Appalachian Indian Frontier: The Edmond Atkin Report and Plan of 1755* (Lincoln: University of Nebraska Press, 1967).

23. Estimates of the non-Native population of Georgia are in Coleman, *Colonial Georgia*, pp. 223, 226–28; E. Merton Coulter, *Georgia, A Short History,* 3d ed. (Chapel Hill: University of North Carolina Press, 1960), p. 100. A tabulation of estimates of Creek population is in Swanton, *Early History,* p. 442. While the figures reflect devastation by smallpox in 1760 and 1764 (Duffy, *Colonial Epidemics,* pp. 92, 98), they are almost certainly far too low. A careful United States census of the Creeks taken in 1832 revealed 21,759 people, and that count probably missed many individuals. Swanton, *Early History,* p. 443.

24. Clarence Carter, "British Policy towards the American Indians in the

South, 1763–1768," *English Historical Review* 33 (January 1918): 37–56; Helen Louise Shaw, *British Administration of the Southern Indians, 1756–1783* (Lancaster: Lancaster Press, 1931), chap. 1; Alden, *Southern Colonial Frontier*, passim.

25. Alden, *Southern Colonial Frontier*, pp. 180–85.

26. DeVorsey, *Indian Boundary*, chaps. 7–9; Alden, *Southern Colonial Frontier*, pp. 205–7, 230–31, 302–8, 321–22; Corkran, *Creek Frontier*, pp. 237–41, 247–52, 259–62, 278–81. An eyewitness account of the 1765 Picolata conference is in John Bartram, "Diary of a Journey through the Carolinas, Georgia, and Florida from July 1, 1765, to April 10, 1766," American Philosophical Society *Transactions*, n.s. 33 (December 1942): 51. His son, William Bartram, accompanied the Creek and Georgia surveying party to mark the boundaries of the 1773 cession. See his description in "Travels in Georgia and Florida, 1773–74: A Report to Dr. John Fothergill," ibid., 33, pt. 2 (November 1943): 138–41.

27. Alden, *Southern Colonial Frontier*, chap. 14.

28. For the role of the Creeks in the American Revolution, see particularly Corkran, *Creek Frontier*, chaps. 16–18; Homer Bast, "Creek Indian Affairs, 1775–1778," *Georgia Historical Quarterly* 33 (March 1949): 1–25; and Debo, *Road to Disappearance*, pp. 37–38. Important general accounts include James H. O'Donnell III, *Southern Indians in the American Revolution* (Knoxville: University of Tennessee Press, 1973); idem, "The Florida Revolutionary Indian Frontier: Abode of the Blessed or Field of Battle?" in *Eighteenth-Century Florida: Life on the Frontier* ed. Samuel Proctor (Gainesville: University of Florida Press, 1976), pp. 60–74; R. S. Cotterill, *The Southern Indians: The Story of the Civilized Tribes before Removal* (Norman: University of Oklahoma Press, 1954) chap. 3; Walter H. Mohr, *Federal Indian Relations, 1774–1788* (Philadelphia: University of Pennsylvania Press, 1933), chap. 2. My own interpretation of the role of the Creeks in the American Revolution is "The Creek Confederacy in the American Revolution: Cautious Participants," a paper presented at the ninth Gulf Coast History and Humanities Conference, Pensacola, May 1981, to be published in the *Proceedings* of the Conference.

29. Hawkins, *Sketch*, pp. 26–27; Corkran, *Creek Frontier*, p. 307; Alexander McGillivray to Pedro Favrot, 8 November 1786, in John W. Caughey, *McGillivray of the Creeks* (Norman: University of Oklahoma Press, 1938), p. 136.

30. James H. O'Donnell III, "Alexander McGillivray: Training for Leadership, 1777–1783," *Georgia Historical Quarterly* 49 (June 1965): 172–86.

31. Arthur P. Whitaker, "Alexander McGillivray, 1783–1789," *North Carolina Historical Review* 5 (April 1928): 181–85; Caughey, *McGillivray*, pp. 3–16; Swan, "State of Manners in the Creek Nation," p. 279.

32. McGillivray to Estaban Miro, 28 March 1784, in Caughey, *McGillivray*, p. 73; Swan, "State of Manners in the Creek Nation," pp. 279, 281–82; Albert James Pickett, *History of Alabama, and Incidentally of Georgia and Mississippi from the Earliest Period* 2 vols. (Charleston: Walker and James, 1851)

2:33. Spanish-Creek treaty relations are analyzed in Jack D. L. Holmes, "Spanish Treaties with West Florida Indians, 1784–1802," *Florida Historical Quarterly* 48 (October 1979): 140–42. The Creek-Spanish treaty of Pensacola, 1 June 1784, is printed in *American State Papers: Foreign Relations,* 1:278–79. My "Alexander McGillivray," in *American Indian Leaders: Studies in Diversity,* ed. R. David Edmunds (Lincoln: University of Nebraska Press, 1980), pp. 41–63, is the most recent attempt to interpret this complex Creek.

33. Swan, "State of Manners in the Creek Nation," 5: 281–82; McGillivray to Arturo O'Neill, 3 January 1784, in Caughey, *McGillivray,* p. 67; Miro to McGillivray, 7 June 1784, ibid., p. 77.

34. Caleb Swan noted in 1790 that McGillivray was "eminent . . . only for his superior talents and political abilities. . . . [His] influence . . . consists in the privilege of advising and not in the power of commanding." "State of Manners in the Creek Nation," 5:279.

35. Report of Henry Knox, Secretary of War, to the President, 6 July 1789, *ASP:IA,* 1:15–16; McGillivray to Miro, 1 May 1786, in Caughey, *McGillivray,* pp. 106–10; McGillivray to Miro, 12 June 1788, ibid., pp. 205–7. Louise Frederick Hays, *Hero of Hornet's Nest: A Biography of Elijah Clark, 1733 to 1799* (New York: Stratford House, 1946), is a colorful account of the border warfare of the 1780s. A full and careful analysis of Bowles and his activities in the Creek Nation is J. Leitch Wright, Jr., *William Augustus Bowles: Director General of the Creek Nation* (Athens: University of Georgia Press, 1967), especially chap. 2. The treaties of Augusta (1783), Galphinton (1785), and Shoulderbone (1786) are conveniently reprinted in Linda Grant DePauw, ed., *Senate Executive Journal and Related Documents* (Baltimore: Johns Hopkins University Press, 1974), pp. 165–69, 179–83.

36. The Treaty of New York, 7 August 1790, is in Charles J. Kappler, comp., *Indian Affairs: Laws and Treaties* 5 vols. (Washington, D.C.: Government Printing Office, 1904–41), 2:25–28. McGillivray's description of the treaty is in McGillivray to Carlos Howard, 11 August 1790, in Caughey, *McGillivray,* pp. 273–75. The treaty is analyzed in Whitaker, "McGillivray, 1789–1793," *North Carolina Historical Review* 5 (July 1928): 298–301; Randolph C. Downes, "Creek-American Relations, 1782–1790," *Georgia Historical Quarterly* 21 (June 1937): 182–84; Caughey, *McGillivray,* pp. 40–46; and J. Leitch Wright, Jr., "Creek-American Treaty of 1790: Alexander McGillivray and the Diplomacy of the Old Southwest," *Georgia Historical Quarterly* 51 (December 1967): 379–400.

37. McGillivray to William Panton, 28 October 1791, in Caughey, *McGillivray,* pp. 298–300; Panton to Baron Francis Hector de Carondelet, 20 February 1793, ibid., p. 354. For an assessment of McGillivray's final year, see Caughey, *McGillivray,* pp. 46–53, and Whitaker, "McGillivray, 1789–1793," pp. 301–6.

38. Caughey, *McGillivray,* p. 55; Merritt B. Pound, *Benjamin Hawkins: Indian Agent* (Athens: University of Georgia Press, 1951), p. 163. James F. Doster, *The Creek Indians and Their Florida Lands, 1740–1823,* 2 vols. (New York: Garland Publishing Co., 1974), 1:190.

39. Pound, *Hawkins,* pp. 99–101, 103, 112–13, 116, chap. 8; Doster, *Creek Indians,* 2:9–10.

40. Hawkins to Secretary of War James McHenry, 6 January 1797, in Hawkins, *Letters of Hawkins,* pp. 57–58.

41. Hawkins, *Sketch,* pp. 51–52, 67–68; Hawkins to James Burges, 1 February 1797, in Hawkins, *Letters of Hawkins,* p. 68; Hawkins to Alexander Cornells, 10 February 1797, ibid., p. 78; Annual Report of Benjamin Hawkins, 1801, *ASP:IA,* 1:647–48; Doster, *Creek Indians,* 2:27–28.

42. Hawkins, *Sketch,* p. 68; Doster, *Creek Indians,* 2:276. See John Phillip Reid, *A Law of Blood: The Primitive Law of the Cherokee Nation* (New York: New York University Press, 1970), for an analysis of the function of the clans in the legal system of a nation neighboring the Creek Confederacy.

43. Doster, *Creek Indians,* 2:14, 17, 20, 28.

44. Ibid., 2:4, 20.

45. Big Warrior and Alexander Cornells to Hawkins, 26 April 1813, *ASP: IA,* 1:843; Doster, *Creek Indians,* 2:10, 33, 36–37; Pound, *Hawkins,* pp. 209–10. The records of the negotiations of the 1802 treaty between the United States and the Creeks are in *ASP:IA,* 1:668–81. The treaties of 1802 and 1805 are in Kappler, *Laws and Treaties,* 2:58–59, 85–86.

46. Hawkins, *Sketch,* p. 29; Hawkins to Armstrong, 26 April 1813, *ASP:IA,* 1:841.

47. Nunez, "Creek Nativism," p. 4; Doster, *Creek Indians,* 2:1, 14, 40, 72; Peter A. Brannon, "Fort Bainbridge," *Arrow Points* 5 (5 August 1922): 24, 26; idem, "Tuckabahchi Chiefs," ibid., 14 (10 May 1929): 33; Reginald Horsman, *Expansion and American Indian Policy, 1783–1812* (East Lansing: Michigan State University Press, 1967), pp. 160–64.

48. Big Warrior and Alexander Cornells to Hawkins, 26 April 1813, *ASP:IA,* 1:843; Hawkins to Secretary of War John Armstrong, 26 April 1813, ibid., 1:841; Hawkins to Tustunnuggee Thlucco, Cornells, and McIntosh, 24 April 1813, ibid., 1:842; Stiggins, "Historical Narrative," pp. 159, 298. Stiggins says the Alabamas "done more murder and other mischief in the time of their hostilities in the year 1813 than all the other tribes together." Ibid., p. 21.

49. Big Warrior, Alexander Cornells, and William McIntosh to Hawkins, 26 April 1813, *ASP:IA,* 1:841.

50. Hawkins to Tustunnuggee Thlucco, Oche Haujo, and every chief of the Upper Creeks, 29 March 1813, ibid., 1:839; Nimrod Doyell to Hawkins, 3 May 1813, ibid., 1:843–44; Stiggins, "Historical Narrative," p. 145.

51. Stiggins, "Historical Narrative," pp. 146–50, 152–53, 155, 167; Thomas S. Woodward, *Reminiscences of the Creeks, or Muscogee Indians* (Montgomery: Barrett and Wimbish, 1859): reprinted as *The American Old West* (Mobile: Southern University Press, 1965) p. 84. Woodward calls High-head Jim, Jim Boy. For evidence of the Prophet's reign of terror, see Alexander Cornells to Hawkins, 22 June 1813, *ASP:IA,* 1:845–46; Talosee Fixico to Hawkins, 5 July 1813, ibid., 1:847; Hawkins to Secretary of War, 28 July 1813, ibid., 1:849–50.

52. Stiggins, "Historical Narrative," pp. 155–57, 163–67; Woodward,

Reminiscences, pp. 85–86. The best general history of the Creek War remains Henry S. Halbert and T. H. Ball, *The Creek War of 1813 and 1814* (Chicago: Donohue and Henneberry, 1895), supplemented with Pickett, *History of Alabama*, vol. 2, chaps. 31–39. A short but useful recent interpretation is Doster, *Creek Indians*, 2, chaps. 3–4. The most complete account of Fort Mims is Frank L. Owsley, Jr., "The Fort Mims Massacre," *Alabama Review* 24 (July 1971): 192–204. See Ross Hassig, "Internal Conflict in the Creek War of 1813–1814," *Ethnohistory* 21 (Summer 1974): 251–71, for an attempt to analyze the dimensions of factionalism in the Creek civil war. Admitting that the sources are inconclusive, Hassig suggests that one factor in the civil war was a conflict between the young and upwardly mobile against the older, entrenched leaders.

53. Andrew Jackson to William H. Crawford, 10 June 1816, in John S. Bassett, ed., *Correspondence of Andrew Jackson* 7 vols. (Washington, D.C.: Carnegie Institute, 1926–1935), 2:244; John C. Calhoun to John Crowell, 29 September 1821, SW, LSIA, RG 75, E:160.

54. Message from the speaker of the Upper and Lower Towns (Big Warrior) to Benjamin Hawkins, 7 August 1814, DRT, RG 75, 1:190–91; Grant of land to Andrew Jackson and others, 9 August 1814, ibid., 1:193. The Treaty of Fort Jackson is in Kappler, *Laws and Treaties*, 2:107–10. Andrew Jackson's perspective on the Creek War is well summarized in Robert V. Remini, *Andrew Jackson and the Course of American Empire, 1767–1821* (New York: Harper and Row, 1977), chaps. 13–14.

Chapter 3

1. Remini, *Andrew Jackson*, chap. 19, suggests a new view of the significance of the War of 1812, especially Jackson's victories over the Creeks and British and his humiliation of the Spanish, in the history of the United States expansion in the South. The post War-of-1812 mood of enthusiastic nationalism has been described by many scholars. One convenient source is George Dangerfield, *The Awakening of American Nationalism, 1815–1828* (New York: Harper and Row, 1965). John William Ward's *Andrew Jackson: Symbol for an Age* (New York: Oxford University Press, 1962), shows how Jackson personified this enthusiastic postwar nationalism. The best short discussion of "The Great Migration" is chap. 16 of Thomas P. Abernethy, *The South in the New Nation, 1789–1819* (Baton Rouge: Louisiana State University Press, 1961). Calhoun's letter is John C. Calhoun to the House of Representatives, 5 December 1818, *ASP:IA*, 2:183.

2. The standard histories of the factory system are Royal B. Way, "The United States Factory System for Trading with the Indians, 1796–1822," *Journal of American History* 6 (September 1919): 220–35, and Edgar B. Wesley, "The Government Factory System Among the Indians, 1795–1822," *Journal of Economic and Business History* 4 (May 1932): 487–511. These should be supplemented with the more detailed work of Ora Brooks Peake, *A History of*

the United States Indian Factory System, 1795–1822 (Denver: Sage Books, 1954). Francis Paul Prucha, *American Indian Policy in the Formative Years: The Indian Trade and Intercourse Acts, 1790–1834* (Cambridge: Harvard University Press, 1962), pp. 84–92, analyzes the legislative history of the factory system and the trade regulation efforts which followed it. For a recent and insightful account of the factory system as an engine for reform, and the battle to preserve it after the War of 1812, see Herman J. Viola, *Thomas L. McKenney, Architect of America's Early Indian Policy: 1816–1830* (Chicago: Swallow Press, 1974), chaps. 3–4.

3. "An Act regulating trade and intercourse with the Indian tribes and for preserving peace on the frontier," 30 March 1802, *United States Statutes at Large,* 2:139–46. See especially sec. 13.

4. President James Monroe, First Annual Message, 2 December 1817, in James D. Richardson, comp., *A Compilation of the Messages and Papers of the Presidents,* 20 vols. (New York: Bureau of National Literature, 1897), 2:585.

5. "An Act making provision for the civilization of the Indian tribes adjoining the frontier settlements," 3 March 1819, *United States Statutes at Large,* 3:516–17. For a more elaborate analysis of the background of the "Civilization Act," see Prucha, *Indian Policy in the Formative Years,* pp. 219–24.

6. The Committee of Friends on Indian Concerns refused to accept money from the "civilization" fund because they "feared to place themselves under any other control than their own consciences, not knowing but that circumstances might hereafter occur, in which the views of the government, might conflict with those religious principles which govern us." Philip E. Thomas to Calhoun, 27 April 1820, in W. Edwin Hemphill, ed., *The Papers of John C. Calhoun,* vol. 5 (Columbia: University of South Carolina Press, 1971), p. 79.

7. Calhoun to Thomas L. McKenney, 16 February 1818, in Hemphill, *Calhoun Papers,* 2:141; Samuel Worcester to Calhoun, 6 February 1818, ibid., 2:124–25; Worcester to Calhoun, 2 March 1818, ibid., 2:171; Return J. Meigs to Calhoun, 10 June 1818, ibid., 2:336. For a more extended discussion of the partnership between government and missionaries see R. Pierce Beaver, *Church, State, and the American Indians: Two and a Half Centuries of Partnership in Missions between Protestant Churches and Government* (St. Louis: Concordia Publishing House, 1966). A penetrating analysis of the impact of mission activities on Native American societies is Robert F. Berkhofer, Jr., *Salvation and the Savage: An Analysis of Protestant Missions and American Indian Responses, 1787–1862* (Lexington: University of Kentucky Press, 1965).

8. Andrew Jackson to President James Monroe, 4 March 1817, in John S. Bassett, ed., *Correspondence of Andrew Jackson,* 2:277–82. Francis Paul Prucha, "Andrew Jackson's Indian Policy: A Reassessment," *Journal of American History* 56 (December 1969): 527–39, correctly argues that Jackson was far too complex to be dismissed as a western frontiersman with a knee-jerk hatred for Indians. But Prucha leans too far in his effort to offset the standard interpretation of the general and fails to detect the broader implications of

Jackson's advice to his superiors in Washington. See also Jackson to Calhoun, 2 September 1820, in Bassett, *Correspondence of Jackson,* 3:32, in which Jackson urges that "the arm of Government is sufficiently strong to carry into effect any law that Congress may deem necessary and proper to pass for the welfare and happiness of the Indian and for the convenience and benefit of the U. States."

9. Monroe to Jackson, 5 October 1817, ibid., 2:331–32; Calhoun to Jackson, 16 November 1821, ibid., 3:132; Calhoun to the House of Representatives, 5 December 1818, *ASP:IA,* 2:183. My interpretation of Calhoun differs sharply from that of Arthur H. DeRosier, Jr., *The Removal of the Choctaw Indians* (Knoxville: University of Tennessee Press, 1970), who seems immoderately impressed by Calhoun's Indian "policy of moderation."

10. Ulrich B. Phillips, *Georgia and State Rights* (1901; rpt. ed., Yellow Springs: The Antioch Press, 1968), p. 52; "Joseph McMinn, *"Dictionary of American Biography,"* 12:146; Committee on Public Lands to the Senate, 9 January 1817, *ASP:IA,* 2:123–24.

11. Kappler, *Laws and Treaties,* 2:140–44; Charles C. Royce, *The Cherokee Nation of Indians* (1887; rpt. ed., Chicago: Aldine Publishing Co., 1975) pp. 84–91.

12. Monroe, First Annual Message, 2 December 1817, in Richardson, *Messages and Papers,* 2:585; C. Vanderventer to Lewis Cass, 29 June 1818, *ASP:IA,* 2:175. The classic history of the removal policy is Annie H. Abel, "The History of Events Resulting in Indian Consolidation West of the Mississippi," American Historical Association *Annual Report for 1906* (Washington, D.C.,: Government Printing Office, 1908), 1:233–450.

13. Committee on Public Lands to the Senate, 9 January 1817, *ASP:IA,* 2:124.

14. Jackson had the temerity to argue in his letter to Monroe, 4 March 1817, Bassett, *Correspondence of Jackson,* 2:281, that the abolition of the treaty system would have the reforming result of ending the practice of corrupting Native leaders through bribery. His acquaintance with that device was intimate. See Jackson, David Meriwether, and Jesse Franklin to Crawford, 20 September 1816, *ASP:IA,* 2:105.

15. R. S. Cotterill, "Federal Indian Management in the South, 1789–1825," *Journal of American History* 20 (December 1933): 335–36, 340–42, 346–47; Martin Abbott, "Indian Policy and Management in the Mississippi Territory, 1798–1817, " *Journal of Mississippi History* 14 (July 1952): 156–62; Virginia L. Close, "Silas Dinsmoor, Not Dinsmore," *Dartmouth College Library Bulletin* 15 (November 1974): 23–32; James Mooney, *Historical Sketch of the Cherokee,* (1900; rpt. ed., Chicago: Aldine Publishing Co., 1975), pp. 222–23; Henry T. Malone, *Cherokees of the Old South: A People in Transition* (Athens: University of Georgia Press, 1956), chap. 5; Pound, *Hawkins;* Ruth A. Gallaher, "The Indian Agent in the United States before 1850," *Iowa Journal of History and Politics* 14 (January 1916): 3–32; Prucha, *Indian Policy in the Formative Years,* pp. 51–56.

16. Michael D. Green, "Federal-State Conflict in the Administration of Indian Policy: Georgia, Alabama, and the Creeks, 1824–1834" (Ph.D. diss., University of Iowa, 1973), pp. 87–145.

17. Pound, *Hawkins,* p. 188.

18. George Graham to David B. Mitchell, 27 January 1817, David B. Mitchell Papers, Ayer Collection, Newberry Library, Chicago. Mitchell's biography is in *Dictionary of American Biography,* 13:40–41. For evidence that Mitchell's was not a unique appointment, see R. S. Cotterill, *The Southern Indians: The Story of the Civilized Tribes before Removal* (Norman: University of Oklahoma Press, 1954), pp. 205, 216; Cotterill, "Federal Indian Management," p. 347; Abel, "Indian Consolidation," pp. 282–83, 286 n., 335 n., 371–72. DeRosier, *Removal of the Choctaws,* pp. 43–44, noticed the same transition of agency personnel, but he argues that the replacement of Hawkins by Mitchell (Creeks), of Meigs by Tennessee governor Joseph McMinn (Cherokees), and Dinsmoor by John McKee and William Ward (Choctaws) represented the removal of "undesirable Indian agents" and the appointment of "men of higher character." On pp. 135–37, however, DeRosier describes the particularly nefarious activities of William Ward.

19. William Baldwin to William Darlington, 19 April 1817, in William Darlington, comp., *Reliquiae Baldwinianae; Selections from the Correspondence of the late William Baldwin, M.D.* (Philadelphia: Kimber and Sharpless, 1843), pp. 216–17.

20. Paul Murray, "Party Organization in Georgia Politics, 1825–1853," *Georgia Historical Quarterly* 29 (December 1945); 195; Phillips, *Georgia and State Rights,* chap. 4. John Quincy Adams made some characteristically trenchant comments on the nature of Georgia politics in his diary. See Charles Francis Adams, ed., *Memoirs of John Quincy Adams, Comprising Portions of his Diary from 1795 to 1848,* 12 vols. (Philadelphia: J. B. Lippincott and Co., 1875), 5:21–22 (13 March 1820) and 5:211–12 (3 December 1820).

21. For Crawford's use of patronage, see Adams, *Adams Memoirs,* 5:185 (5 October 1820); for correspondence regarding Mitchell's appointment as Creek agent, see Crawford to Mitchell, 2 October, 28 October, 22 November 1816, Mitchell Papers; on Mitchell's land speculations, see Crawford to Mitchell, 6 June 1817, and Mitchell to Crawford, 30 December 1818, ibid., and Alexander Pope to Josiah Meigs, 4 March 1819, in Clarence E. Carter, ed., *The Territorial Papers of the United States, XVIII, Alabama* (Washington, D.C.: Government Printing Office, 1952), pp. 573–74; complaints about Mitchell's involvement in trade are in Daniel Hughes to McKenney, 28 December 1817, 23 March 1818, in Carter, *Territorial Papers, Alabama,* pp. 275, 282–85. The earliest formal charges against Mitchell for slave smuggling are in Jackson to Calhoun, 14 February 1818, in Bassett, *Correspondence of Jackson,* 2:354–55. John Clark, Mitchell's most bitter political foe and thus a virtually worthless source, reported that Mitchell was heard to say, as he embarked for the Creek Nation, that he had "served the public long enough, and he would be d——d if he did not now serve himself." John Clark, *Considerations on the Purity of the Prin-*

ciples of William H. Crawford (Augusta: Georgia Advertiser office, 1819), p. 313, quoted in Antonio J. Waring, *Laws of the Creek Nation* (Athens: University of Georgia Press, 1960), p. 3 n. 4.

22. Adams, *Adams Memoirs,* 5:186 (14 October 1820), 5:514–15 (2 May 1822). Andrew Jackson's role in the campaign to discredit Crawford and Mitchell can be traced in his correspondence with John Clark throughout 1819. See especially Bassett, *Correspondence of Jackson,* 2:416–18, 419–21, 424–26, and 442–43. Also important is Jackson to Monroe, 28 September 1819, ibid., 2:433–47. The bulk of the evidence relating to the charge that Mitchell engaged in smuggling slaves is in SW, LRIA, RG 75, 3:558–749 and 3:819–79. Attorney General William Wirt's analysis and opinion in the case is in Wirt to Monroe, 21 January 1821, *American State Papers: Miscellaneous,* 2:957–75. The Crawford–Mitchell correspondence on the slave-smuggling investigation shows Crawford as Mitchell's chief adviser on the gathering and preparing of evidence. See especially, Crawford to Mitchell, 29 April 1820, Mitchell to Crawford, 29 May, 1 June 1820, Mitchell papers, Crawford to Mitchell, 6 November, 2 December, ibid., reveal Crawford's anxiety over the political harm Mitchell was doing him and his decision to abandon the Creek agent. Calhoun's note dismissing Mitchell is Calhoun to Mitchell, 16 February 1821, SW, LSIA, RG 75, E:54.

23. William McIntosh to Jefferson, 3 November 1805, SW, LSIA, RG 75, B:154–60. James C. Bonner is the major source of biographical information on McIntosh. See his "Tustunugee Hutkee and Creek Factionalism on the Georgia-Alabama Frontier," *Alabama Review* 10 (April 1957): 111–25; idem., "William McIntosh," in *Georgians in Profile: Historical Essays in Honor of Ellis Merton Coulter,* ed. Horace Montgomery (Athens: University of Georgia Press, 1958): and idem., *Georgia's Last Frontier: The Development of Carroll County* (Athens: University of Georgia Press, 1971), chap. 1.

24. *Niles' Weekly Register,* 15 (7 November 1818): 176.

25. William McIntosh, Yoholo Mico, and others to the Secretary of War, 8, 10, 15 March 1817, SW, LRIA, RG 75, 2:52–56, 57–60, 61–64; McIntosh to the Secretary of War, 23 February, 9 March 1819, ibid., 2:1237–40, 1242–46; McIntosh to Calhoun, 31 December 1819, ibid., 3:423–24; Calhoun to Creek deputies, 28 March 1819, SW, LSIA, RG 75, D:278–80; Calhoun to McIntosh, 6 January 1820, ibid., D:352–53. Congress appropriated $85,000 to cover Creek claims totaling $195,000. See Mitchell to Calhoun, 18 January 1818, *ASP:IA,* 2:494–95.

26. Crawford to Mitchell, 30 October 1817, Mitchell Papers; Calhoun to Andrew Pickens and Thomas Flournoy, 8 August 1820, SW, LSIA, RG 75, E:3–4. The treaty is in Kappler, *Laws and Treaties,* 2:155–56.

27. Graham to Mitchell, 20 March 1817, SW, LSIA, RG 75, D:17–18; Mitchell to Calhoun, 28 January 1818, DRT, RG 75, 1:307–8. In mid-1819, Calhoun received a recommendation from his superintendent of Indian Trade that the Creek factory be closed. The "Cheifs, and those with whom they appear to be associated, seem to have monopolized every thing like trade in that quarter" and the Creeks were thus "independent of the U. S. supplies."

McKenney to Calhoun, 26 July 1819, in Hemphill, *Papers of Calhoun,* 4:181–82.

28. Samuel G. Drake, *Biography and History of the Indians of North America from its First Discovery,* 11th ed. (Boston: B. B. Mussey, 1851), p. 394; Graham to Mitchell, 20 March 1817, SW, LSIA, RG 75, D:17; Expenditures for the Indian Department since the Declaration of Independence, 7 December 1820, ASP:IA, 2:216.

29. Jackson described to Calhoun the annuity swindle of McIntosh and Mitchell in a letter of 12 January 1822, in Hemphill, *Papers of Calhoun,* 6:618–19. The secretary had known and tolerated the outrage for sometime. See Hughes to McKenney, 28 December 1817, in Carter, *Territorial Papers, Alabama,* pp. 282–83; Calhoun to Mitchell, 26 October 1818, in Hemphill, *Papers of Calhoun,* 3:236. Waring, *Laws of the Creek Nation,* pp. 2–3, thinks Mitchell corrupted McIntosh. The full dimensions of the annuity swindle are not clear, but there is a hint that Big Warrior and Little Prince, and perhaps other headmen, were also on the take. See the unspecified order signed by Big Warrior and Little Prince, 10 May 1819, Mitchell Papers, which authorized Mitchell to pay McIntosh $15,000 from the annuity money, and McIntosh's statement of 14 June 1819, ibid., that he had received it. It strains credulity to think that these headmen, themselves astute entrepreneurs, were ignorant of the McIntosh-Mitchell operation. Certainly they discovered it. Little Prince testified in later years that McIntosh and Mitchell, "in cheating the nation out of their annuity, . . . used to steal all our money, because they could write." Questions Put to the Chiefs . . . by General E. P. Gaines, 29 June 1825, HR 98, 19th Cong., 2d sess., serial 161. Hereafter cited as HR 98, 19/2 (161).

30. Calhoun to Pickens and Flournoy, 8 August 1820, SW, LSIA, RG 75, E:3–4; Adams, *Adams Memoirs,* 5:21 (13 March 1820).

31. "Copy of a talk delivered by the U. States Commissioners during the negotiations of the Treaty of Indian Springs," 8 January 1821, DRT, RG 75, 1:504–05; "Answers of the Chiefs to the Commissioners from Georgia," undated, ibid., 1:499–502; Daniel M. Forney and David Meriwether to Calhoun, 9 January 1821, ibid., 1:507–10; Calhoun to Duncan G. Campbell and James Meriwether, 16 July 1824, OIA, LS, RG 75, 1:138–39. The Upper Town headmen were angry that the negotiations were at McIntosh's Indian Springs tavern, and they probably boycotted the meeting in protest. See Mitchell to Calhoun, 21 November 1820, Mitchell Papers. McIntosh, needless to say, was quite pleased. McIntosh to Mitchell, 25 November 1820, ibid.

32. David Adams and Daniel Newnan to John Clark, 31 December 1820, Governor John Clark File, Georgia State Department of Archives and History, Atlanta, quoted in Waring, *Laws of the Creek Nation,* 4 n. 6.

33. Kappler, *Laws and Treaties,* 2:195–96; Forney and Meriwether to Calhoun, 9 January 1821, DRT, RG 75, 1:507–10. The correspondence relating to the 1821 Treaty of Indian Springs is conveniently gathered in *ASP:IA,* 2:248–57.

34. Biographical information on Creek headmen is limited and widely scattered. Some material on Big Warrior is collected in "'Tukabahchi Chiefs,"

Arrow Points 14 (10 May 1929): 33–34; and Woodward, *Reminiscences of the Creeks,* pp. 100–101 and passim. Material on Little Prince is even more dispersed. Evidence of his senility is in James R. Vinton, "Journal of My Excursion to Georgia, and the Creek Nation—1827," James Rogers Vinton Papers, Perkins Library, Duke University. In his entry for 2 March 1827, Vinton writes that Little Prince's "virtues, whatever they may have been, are paralyzed by extreme age." Vinton's journal has been edited by James C. Bonner and published in *Georgia Historical Quarterly* 44 (March 1960): 74–84.

35. Crowell is only slightly better known then his Creek associates. For skeletal biographies see *Biographical Directory of the American Congress, 1774–1971* (Washington, D.C.: Government Printing Office, 1971), p. 806; and Peter A. Brannon, "Fort Mitchell Cemetery," *Alabama Historical Quarterly* 21 (1959): 68–71. Thomas M. Owen, *History of Alabama and Dictionary of Alabama Biography* (Chicago: S. J. Clarke Publishing Co., 1921), 1:202, 2:1224, contains a description of early St. Stephens.

36. One of the many charges of complicity in the trade leveled against Agent Crowell is James Beddo to Calhoun, 3 August 1824, OIA, LR, CA, RG 75, reel 219:1–5. There is no solid evidence to convict or acquit Crowell of the charge, but circumstantial evidence points to some involvement.

37. When Crowell became agent, the Creek agency was on the east bank of the Flint River near the present-day town of Knoxville, Georgia. In 1826 it was relocated at Fort Mitchell, Alabama, adjacent to present-day Phenix City, where it remained until the transfer to Indian Territory in 1836.

38. Brannon, "Fort Mitchell Cemetery," p. 70. A copy of the portrait of Crowell's horse, John Bascomb, is in ibid., p. 114. Crowell's portrait, the original of which hangs in the Alabama Department of History and Archives, Montgomery, is in ibid, p. 57. Crowell's will, dated 19 December 1845, is from the Russell County, Alabama, Probate Records, Phenix City, Alabama. Crowell died 20 June 1846.

39. Samuel Hawkins to George M. Troup, 12 April 1825, HR 98, 19/2 (161), pp. 373–74. There are no specific denials of the described swindle. Several witnesses testified that Crowell always paid in money, Mitchell paid in goods, and the Creeks much preferred the former to the latter method. Those who testified against Crowell were friends of McIntosh; those who defended Crowell hated McIntosh. There seems no way to sort out the truth at this late date. For examples of testimony on this question, see Affidavit of Nimrod Doyell, 5 July 1825, ibid., pp. 419–20; Testimony of Thomas Triplett, 20 July 1825, ibid., pp. 389–90. The National Council's evaluation of the relative merits of Crowell and Mitchell and their methods of distributing the annuity is in "Questions of Maj. Andrews and Gen. Gaines Put to the Creek Chiefs," 29 June 1825, OIA, LR, CA, RG 75, reel 219:1072–73.

40. "An Act regulating trade and intercourse with the Indian tribes and for preserving peace on the frontier," 30 March 1802, *United States Statutes at Large,* 2:142.

41. Crowell to Little Prince, 25 July 1823, OIA, LR, CA, RG 75, reel 220:1820; Crowell to William Hambly, 22 August 1823, ibid., reel 220:1821–22.

42. U.S. District Court, Savannah, Georgia, Record Book 260:192–93, 197–98, 200–1. National Archives Records Center, Atlanta; Crowell to Calhoun, 23 November 1824, OIA, LR, CA. RG 75, reel 219:123–26; Jeremiah Cuyler to Calhoun, 14 July 1825, HR 98, 19/2 (161), p. 388. The Treaty of Fort Jackson is in Kappler, *Laws and Treaties*, 2:108–9.

43. Crowell to Calhoun, 23 November 1824, OIA, LR, CA, RG 75, reel 219:125.

44. See Bonner, "William McIntosh," pp. 114–43, especially pp. 126–32. Bonner's "Tustunugee Hutkee and Creek Factionalism" covers much the same ground with a sharper focus on Creek politics. Doster, *The Creek Indians* 2:275, suggests that their rivalry began during the Creek Civil War when McIntosh was "staunch and courageous" and Big Warrior was "trembling." Incidents frequently occurred. During the summer of 1822, McIntosh, as head of the law menders, enforced a national law prohibiting slaves to own property by confiscating goods owned by Big Warrior's slaves. Big Warrior resisted. The press called it "hostilities in the Creek Nation." See *Montgomery Republican,* 23 August, 6 September 1822.

45. William Capers to Calhoun, 8 January 1824, HR 98, 19/2 (161), pp. 24–25.

46. "A Report made before the Bishops and South Carolina Conference of the Methodist Episcopal Church by the Missionary Committee," 21 February 1822, ibid., pp. 68–69. Capers had originally planned only one school, at Coweta, but Big Warrior asked for one at his town as well, and Capers, for political reasons, agreed while having full knowledge that the South Carolina Methodists could not afford a second institution.

47. Capers to Calhoun, 8 January 1824, ibid., pp. 25–29; Crowell to Calhoun, 18 March 1824, ibid., pp. 48–49.

48. Statement of William Walker, 2 June 1824, in "Crowell-Capers Controversy, 1824," *Arrow Points* 5 (5 October 1922): 77–78; Statement of William Hambly, 3 June 1824, ibid., pp. 75–76.

49. A. Hamill to Capers, 25 March 1823, HR 98, 19/2 (161), p. 43; Mitchell to McIntosh, 1 May 1822, Mitchell Papers.

50. Capers to Calhoun, 8 January 1824, HR 98, 19/2 (161), pp. 24, 32.

51. "Second Annual Report of the Missionary Committee of the South Carolina Conference," 26 February 1823, ibid., p. 36; Capers to Calhoun, 8 January 1824, ibid., p. 30; Crowell to Calhoun, 18 March 1824, ibid., pp. 51–52.

52. Capers to Calhoun, 8 January 1824, ibid., pps. 28–29; "Report before the Bishops and South Carolina Conference," 21 February 1822, ibid., p. 73; Capers to Calhoun, 9 January 1824, ibid., p. 47.

53. "George M. Troup," *Dictionary of American Biography,* 18:650–51; Edward J. Harden, *Life of George M. Troup* (Savannah: E. J. Purse, 1859); Porter L. Fortune, Jr., "George M. Troup: Leading State Rights Advocate" (Ph.D. diss., University of North Carolina, 1949), pp. 3–146. The history of the Troupite–Clarkite confrontation is neatly summarized as chap. 4 of Phillips, *Georgia and State Rights*.

54. Troup to Calhoun, 16 January 1824, HR 98, 19/2 (161), p. 23.

55. Affidavit of Nimrod Doyell, 5 July 1825, ibid., p. 420.

Chapter 4

1. "Laws of the Creek Nation proclaimed at Broken Arrow," 12 June 1818, SW, LRIA, RG 75, 2:772-75. The laws were signed by William McIntosh, "Brig. Gen. & Commander Creek Warriors" (meaning the law menders), and by George Lovett and Noble Kinard, colonels, and Samuel Hawkins and Cohause Emauthlau, lieutenant colonels. An excellent analysis of the legal history of the Creeks' close neighbors, the Cherokees, is Rennard Strickland, *Fire and the Spirits: Cherokee Law from Clan to Court* (Norman: University of Oklahoma Press, 1975). See especially chaps. 3–6. Reid's *Law of Blood* is an elaborate analysis of Cherokee traditional law. The clan as judicial institution is discussed particularly in chap. 5. A much elaborated code of fifty-six laws was reduced to writing, 15 March 1824. A careful analysis of these statutes is Waring, *Laws of the Creek Nation*. The law menders also enforced orders issued by the agent. On 15 June 1818, Mitchell prohibited the "introduction of Spirits into the Creek Nation" and authorized "the warriors of each town, appointed by the Nation to execute the Laws, [to] enforce this Order." Clarence E. Carter, ed., *The Territorial Papers of the United States, XVIII, Alabama* (Washington, D.C.: Government Printing Office, 1952), p. 353.

2. William H. Crawford to David B. Mitchell, 24 August 1817, Mitchell Papers; Willis, "Patrilineal Institutions in Southeastern North America," pp. 250–69; Perdue, *Slavery in Cherokee Society,* especially chap. 4.

3. John C. Calhoun to Mitchell, 29 September 1818, SW, LSIA, RG 75, D:218-19.

4. Perdue, *Slavery in Cherokee Society,* p. 50 and passim, argues that the ownership of black slaves is a measure of the extent of Cherokee acceptance of the prevailing Anglo-American culture of the Southeast. Her interpretation can also be applied to the Creeks. In the 1832 federal census of the Creeks, 13,697 Upper Creeks owned 445 slaves; 8,065 Lower Creeks owned 457. The full significance of this imbalance is obscured by the fact that since 1826 over three thousand Creeks, primarily the most assimilated from the Lower Towns, had moved west taking with them an additional but undetermined number of slaves. The census totals are in Documents on the Emigration of the Indians, SD 512, 23d Cong., 1st sess., serials 245, 246. Hereafter cited as SD 512, 23/1 (245, 246).

5. Much has been written about the different rates and effects of assimilationist pressures on the Upper and Lower Creeks. A good introduction to the work on this subject is in Debo, *Road to Disappearance,* pp. 68–71. Her comments apply specifically to the pre-Creek Civil War period, but the conditions she describes prevailed in the 1820s as well. Bonner, "Tustunugee Hutkee and Creek Factionalism," pp. 111–25, also analyzes this phenomenon.

6. *American State Papers: Public Lands,* 1:125; "Memorial of Georgia General Assembly to the President," 22 December 1819, in Harden, *Troup,* p.

196; John Clark to Calhoun, 26 November 1821, Georgia Executive Letter-book, Department of Archives and History, Atlanta, microfilm copy, reel 2:2–3; Memorial of Georgia General Assembly, 22 December 1823, OIA, LR, CA, RG 75, reel 219, 180–82.

7. The headmen of the National Council said the law was proclaimed on the west bank of the Ocmulgee. See "Declaration of Chiefs concerning the death of McIntosh," 14 May 1825, HR 98, 19/2 (161), p. 456. The Affidavit of John Winslett, 29 June 1825, ibid., pp. 414–16, agrees. Waring, *Laws of the Creek Nation,* p. 5, says flatly that the law was first proclaimed in July 1817. The law was not included in the 1818 code.

8. Affidavit of John Winslett, 29 June 1825, HR 98, 19/2 (161), p. 415; Affidavit of William Scott, 8 June 1825, ibid., p. 404.

9. *Boston Recorder,* 21 February 1824, quoted in Thurman Wilkins, *Cherokee Tragedy: The Story of the Ridge Family and the Decimation of a People* (New York: Macmillan, 1970), p. 142.

10. McIntosh to John Ross, 21 October 1823, HR 98, 19/2 (161) pp. 638–39; Path Killer and Cherokee National Council to Big Warrior and Little Prince, 24 October 1823, OIA, LR, CA, RG 75, reel 219:1082–85; Wilkins, *Cherokee Tragedy,* pp. 142–44. The documents relative to the Cherokee negotiations are in *ASP:IA,* 2:464–77. Gary E. Moulton, "John Ross," *American Indian Leaders: Studies in Diversity,* ed. R. David Edmunds (Lincoln: University of Nebraska Press, 1980), p. 91, argues that Ross's public exposure of McIntosh's offer and his own refusal of it significantly enhanced his position in the Cherokee Council and "strengthened his role as a principle spokesman for his people."

11. Affidavit of William Lott, 28 June 1825, HR 98, 19/2 (161), p. 432. The Reverend Isaac Smith of the nearby Asbury Mission saw and heard McIntosh proclaim the law at the ball play. See Testimony of the Reverend Isaac Smith, 5 July 1825, ibid., p. 400.

12. Calhoun to Duncan G. Campbell and James Meriwether, 16 July 1824, OIA, LS, RG 75, 1:138–39; Campbell to Calhoun, 28 August 1824, OIA, LR, CA, RG 75, reel 219:28–29; Calhoun to Campbell, 13 September 1824, OIA, LS, RG 75, 1:195.

13. Answers of Elijah M. Amos, 6 June 1825, HR 98, 19/2 (161), pp. 209–10; Affidavit of Colonel William Hambly, 4 July 1825, ibid., p. 398.

14. The Tuckabatchee talk, first printed in the *Montgomery Republican,* appeared nationally in the *Niles' Weekly Register,* 27 (4 December 1824): 223–23. For the comparable Cherokee documents, see *ASP:IA,* 2:472–73. A list of Cherokee documents in the hands of the Creeks is in Crowell to Campbell and Meriwether, 14 December 1824, HR 98, 19/2 (161), p. 111. Debo, *Road to Disappearance,* p. 88, says the Tuckabatchee talk "was probably reduced to writing by John Ridge and David Vann." On pp. 87–88 she describes Creek-Cherokee cooperation against Georgia.

15. The Pole Cat Spring talk is in the *Niles' Weekly Register,* 27 (4 December 1824): 223–24. There is a brief account of William Walker in "Tuka-

bahchi Sons-in-Law," *Arrow Points* 14 (10 May 1929): 43. See also Peter A. Brannon, "Pole Cat Springs Agency," ibid., 10 (February 1925): 24–26.

16. *Niles' Weekly Register,* 27 (4 December 1824): 222–23.

17. Campbell to Crowell, 27 July 1824, DRT, RG 75, 1:627.

18. Having pled ignorance of the Compact of 1802 two days before, the Creeks developed a response to it with amazing speed, suggesting that Cherokees were advising them. The Cherokees had long since issued a response to Georgia's assertions based on the compact. Wilkins, *Cherokee Tragedy,* p. 164, suggests that Major Ridge was probably at Broken Arrow during the talks. President James Monroe's 30 March 1824 address to Congress shows that he was in closer agreement with the Creeks than with his commissioners. See Richardson, *Messages and Papers of the Presidents,* 2:804.

19. "Journal of the Proceedings of the Commissioners Appointed to Treat with the Creek Indians, July 16–December 18, 1824," DRT, RG 75, 1:625–49 (printed in *ASP:IA,* 2:564–84 and HR 98, 19/2 (161), pp. 98–113).

20. Affidavit of Nimrod Doyell, 5 July 1825, HR 98, 19/2 (161), p. 419; Affidavit of Colonel William Hambly, 4 July 1825, ibid., p. 395; Affidavit of Drury Spain, 8 July 1825, ibid., p. 439; Testimony of Joel Baley, 14 July 1825, ibid., p. 443–44.

21. Affidavit of Colonel William Hambly, 4 July 1825, ibid., p. 395.

22. Ibid., p. 393; Affidavit of Nimrod Doyell, 5 July 1825, ibid., p. 418; Affidavit of John Winslett, 29 June 1825, ibid., p. 415; Affidavit of Solomon Betton, 26 July 1825, ibid., p. 447.

23. Ibid.

24. Testimony of Joel Baley, 14 July 1825, ibid., p. 444. The amount promised above the $25,000 payment is not certain. Ten days before the gathering at Indian Springs, former Creek agent Mitchell, still McIntosh's confidante, assured one of McIntosh's creditors that the forthcoming treaty would "put into his (McIntosh's) pocket about fifty thousand dollars." Affidavit of Richard J. Nichols, 22 July 1825, ibid., p. 442. McIntosh's reserves are described in Kappler, *Laws and Treaties,* 2:216–17. The payment was far in excess of the current price of the best land in the area.

25. Troup to Campbell and Meriwether, 9 December 1824, HR 98, 19/2 (161), p. 108.

26. Campbell and Meriwether to Troup, 14 December 1824, ibid., p. 109.

27. Troup to the President, 23 December 1824, OIA, LR, CA RG 75, reel 219:229–32.

28. Campbell to Calhoun, 8 January 1825, DRT, RG 75, 1:662–74. A few days later Calhoun specifically invited Campbell to press charges against Crowell. Again he refused. Calhoun to Campbell, 13 January 1825, OIA, LS, RG 75, 1:301–2; Campbell to Calhoun, 14 January 1825, HR 98, 19/2 (161), pp. 117–19.

29. Campbell to Calhoun, 11 January 1825, ibid., p. 113; Calhoun to Campbell, 13 January 1825, OIA, LS, RG 75, 1:300–301.

30. Calhoun to William Walker, 11 January 1825, ibid., 1:298; Calhoun to

Campbell, 18 January 1825, ibid., 1:310–11; Campbell to Troup, 31 January 1825, *ASP:IA*, 2:754.

31. "Memorial of the McIntosh Party to the President," 25 January 1825, *ASP:IA*, 2:579.

32. Ibid.

33. "Instruction to Creek Delegates," 25 January 1825, ibid., 2:579–80.

34. Robert W. McCluggage, "The Senate and Indian Land Titles, 1800–1825," *Western Historical Quarterly* 1 (October 1970): 415–25, describes the Senate's "consistant and clear determination to deny the Indians the security of fee simple title to land either severally or as a group."

35. Affidavit of Major J. H. Brodnax, 7 July 1825, HR 98, 19/2 (161), p. 440.

36. Testimony of Thomas Triplett, 20 July 1825, ibid., p. 392; Affidavit of Major J. H. Brodnax, 7 July 1825, ibid., p. 441; Affidavit of Colonel William Hambly, ibid., p. 395. The political hostility of the two is largely explained by the fact that Duncan Campbell was the brother-in-law of John Clark, leader of the party in opposition to Mitchell's. See Jack Nelson Averitt, "The Democratic Party in Georgia, 1824–1837" (Ph.D. diss., University of North Carolina, 1956), p. 177.

37. Proceedings of the Negotiations at Indian Springs, 11 February 1825, HR 98, 19/2 (161), pp. 129–30; Testimony of Thomas Triplett, 20 July 1825, ibid., pp. 391–92.

38. "List of Chiefs present at the Treaty of Indian Springs, in February 1825, which positively refused to assign the Treaty," 21 February 1825, ibid., pp. 135–36.

39. Treaty of Indian Springs, 12 February 1825, in Kappler, *Laws and Treaties*, 2:214–17.

40. Proceedings of the Negotiations at Indian Springs, 12 February 1825, HR 98, 19/2 (161), p. 130; Testimony of Thomas Triplett, 20 July 1825, ibid., p. 392.

41. Affidavit of Major J. H. Brodnax, 7 July 1825, ibid., p. 441.

42. Major Timothy P. Andrews's report to the Secretary of War, 1 August 1825, ibid., p. 315; "List of signers to the treaty of Indian Springs," 30 June 1825, ibid., pp. 254–56.

43. Campbell and Meriwether to Troup, 13 February 1825, *Niles' Weekly Register*, 28 (12 March 1825):18.

44. Campbell to Calhoun, 16 February 1825, *ASP:IA*, 2:584.

45. Crowell to Calhoun, 13 February 1825, HR 98, 19/2 (161), pp. 132–33.

46. Crowell to James Barbour, 12 March 1825, ibid. p. 137; Defense of Col. Crowell, Indian Agent, 30 July 1825, ibid. pp. 481, 505–6; Testimony of Thomas Triplett, 20 July 1825, ibid. p. 391; Affidavit of Colonel William Hambly, 4 July 1825, ibid., p. 396. The offending article is in Kappler, *Laws and Treaties*, 2:215.

47. Creek Chiefs to the President, 21 February 1825, HR 98, 19/2 (161), pp. 133–34.

48. Talk of McIntosh party with Governor Troup, 17, 19, 20 February 1825, in Harden, *Troup,* pp. 264–66.

49. Troup to Chiefs of Tuckabatchee and Cusseta, 26 February 1825, OIA, LR, CA, RG 75, reel 219:1092–93.

50. Troup to Henry G. Lamar, 26 February 1825, in Harden, *Troup,* pp. 267–68; Lamar to Troup, 10 March 1825, ibid., pp. 268–69; Affidavit of Colonel William Hambly, 4 July 1825, HR 98, 19/2 (161), p. 398.

51. Chilly McIntosh to Troup, 3 March 1825, in Harden, *Troup,* pp. 269–70; Troup to Chilly McIntosh, 5 March 1825, ibid., p. 270.

52. Report of the Select Committee of the House of Representatives on the Georgia Controversy, 3 March 1827, HR 98, 19/2 (161), p. 7; Adams, *Adams Memoirs,* 7:12 (20 May 1825); Crowell to Barbour, 12 March 1825, HR 98, 19/2 (161), p. 137; Thomas L. McKenney to Crowell, 19 March 1825, OIA, LS, RG 75, 1:420.

53. Milton S. Heath, *Constructive Liberalism: The Role of the State in Economic Development in Georgia to 1860* (Cambridge: Harvard University Press, 1954), pp. 143–47; Samuel G. McLendon, *History of the Public Domain of Georgia* (Atlanta: Foote and Davies, 1924), pp. 121–29.

54. Special Commissioner Major Timothy P. Andrews reported from Milledgeville to Secretary of War Barbour in June 1825 that because of Georgia's lottery system, "most, if not all, public men in Georgia seek to recommend themselves to their fellow citizens by a display of zeal in procuring lands to be thus disposed of among the people." Andrews to Barbour, 2 June 1825, HR 98, 19/2 (161), p. 171.

55. Proclamation of Governor Troup, 21 March 1825, ibid. pp. 138–39.

56. Troup to McIntosh, 29 March, 4 April 1825, *Niles' Weekly Register,* 28 (20 August 1825):399; Troup to the President, 31 March 1825, HR 98, 19/2 (161), p. 138.

57. McIntosh to Troup, 6 April 1825, *Niles' Weekly Register,* 28 (20 August 1825): 399; Troup to McIntosh, 9 April 1825, Georgia Executive Letterbook, reel 2: 283–84; McIntosh to Troup, 12 April 1825, *ASP:IA,* 2:759.

58. Troup to McIntosh, 18 April 1825, Georgia Executive Letterbook, reel 2:290. McIntosh knew very well that Big Warrior, Little Prince, and most of the national leaders had not been "Red Sticks" in 1812–14. It is therefore tempting to speculate, without the tiniest shred of evidence, that Troup suggested using the lie to cast an even darker shadow on the uncontrollable National Council. It would have not been beneath Troup's doing.

59. Proclamation of Governor Troup, 18 April 1825, HR 98, 19/2 (161), pp. 141–42; McIntosh to Troup, 25 April 1825, *Niles' Weekly Register,* 28 (20 August 1825):400.

60. Chilly McIntosh to Troup, 3 March 1825, in Harden, *Troup,* pp. 269–70; William McIntosh to Troup, 12 April 1825, *ASP:IA,* 2:759; Affidavit of Colonel William Hambly, 4 July 1825, HR 98, 19/2 (161), pp. 397–98.

61. Wilkins, *Cherokee Tragedy,* p. 166, says this vow of passive resistance was the result of Cherokee influence.

62. Crowell to Barbour, 27 April 1825, HR 98, 19/2 (161), pp. 140–41; Affidavit of Hambly, 4 July 1825, ibid., pp. 397–98; Testimony of the Reverend Isaac Smith, 5 July 1825, ibid., p. 400.

63. Testimony of Thomas Triplett, 20 July 1825, ibid., pp. 392–93. Crowell's description of the execution is in Crowell to Barbour, 2 May 1825, ibid., p. 143. Two particularly graphic and poignant accounts of the execution by the wives of the victims are Peggy and Susannah McIntosh to Campbell and Meriwether, 3 May 1825, OIA, LR, CA, RG 75, reel 219:636–38, and Laura Hawkins to Campbell and Meriwether, 3 May 1825, ibid., reel 219:639–41. In his statement, Agent Crowell (ibid., 781) says none of these women could write, they could barely speak English, and their accounts, therefore, could easily have been tampered with. The evidence suggests that they were. Several historians have described the execution. See particularly Bonner, "William McIntosh," pp. 142–43; Doster, *The Creek Indians and their Florida Lands, 1740–1823* 2:274–84. Andrew J. Pickett, "The Death of McIntosh, 1825," *Arrow Points* 10 (February 1925): 31–32, is based on an interview in 1848 with James Moore, a neighbor of McIntosh.

Chapter 5

1. Alexander Ware to George M. Troup, 1 May 1825, HR 98, 19/2 (161), p. 147; Charles McDonald to Troup, 6 May 1825, ibid., p. 150. Ware unwittingly supplied evidence of the minority status of McIntosh's followers. While the "hostiles" had four thousand warriors at the ready, he reported, the "friendly party amount now to only about 500."

2. Troup to Joseph Marshall, 3 May 1825, ibid., p. 145; Troup to Ware, 5 May 1825, Georgia Executive Letterbook, reel 2:293–94; Troup to Generals Wimberley, Miller, and Shorter, 5 May 1825, ibid., reel 2:294–95; Troup to McDonald, 7 May 1825, HR 98, 19/2 (161), pp. 148–49; Seaborn Jones, Aide de Camp, Orders to Mobilize the Militia, 5 May 1825, Georgia Executive Letterbook, reel 2:295.

3. Affidavit of Dr. M. Bartlett, 14 June 1825, HR 98, 19/2 (161), pp. 405–6; Affidavit of Solomon Betton, 26 July 1825, ibid., pp. 446–47.

4. Troup to the President, 3 May 1825, Georgia Executive Letterbook, reel 2:291–92.

5. Chilly McIntosh and others to James Barbour, 17 May 1825, OIA, LR, CA, RG 75, reel 219:1616–17.

6. Duncan Campbell to Barbour, 4 May 1825, HR 98, 19/2 (161), pp. 145–46. On 15 May Campbell explained to Barbour his confidence of eleven days before. "From the very prompt, and apparently, ingenuous manner in which the opposing Chiefs disavowed all feeling of resentment against the signers of the Treaty, all apprehensions of hostility were quieted and we believed the nation to be in a state of repose." Significantly, Campbell did not attempt to blame Crowell at that time for the execution of McIntosh. See Campbell to Barbour, 15 May 1825, OIA, LR, CA, RG 75, reel 219:634–35.

7. Adams, *Adams Memoirs,* 7:3–4 (15 May 1825); Troup to the President, 3 May 1825, Georgia Executive Letterbook, reel 2:291–92; John Crowell to Barbour, 2 May 1825, HR 98, 19/2 (161), p. 143.

8. Adams, *Adams Memoirs,* 7:4–5 (16 May 1825). *Niles' Weekly Register,* 28 (28 May, 4 June 1825): 197, 212, printed editorial comments from the South which explained the execution of McIntosh as the legal act of an established government which ought not attract the attention or interference of the United States or Georgia. One such commentator, describing McIntosh as a criminal deserving punishment, concluded that "the manner of punishment is nothing: that depends on the custom of the country. The Indians employ the rifle and the tomahawk; we use the gibbet."

9. In addition to the note of Chilly McIntosh and others to Barbour, 17 May 1825, cited earlier, see two others of the same date in OIA, LR, CA, RG 75, reel 219:1619–20, 1622–23.

10. Adams, *Adams Memoirs,* 7:3–8, 11–12 (15–20 May 1825); Barbour to McIntosh and others, 17 May 1825, OIA, LS, RG 75, 2:14. By 19 May, Adams and Barbour had decided Troup was a liar as well as a "madman." They spent a few minutes that day discussing Troup's "false and fabricated intelligence" about Crowell. See Adams, *Adams Memoirs,* 7:11 (19 May 1825).

11. Ibid., 7:6, 8, 11–12 (17, 19, and 20 May 1825); Barbour to Edmund P. Gaines, 18 May 1825, SW, LSMA, RG 107, 12:152–55; Barbour to Troup, 18 May 1825, OIA, LS, RG 75, 2:15–16; Barbour to Timothy P. Andrews, 19 May 1825, ibid., 2:18–19.

12. Adams, *Adams Memoirs,* 7:12 (20 May 1825); Barbour to Troup, 18 May 1825, OIA, LS, RG 75, 2:15–16.

13. For a solid analysis of Troup's political style and thinking, see Fortune, "George M. Troup," especially pp. 132, 147, 191–92. Fortune, pp. 234–39, 247, argues that a major reason for Troup's anxiety to expel the Indians, aside from his own electoral ambitions, was his desire to push forward with a massive river and canal project. This could not be done without the dismemberment of the Creek and Cherokee nations because their property separated Georgia from the Tennessee River.

14. Troup to the Georgia General Assembly, 23 May 1825, *Niles' Weekly Register,* 28 (11 June 1825): 238–40.

15. Troup to Barbour, 3 June 1825, OIA, LR, CA, RG 75, reel 220:1728–34.

16. "Report and Resolution of the Committee on the State of the Republic, in reference to the conduct of the Creek Indian Agent, Capt. John Crowell," 10 June 1825, HR 98, 19/2 (161), pp. 188–96. The Georgia senate approved the report by a margin of 31 votes to 18; the House, 64 votes to 18. Ibid., p. 211.

17. "An Act to dispose of and distribute the lands lately acquired by the United States, for the use of Georgia, of the Creek nation of Indians, by a Treaty made and concluded at the Indian Springs on the twelfth day of February, 1825," 9 June 1825, ibid., pp. 214–24. See also Edward J. Harden, Troup, pp. 189–93, 311–12; Martha Lou Houston, comp., *Reprint of Official Register*

of Land Lottery of Georgia, 1827 (Columbus: Walton-Forbes Co., 1929); Andrews to Barbour, 12 June 1825, HR 98, 19/2 (161), p. 182. For a discussion of the impact of state jurisdiction on Native nations, see Michael Paul Rogin, *Fathers and Children: Andrew Jackson and the Subjugation of the American Indian* (New York: Vintage Books, 1975), especially pp. 212–18. On the day after the law was passed, Troup ordered Captain James Harrison of Twiggs Cavalry to the frontier. The task of the unit, Troup stressed, was defensive, but, "Remember," he wrote, "our jurisdiction is now over the ceded territory so you can enter it to arrest offenders." Troup to Harrison, 10 June 1825, Georgia Executive Letterbook, reel 2:308–309.

18. Troup to Georgia House of Representatives, 6 June 1825; Captain William Howard to Troup, 2 June 1825; Major John Richardson to Troup, 3 June 1825 (these letters, plus editorial comment, were originally published in the Milledgeville *Georgia Journal* and the Milledgeville *Southern Recorder*), HR 98, 19/2 (161), pp. 180–81; Troup to Ware, 11 June 1825, *ASP:IA*, 2:819.

19. Andrews to Barbour, 2, 6, 12 June 1825, HR 98, 19/2 (161), pp. 170–73, 178–79, 182; Troup to the Georgia General Assembly, 9 June 1825, ibid., p. 187. As early as 2 June 1825, Andrews predicted to Barbour that if federal troops were not nearby, "a large militia force would be called out and marched against the Indians. Pretexts would not be wanting."

20. Crowell to Barbour, 8 May 1825, OIA, LR, CA, RG 75, reel 219:701–3; "Declaration of Chiefs concerning the death of McIntosh," 14 May 1825, ibid., reel 219:1099–1102.

21. "Journal of Events, consequent on an order from the General in Chief to Major General Gaines, dated Washington, May 18, 1825, directing him to repair to Milledgeville," HR 98, 19/2 (161), p. 588 (18 September 1825).

22. James W. Silver, *Edmund Pendleton Gaines, Frontier General* (Baton Rouge: Louisiana State University Press, 1949), is an excellent biography of a complex and colorful figure.

23. Troup to Gaines, 13 June 1825, *Niles' Weekly Register,* 28 (20 August 1825): 392; Gaines to Troup, 14 June 1825, ibid.; Gaines to Barbour, 15 June 1825, HR 98, 19/2 (161), p. 226. General Jacob Brown, commanding general of the Army, had described Gaines to President Adams as a "fair, honorable and virtuous man, but excitable." Adams, *Adams Memoirs,* 7:8 (19 May 1825).

24. Marshall, McIntosh, and others to Gaines, 19 June 1825, HR 98, 19/2 (161), pp. 596–98.

25. Gaines to Indian Chiefs, 19 June 1825, ibid., pp. 599–600.

26. Marshall, McIntosh, and others to Gaines, 20 June 1825, ibid., pp. 605–9.

27. Gaines to Barbour, 22, 27 June 1825, ibid., pp. 233, 245–46; Gaines to Barbour, 4 October 1825, OIA, LR, CA, RG 75, reel 219:1470–71; Andrews to Barbour, 4 July 1825, HR 98, 19/2 (161), pp. 252–53; "Journal of Events," ibid., p. 577 (22 June 1825). The second, and to Gaines offensive, communication contains whole sections identical to an undated memorial from the McIntosh party to the Georgia legislature sitting in special session from late in

May to mid-June. The memorial expressed great fear at going west without McIntosh and offered to pay four hundred thousand dollars (the purchase price promised in the Treaty of Indian Springs) for a tract twenty by forty miles on the east bank of the Chattahoochee. The document, written by former congressman John A. Cuthbert, was "suppressed" in Milledgeville. See John H. Brodnax to Andrews, 11 July 1825, ibid., p. 842 and "Memorial of the Headmen and Warriors of Coweta to the Chief men of Georgia," n.d., ibid., pp. 842–44.

28. *Niles' Weekly Register,* 28 (19 March 1925): 48.

29. "Journal of Events," HR 98, 19/2 (161), pp. 581–82 (28 June 1825).

30. Gaines to Creek Council, 28 June 1825, ibid., pp. 614–15; "Journal of Events," ibid., pp. 579–81 (28 June 1825).

31. "Journal of Events," ibid., pp. 582–86 (30 June–2 July 1825); "Resolution of the Creek Council," 29 June 1825, ibid., pp. 619–20.

32. "Journal of Events," ibid., pp. 579–81 (28 June 1825); Agreement with the Creeks, 29 June 1825, in Kappler, *Laws and Treaties,* 2:1034–35.

33. Creek Chiefs to Gaines, 29 June 1825, ibid., pp. 616–19; "Journal of Events," 582–83 (29, 30 June, 1 July 1825).

34. "Journal of Events," ibid., pp. 583–84 (1 July 1825); Gaines to McIntosh party, 3 July 1825, ibid., pp. 625–26.

35. Edward G. W. Butler to Frances Parke Lewis, 1 July 1825, Edward George Washington Butler Papers, Perkins Library, Duke University; Gaines to Barbour, 10, 18 July 1825, HR 98, 19/2 (161), pp. 272–73, 277. See James W. Silver, "A Counter-Proposal to the Indian Removal Policy of Andrew Jackson," *Journal of Mississippi History* 4 (October 1942): 207–15, and Calvin Lee Reese, "The United States Army and the Indian: Low Plains Area, 1815–1854" (Ph.D. diss., University of Southern California, 1963), pp. 163–66 for discussions of Gaines's developing views on United States Indian policy.

36. Butler to Lewis, 11 July 1825, Butler Papers; Gaines to Troup, 10 July 1825, *Niles' Weekly Register,* 28 (6 August 1825): 366–67; Testimony of William Edwards and Joseph Marshall, 9 July 1825, ibid., p. 367; Gaines to Barbour, 10 July 1825, HR 98, 19/2 (161), pp. 272–74.

37. These reports Gaines sent to Washington were drafted in proper language. His aide-de-camp, Lieutenant Butler, was more colorful in his private correspondence. "The only enemies we shall have to contend with," he assured his fiance, "will be the crazy governor and his corrupt and designing politicians. He is now raising an army to force the survey of the Indian land contrary to the Treaty and the orders of the President." Butler to Lewis, 11 July 1825, Butler Papers.

38. Adams, *Adams Memoirs,* 7:33–35 (20, 21 July 1825); Barbour to Troup, 21 July 1825, OIA, LR, CA, RG 75, reel 220:1839–41; Barbour to Gaines, 21 July 1825, SW, LSMA, RG 107, 12:170–71.

39. Lieutenant Butler was surprised. Raised by Andrew and Rachel Jackson, he had no particular faith in the vigor of John Quincy Adams. "If Andrew Jackson were president, I would say to you the Governor will immediately de

sist from his project or lose his life." Butler to Lewis, 11 July 1825, Butler Papers. In an unguarded moment Gaines may have said something similar. Later in 1825, Troup gathered affidavits from three men who claimed to have overheard, in August, the general call the governor a "demagogue" and a "traitor" and boast that if Troup pressed on with the survey, "he would be tried for treason and hung." See Affidavits of Michael Watson, Christopher B. Strong, and Joel Bailey, 10 November 1825, in Harden, *Troup,* pp. 393–94.

40. Gaines to Barbour, 9 August 1825, OIA, LR, CA, RG 75, reel 219:1412–13. As a young officer, Gaines had arrested Aaron Burr following the exposure of his "conspiracy."

41. Troup to Barbour, 15 August 1825, ibid., reel 220:1918–22.

42. Troup to Adams, 31 August 1825, *Niles' Weekly Register,* 29 (10 December 1825), p. 228. Fortune, "Troup," p. 206 n., says that it was "public knowledge" throughout Georgia that Gaines was openly and actively campaigning for John Clark, Troup's opponent in the coming gubernatorial election.

43. Barbour to Gaines, 19 September 1825, *National Intelligencer* (Washington, D.C.), 6 December 1825. The conflict between Gaines and Troup, the barest outline of which appears here, has been analyzed by James W. Silver in "General Gaines Meets Governor Troup. A State–Federal Clash in 1825," *Georgia Historical Quarterly* 27 (September 1943): 248–70, and idem., *Gaines,* pp. 113–29. Virtually all the correspondence in question appeared in the *Niles' Weekly Register* during the late summer and fall of 1825, thus giving it national exposure.

44. Gaines to Barbour, 12 September 1825, HR 98, 19/2 (161), pp. 554–55; General Orders, 12 September 1825, ibid., p. 558.

45. Andrew Jackson to Butler, 25 July 1825, in Bassett, *Correspondence of Jackson,* 3:288–89.

46. Gaines to Barbour, 4 August 1825, OIA, LR, CA, RG 75, reel 219:1375–78; C. Vandeventer to Gaines, 30 August 1825, SW, LSMA, RG 107, 12:179.

47. Barbour to Gaines, 16 September 1825, ibid., 12:182. For an interesting analysis of Adams's views on Indians and Indian policy and how they changed during the 1820s, see Lynn Hudson Parsons, " 'A Perpetual Harrow Upon My Feelings': John Quincy Adams and the American Indian," *The New England Quarterly* 46 (September 1973): 339–79.

48. Butler to Crowell, 9 October 1825, OIA, LR, CA, RG 75, reel 219:598; Gaines to Barbour, 11 October 1825, ibid., reel 219:1586–89.

49. Butler to Barbour, 18 November 1825, ibid., reel 219:583.

50. "Journal of a Meeting between General Gaines and the Creek Nation, 30 October–1 November 1825," HR 98, 19/2 (161), pp. 708–12; Powers of the Creek Delegation, 1 November 1825, OIA, LR, CA, RG 75, reel 219:583.

51. A detailed account of the negotiations and treaty is Richard J. Hryniewicki, "The Creek Treaty of Washington, 1826," *Georgia Historical Quarterly* 48 (December 1964): 425–41.

52. Draft Treaty, 3 December 1825, DRT, RG 75, 1:821–24.

53. Opothle Yoholo and others to Barbour, 3 December 1825, HR 98, 19/2 (161), pp. 717–19.

54. Adams, *Adams Memoirs,* 7:66, 73–74 (1, 7 December 1825).

55. Opothle Yoholo and others to Barbour, 3 December 1825, HR 98, 19/2 (161), p. 719; Adams, *Adams Memoirs,* 7:72–73, 79, 102 (6, 13 December 1825, 9 January 1826); Gaines to Barbour, 11 December 1825, HR 98, 19/2 (161), pp. 726–29; Barbour to Georgia Senators and Congressmen, 24 December 1825, SW, LSMA, RG 107, 12:202; Georgia Congressmen and Senators to Barbour, 7 January 1826, HD 59, 19/2 (151), pp. 54–56; Troup to Georgia Congressmen and Senators, 9 January 1826, Georgia Executive Letterbook, reel 2:362–63.

56. John Ridge to Thomas L. McKenney, 18 January 1826, HR 98, 19/2 (161), pp. 763–64; McKenney to Barbour, 11 May 1826, OIA, LS, RG 75, 3:71–74.

57. McKenney to Ridge, 19 January 1826, HR 98, 19/2 (161), p. 765; Ridge to McKenney, 19 January, 1826, ibid., p. 765; Treaty of Washington, 24 January 1826, in Kappler, *Laws and Treaties,* 2:264–67.

58. Adams to the Senate, 31 January 1826, in Richardson, *Messages and Papers of the Presidents* 2:890–92. Parsons, " 'A Perpetual Harrow Upon My Mind'," p. 353, argues that Adams, "whose constitutional nationalism was more thoroughgoing than that of any other nineteenth-century President," was strongly influenced by "the fact that the integrity of the federal government now was closely tied to the protection of the Indians."

59. Supplemental Article to the Creek Treaty of the 24th January, 1826, 31 March 1826, Kappler, *Laws and Treaties,* 2:267–68.

60. Barbour to the President, 25 June 1826, SW, LSP, RG 107, 2:156–57.

61. Kappler, *Laws and Treaties,* 2:265–66.

62. Ibid., 2:265; McKenney to Barbour, 11 May 1826, OIA, LS, RG 75, 3:71–74; Thomas Hart Benton and Louis McLane to Barbour, 15 May 1826, OIA, LR, CA, RG 75, reel 220:29–31.

63. Debo, *Road to Disappearance,* p. 92.

64. Peter A. Brannon, "Fort Bainbridge," *Arrow Points* 5 (5 August 1922): 21–28, calls Little Prince a "property owner of some means," and describes Big Warrior's two plantations, three hundred slaves, and two taverns, most of which Tuskeneah inherited. Mrs. Clement C. Clay, "Recollections of Opothleyoholo," ibid. 4 (5 February 1922): 35–36, describes Opothle Yoholo's wealth. John Bartlett Meserve, "Chief Opothleyohola," *Chronicles of Oklahoma* 9 (December 1931): 452, says that in 1860 Opothle Yoholo was "considered to be the richest member of the Creek tribes." The Cornells and the Stedhams were among the oldest and most influential mixed-blood families in the Nation, tracing their roots back to eighteenth-century traders.

65. Thomas Hart Benton, *Thirty Years' View* 2 vols. (New York: Appleton, 1854–56), 1:59–60; Wilkins, *Cherokee Tragedy,* pp. 175–76.

Chapter 6

1. Vinton, "Journal of My Excursion to Georgia," John Rogers Vinton Papers, Perkins Library, Duke University, 12 (19 February 1827).

2. John Crowell's defense, dated 30 July 1825, is in manuscript form in OIA, LR, CA, RG 75, reel 219:706–830 and published in HR 98, 19/2 (161), pp. 457–508. Major Timothy Andrews's report to Secretary James Barbour, 1 August 1825, is printed in ibid., pp. 305–47. Crowell discusses the question of his resignation in Crowell to Barbour, 18 December 1825, OIA, LR, CA, RG 75, reel 219:1191–94.

3. George M. Troup to Georgia General Assembly, 8 November 1825, *Niles' Weekly Register*, 29 (26 November 1825): 204; Troup to Georgia Congressmen and Senators, 9 January 1826, Georgia Executive Letterbook, reel 2:362–63.

4. Fortune, "George M. Troup," pp. 146–55. Averitt, "The Democratic Party in Georgia," pp. 17–19, 53–62, argues that Troup's states' rights extremism, the central issue of the 1825 campaign, split the Clark party. Clark had argued a moderate states' rights line and had been critical of Troup's handling of the "Creek Crisis." Many Clark supporters, however, preferred extremism to moderation.

5. Troup to Dr. W. C. Daniell, 8 June 1826, in Harden, *Troup,* pp. 453–54.

6. Barbour to Troup, 16 September 1826, OIA, LS. RG 75, 3:169–70; J. H. Rooker to Barbour, 17 August 1826, OIA, LR. CA, RG 75, reel 220:485–87; Crowell to Barbour, 26 August 1826, ibid., reel 220:267–69; Solomon Betton, 27 August 1826, ibid., reel 220:44–46.

7. Proclamation of Governor Troup, 26 August 1826, in Harden, *Troup,* p. 463 n; Troup to Barbour, 26 August 1826, in ibid., pp. 456–59.

8. Barbour to Troup, 16 September 1826, OIA, LS, RG 75, 3:169–70; Barbour to Crowell, 16 September 1826, ibid., 3:171.

9. Crowell to Barbour, 12 October 1826, OIA, LR, CA, RG 75, reel 220:279–81.

10. Crowell to Barbour, 30 September 1826, ibid., reel 220:274–77; Crowell to Barbour, 6 November 1826, ibid., reel 220:286.

11. The Cherokees began to restructure their National Council in 1817 with the establishment of a thirteen-member executive committee charged with conducting relations with the United States. In 1820, the Council divided the Nation into eight representative districts and streamlined procedures for electing delegates. In 1823, the executive committee gained the power to review all Council decisions. Two years later, in an elaborate code, the Council reaffirmed its authority over the national domain, prohibited individual headmen from selling public property, and forbade any Cherokee to sell his privately owned improvements to a non-Cherokee. Then, in 1827, the Council called a constitutional convention. The document, patterned after that of the United States, was ratified by popular vote in 1828. V. Richard Persico, Jr., "Early Nineteenth-Century Cherokee Political Organization," in *The Chero*

kee Indian Nation: A Troubled History, ed. Duane H. King (Knoxville: University of Tennessee Press, 1979), pp. 92-109, is a convenient source for the details.

12. Creek Chiefs to John Ridge, 16 December 1826, Report on the Indian Agent, 15 April 1828, HD 248, 20th Cong., 1st. sess., serial 174, pp. 7-8. Hereafter cited as HD 248, 20/1 (174). Ridge to Barbour, 20 December 1826, ibid., pp. 6-7. For correspondence on whites killed by Creeks, see Troup to Crowell, 30 November 1826, OIA, LR, CA, RG 75, reel 220:632; Crowell to Troup, 17 December 1826, ibid., reel 220:594-95; Captain J. S. McIntosh to Barbour, 18 January 1827, OIA, LR, CA, RG 75, reel 221:380-82.

13. Troup to Barbour, 6 October 1826, in Harden, *Troup,* pp. 460-63; Troup to Georgia General Assembly, 7 November 1826, ibid., pp. 466, 469-70; Troup to Georgia General Assembly, 9 December 1826, *ASP:IA,* 2:749.

14. Crowell to Barbour, 15 January 1827, OIA, LR, CA, RG 75, reel 221:183-84; Troup to the President, 27 January 1827, ibid., reel 221:525-26; Little Prince and others to Georgia Surveyors, 12 January 1827, ibid., reel 221: 527-28; Wiley Williams to Troup, 22 January 1827, ibid., reel 221:529-30; James A. Rogers to Troup, 23 January 1827, ibid., reel 221:531-32. All these letters were published in the *National Intelligencer* (Washington, D.C.), 8, 10 February 1827.

15. Thomas L. McKenney to David Brearley, 13 May 1826, OIA, LS, RG 75, 3:76; Brearley to Barbour, 2 December 1826, OIA, LR, CE, RG 75, reel 237:12-14; McKenney to William R. King and George W. Owen, 26 January 1827, OIA, LS, RG 75, 3:340. See also Debo, *Road to Disappearance,* p. 95, and Mooney, *Historical Sketch of the Cherokees,* pp. 93-97.

16. Creek Chiefs to Barbour, 17 February 1827, OIA, LR, CA, RG 75, reel 221:176-81. This document, drafted by John Ridge, "secy pro tem," carried about one hundred seventy-five signatures.

17. Crowell to Barbour, 21 June 1827, ibid, reel 221:212-19; Barbour to Headmen of Cherokee Nation, 5 June 1827,OIA, LS, RG 75, 4:83; McKenney to Barbour, 24 March 1828, ibid., 4:354-63.

18. Adams, *Adams Memoirs,* 7:219-20 (27, 29 January 1827); Barbour to Troup, 29 January 1827, SW, LSMA, RG 107, 12:270; Barbour to John H. Morel, ibid.; Barbour to R. W. Habersham, ibid., 12:271; Troup to Barbour, 17 February 1827, *National Intelligencer* (Washington D.C.), 3 March 1827; General Orders, 17 February 1827, Harden *Troup,* p. 487; Circular to State Attorney and Solicitor General, 17 February 1827, *National Intelligencer,* (Washington, D.C.), 3 March 1827. See Vinton, "Journal of My Excursion to Georgia," for a colorful description of Troup, Milledgevile, Georgia politics, and public opinion on the Creeks and the federal government.

19. Adams, *Adams Memoirs,* 7:221 (4 February 1827); President John Quincy Adams to Congress, 5 February 1827, in Richardson, *Messages and Papers of the Presidents,* 3:936-39. Adams's message did not engender universal respect. John Eaton, in describing the turn of events in Georgia and Washington to his close friend, Andrew Jackson, snorted, "None are so silly to be-

lieve that this Civil administration, and Civil cabinets who so oft have denounced mil. cheiftains will raise the sword against a sovereign State: the thing is too preposterous and absurd for belief. Will he send his little army of 6,000, they will be eat up before they get to Georgia, while the mil'a of the So and west will never arm in such a cause. How idle then for peicable men like our present rulers who so often have denounced mil. cheiftains, to talk of War, and upon their own citisens. If the laws be not strong enough let the laws be amended and the Judiciary settle the matter—not the *bayonette.*" Eaton to Jackson, 8 February 1827, in Bassett, *Correspondence of Jackson,* 3:342.

20. Barbour to Crowell, 31 January 1827, OIA, LS, RG 75, 3:349.

21. McKenney to Vinton, 17 February 1827, OIA, LS, RG 75, 3:493–94; Vinton to Barbour, 7, 30 March 1827, OIA, LR, CA, RG 75, reel 221:605–7, 616–18; Vinton to Barbour, 17 March 1827, HD 248, 20/1 (174), pp. 9–11.

22. Crowell to Barbour, 2, 18 March 1827, OIA, LR, CA, RG 75, reel 221: 197–98, 202–3.

23. Crowell to Barbour, 16 April 1827, ibid., reel 221:205–6; Charles I. Nourse to Crowell, 24 April 1827, OIA, LS, RG 75, 4:29; Barbour to Crowell, 26 April 1827, ibid., 4:31–32.

24. Little Prince to Crowell, 3 June 1827, OIA, LR, CA, RG 75, reel 221:221–22.

25. Creek Chiefs to Barbour, 5 June 1827, ibid., reel 221:165–70.

26. Crowell to Barbour, 21 June 1827, ibid., reel 221:212–19; Barbour to Headmen of Cherokee Nation, 25 June 1827, OIA, LS, RG 75, 4:83; Wilkins, *Cherokee Tragedy,* p. 176.

27. Barbour to Little Prince, 23 June 1827, OIA, LS, RG 75, 4:78–81.

28. Crowell to Barbour, 12 August 1827, OIA, LR, CA, RG 75, reel 221:232–35; Creek Chiefs to Barbour, 2 August 1827, ibid., reel 221:172–74. Crowell's continued failures so disgusted Barbour that he suggested firing him. The agent kept his job largely because neither the secretary nor the president could think of a suitable replacement. See Adams, *Adams Memoirs,* 7:294 (20 June 1827); Barbour to the President, 14 August 1827, SW, LSP, RG 107, 2:182–83.

29. McKenney to Barbour, 24 March 1828, OIA, LS, RG 75, 4:354–63; Col. McKenney's Talk to the Creeks, 14 November 1827, DRT, RG 75, 1:64–76. For a published discussion of the Fort Mitchell Treaty, see Richard J. Hryniewicki, "The Creek Treaty of November 15, 1827, *Georgia Historical Quarterly* 52 (March 1968): 1–15.

30. Opothle Yoholo and Creek Delegates to McKenney, 24 February 1826, OIA, LR, CA, RG 75, reel 220:211. McKenney's *Sketch of a Tour to the Lakes, of the Character and Customs of the Chippeway Indians, and of Incidents connected with the Treaty of Fond Du Lac* (Baltimore: Fielding Lucas, Jr., 1827), recounts the northern leg of his tour. He summarized that material and added a brief commentary on his return home through the southern nations in his *Memoirs, Official and Personal,* ed. Herman J. Viola (Lincoln: University of Nebraska Press, 1973). See also Viola, *Thomas L. McKenney,* pp. 135–67,

206–10. McKenney was severely criticized for "breaking" John Ridge, a man recognized as a chief by the Creek Council. His elaborate and self-serving justification is in McKenney to Barbour, 24 March 1828, OIA, LS, RG 75, 4:354–63. Regardless of McKenney's stated reasons, Debo, *Road to Disappearance,* p. 93, correctly argues that McKenney hated Ridge "not for his exploitation of the Creeks, but for his ability and independence" as their adviser.

31. Thomas L. McKenney and James Hall, *Biographical Sketches and Anecdotes of Ninety-Five of 120 Principal Chiefs from the Indian Tribes of North America,* reprint edition (Washington: U.S. Department of the Interior, Bureau of Indian Affairs, 1967), pp. 209–14.

32. Kappler, *Laws and Treaties,* 2:284–85.

33. Crowell to Barbour, 7 January 1828, OIA, LR, CA, RG 75, reel 221:715–18.

Chapter 7

1. Captain J. S. McIntosh to James Barbour, 18 January 1827, OIA, LR, CA, RG 75, reel 221:380–82.

2. There is a mass of correspondence on this swindle, a brief sense of which can be gained from the following: Barbour to Solomon Betton, 14 June 1827, OIA, LS, RG 75, 4:69–70; John Crowell to Barbour, 17 June 1827, OIA, LR, CA, RG 75, reel 221:243–46; Crowell to S. S. Hamilton (Confidential), 17 August 1827, ibid., reel 221:239–40; Crowell to Barbour, 27 November 1827, ibid., reel 221:280–85; Thomas L. McKenney to Peter Porter, 26 September 1828, OIA, LS, RG 75, 5:125–31.

3. John Forsyth to Colonel Michael Watson, 13 November 1827, OIA, LR, CA, RG 75, reel 221:313–14; McKenney to Crowell, 10 March 1828, OIA, LS, RG 75, 4:332; "An Act to keep the Creeks out of the State," 20 December 1828, OIA, LR, CA, RG 75, reel 222:157–58; Forsyth to Samuel L. Southard, 23 June 1828, ibid., reel 221:793–95; Adjutant General to Colonel Clinch, 3 July 1828, ibid., reel 221:754–55.

4. McKenney to Barbour, 29 November 1827, OIA, LS, RG 75, 4:153–57.

5. McKenney to George W. Owen, 3 January 1828, ibid., 4:226; McKenney to Barbour, 29 November 1827, ibid., pp. 153–57. Robert F. Berkhofer, Jr., *The White Man's Indian: Images of the American Indian from Columbus to the Present* (New York: Random House, 1978), is the newest and best analysis of the mentality displayed here by McKenney.

6. "Statement of the purchases of land made from each Indian tribe," Message Concerning Indian Lands, 20 July 1840, S.D. 616, 26th Cong., 1st. sess., serial 361, p. 4.

7. Israel Pickens to George Troup, 3 July 1825, Alabama Executive Letterbook, Alabama Department of Archives and History, Montgomery, microfilm copy, reel 2:56–57; Edmund P. Gaines to Pickens, 4 July 1825, *Niles' Weekly Register,* 29 (8 October 1825): 83–84; Pickens to Gaines, 28 July 1825, Alabama Executive Letterbook, reel 2:59–60.

8. Alabama Senate *Journal, 1825–26,* Debates (30th. and 31 December 1825, 2d. and 13 January 1826), pp. 100, 105, 106, 155, 157, and 158; Alabama House *Journal, 1825–26,* Debates (2, 7, 12, and 13 January 1826), pp. 149, 184–85, 208, 215; John Murphy to Alabama Legislature, 7 January 1826, Alabama Senate *Journal, 1825–26,* pp. 127–30; ibid., *Journal 1824–25,* Debates, (24th. and 30 November 1824), pp. 25, 43; Alabama House *Journal, 1824–25,* Debates (22, 27, 29, and 30 November 1824), pp. 22, 42, 46, 51.

9. Alabama Senate *Journal, 1826–27,* Annual Message of Governor John Murphy, 21 November 1826, p. 11.

10. Alabama Senate *Journal, 1826–27,* Debates (15, 28, and 30 December 1826), pp. 68, 96, 101–2. The house slightly modified the language and passed the resolution 13 January 1827. See *Acts Passed at the Eighth Annual Session of the General Assembly of the State of Alabama* (Tuscaloosa, 1827), pp. 120–21.

11. Alabama House *Journal, 1826–27,* Debates (20, 28, and 30 December 1826, 5, 9, and 11 January 1827), pp. 142, 167, 183–85, 216, 239, 262; Alabama Senate *Journal, 1826–27,* Debates (7 December 1826, 1st. and 4 January 1827), pp. 51, 104, 114; John G. Aiken, comp., *Digest of the Laws of the State of Alabama* (Philadelphia: Alexander Towar, 1833), p. 223. This act predated by nearly two years the more well-known series of laws passed by the Georgia legislature to extend civil and criminal jurisdiction over the Cherokee Nation. See Phillips, *Georgia and State Rights,* pp. 72–73.

12. Crowell to Barbour, 27 January 1827, OIA, LR, CA, RG 75, reel 221:189; "An Act to prevent Creeks from hunting in settled country," 11 January 1827, ibid., reel 221:192–93.

13. For Lewis's report, see Alabama House *Journal, 1828–29,* Debates (21 January 1829), pp. 220–23. See also Thomas P. Abernethy, *The Formative Years in Alabama, 1815–1828,* 2d edition (University: University of Alabama Press, 1965), pp. 147–48; Ronald W. Faircloth, "The Legislative Career of Dixon Hall Lewis, 1826–1848" (master's thesis, Auburn University, 1965), pp. 15–18. The acts of 1828 and 1829 are in Aiken, *Digest of Alabama Laws,* pp. 223–24. The *Mobile Commercial Register,* one of the most prominent Alabama newspapers, opposed the extension law of 1829 on the grounds that it violated the last article of the Alabama constitution, which obligated the state to "forever disclaim all right or title to the waste or unappropriated lands lying within this State, and the same shall be and remain at the sole and entire disposition of the United States." 13 September 1828, 14 January 1829. Georgia enacted a similar extension law in January 1829. Scholars have commonly argued that the election of Andrew Jackson was the signal to pass the law.

14. See Alabama House *Journal, 1829–30, 1830–31, 1831–32,* passim; Gabriel Moore to the Senate, 16 November 1830, Alabama Senate *Journal, 1830–31,* pp. 12–13; Samuel B. Moore to the Senate, 22 November 1831, ibid., *1831–32,* p. 15; Aiken, *Digest of Alabama Laws,* pp. 224–25. The supreme court of the state of Alabama, on two occasions, upheld the constitutionality of the extension acts. Alabama House *Journal, 1833–34,* Debates (24 December

1833), pp. 132–33. One of the cases, *Caldwell* v. *The State of Alabama,* 1 Stewart and Potter (Alabama) 327 (1832), is printed in Vine Deloria, Jr., ed., *Of Utmost Good Faith* (New York: Bantam Books, 1972), pp. 10–56.

15. Crowell to Barbour, 27 January 1827, OIA, LR, CA, RG 75, reel 221:189; Thomas Cobb to Barbour, 23 February 1827, ibid., reel 221:161–63; Adams, *Adams Memoirs* 7:222, 232 (8, 26 February 1827); Barbour to John Murphy, 2 March 1827, OIA, LS, RG 75, 3:415; "An Act regulating trade and intercourse with the Indian tribes," 30 March 1802, *United States Statutes at Large,* 2:139–46.

16. Crowell to Barbour, 6 December 1827, OIA, LR, CA, RG 75, reel 221:289–91; Debo, *Road to Disappearance,* p. 95.

17. Lee Compere to McKenney, 10 December 1827, OIA, LR, CE, RG 75, reel 237:78–82.

18. McKenney to John Eaton, 11 February 1830, OIA, LS, RG 75, 6:262.

19. Proceedings in the Council at Broken Arrow, 28 June 1825, HR 98, 19/2 (161), p. 262; "Journal of Events," ibid., p. 580 (28 June 1825).

20. William Walker to William R. King, 8 December 1827, OIA, LR, CE, RG 75, reel 237:92–94; Compere to McKenney, 10 December 1827, ibid., 1:78–82; John Davis to Walker, 14 February 1828, OIA, LR, CA, RG 75, reel 221:699.

21. Compere to McKenney, 10 December 1827, OIA, LR, CE, RG 75, reel 237:78–79.

22. Walker to McKenney, 3 March 1828, ibid., reel 237:183.

23. Creek Emigrants to David Brearley, 3 June 1828, ibid., reel 237:154.

24. Walker to McKenney, 3, 8 March 1828, ibid., reel 237:181–84, 174–75; Walker to McKenney, 8 March 1828, OIA, LR, CA, RG 75, reel 221:876; Creek Emigrants to McKenney, 18 July 1828, OIA, LR, CE, RG 75, reel 237:158–59; King to Secretary of War, 23 March 1828, OIA, LR, CA, RG 75, reel 221:827; Crowell to Barbour, 6 June 1828, ibid., pp. 742–44.

25. McKenney to Crowell 23 July 1828, OIA, LS, RG 75, 5:50–51.

26. Brearley to Porter, 6 September 1828, OIA, LR, CE, RG 75, reel 237:131–32; J. W. Freeman to George W. Owen, 25 August 1828, OIA, LR, CA, RG 75, reel 221:837–38.

27. Charles I. Nourse to Major General A. Macomb, 23 September 1828, SW, LSMA, RG 107, 12:377; Nourse to Forsyth, 23 September 1828, ibid., 12:377; Porter to Forsyth, 23 September 1828, OIA, LS, RG 75, 5:118.

28. Nourse to Macomb, 23 September 1828, SW, LSMA, RG 107, 12:377. As Parsons, " 'A Perpetual Harrow Upon My Feelings'," p. 359, points out, "In the last weeks of his presidential term, Adams showed signs of acceding to the white demands upon the Indians."

29. McKenney to Porter, 6 October 1828, OIA, LS, RG 75, 5:146–47. Neither Porter nor Adams took any notice of McKenney's concern, and the troops remained at Tuckabatchee until the end of the year, at which time they returned to the relative comfort of the Fort Mitchell barracks for winter quarters.

30. Thomas Triplett to McKenney, 28 October 1828, OIA, LR, CA, RG 75, reel 221:865–67.

31. Andrew Jackson, First Annual Message, 8 December 1829, in Richardson, *Messages and Papers of the Presidents*, 3:1020–22; Ronald N. Satz, *American Indian Policy in the Jacksonian Era* (Lincoln: University of Nebraska Press, 1975), pp. 12–13 and passim.

32. Jackson to the Creeks, 23 March 1829, OIA, LS, RG 75, 5:373–75.

33. Writ for the arrest of Opothle Yoholo and Jim Boy, 16 February 1829, OIA, LR, CA, RG 75, reel 222:20; Writ for the arrest of Jim Boy, 16 February 1829, ibid., reel 222:28; Writ for the arrest of Opothle Yoholo, 6 March 1829, ibid., reel 222:29–30; *Mobile Commercial Register*, 7 March 1829; *National Intelligencer* (Washington, D.C.), 21 October 1829. The *Montgomery Alabama Journal*, 2 October 1829, published a near verbatim transcript of the arguments. Ibid., 19 March 1830, refers to the mistrial and the Reed case.

34. Creek Chiefs to the President, 20 March 1829, OIA, LR, CA, RG 75, reel 222:14–18.

35. Crowell to Eaton, 7 May 1829, ibid., reel 222:59–61; Crowell to McKenney, 11 May 1829, ibid., reel 222:63–64; Crowell to John Branch, 11 May 1829, ibid., reel 222:66–71.

36. Crowell to Branch, 11 May 1829, ibid., reel 222:70–71; Crowell to Eaton, 18 April, 14 May, 18 September 1829, ibid., reel 222:55–56, 74–75, 123–24; McKenney to Crowell, 15 July 1829, OIA, LS, RG 75, 6:51; Crowell to McKenney, 1 August, 6 October 1829, OIA, LR, CA, RG 75, reel 222:118–19, 129; McKenney to Eaton, 8 September 1829, OIA, LS, RG 75, 6:82.

37. Crowell to Eaton, 10 October 1829, OIA, LR, CA, RG 75, reel 222:138–39.

38. John Coffee to Eaton, 24 December 1829, OIA, LR, CE, RG 75, reel 237:252.

39. McKenney to Eaton, 16 October 1829, OIA, LS, RG 75, 6:121–23.

40. "Memorial of a Deputation from the Creek Nation of Indians," 3 February 1830, SD 53, 21st Cong., 1st sess., serial 193, pp. 1–5.

41. McKenney to Eaton, 16 October 1829, OIA, LS, RG 75, 6:121–23.

42. Creek Chiefs to the President, 12 October, 20 November, 10 December 1829, OIA, LR, CA, RG 75, reel 222:33, 37–40, 42–43.

43. McKenney to Eaton, 16 February 1830, OIA, LS, RG 75, 6:272–73; Paddy Carr to Eaton, 10 December 1829, OIA, LR, CA, RG 75, reel 222:35.

44. Creek Chiefs to the President and Secretary of War, 21 January 1830, OIA, LR, CA, RG 75, reel 222:275–76; McKenney to Eaton, 16 February 1830, OIA, LS, RG 75, 6:272–74.

45. Creek Chiefs to the President, 1 February 1830, OIA, LR, CA, RG 75, reel 222:281–82.

46. Creek Chiefs to the President, 10 December 1829, ibid., reel 222:42–43; McKenney to Eaton, 16 February 1830, OIA, LS, RG 75, 6:272–74.

47. Crowell to McKenney, 4 February 1830, "Report on the Indians," SD 110, 21st Cong. 1st sess., serial 193, p. 15.

48. Creek Chiefs to the Indian Office, 21 January 1830, OIA, LR, CA, RG 75, reel 222:271–73.

49. McKenney to Eaton, 16 February 1830, OIA, LS, RG 75, 6:272–74; McKenney to John Ridge, 26 January 1830, ibid., 6:243; McKenney to Opothle Yoholo, 16 February 1830, ibid., 6:274–75.

50. Eaton to Creek Indians East of the Mississippi, 20 March 1830, ibid., 6:343–46.

51. Creek Chiefs to the President, 20, 25 April 1830, OIA, LR, CA, RG 75, reel 222:285–87, 289, 298–300. See Rolly McIntosh to the Secretary of War, 1 May 1830, ibid., reel 222:369–73, in which the brother of the dead William McIntosh charged that these letters were forgeries concocted by Thomas Crowell to protect his brother's powerful and profitable position. Although he believed Crowell was in every respect unsuited to be agent, McIntosh wrote, he had long since given up hope of ousting him. And rather than follow him west, he would go in spite of the agent.

52. S. C. Benton to Eaton, 8 February 1830, ibid., reel 222:286; Eaton to Major General Macomb, 19 February 1830, SW, LSMA, RG 107, 12:473; John Elliot to Eaton, 4 June 1830, OIA, LR, CA, RG 75, reel 222:349–51. Newspaper coverage was spectacular. The *Montgomery Alabama Journal,* 12, 19 February 1830, was perhaps the most complete, but see also the *National Intelligencer* (Washington, D.C.), 9 March, 6 May 1830, and the *United States Telegraph* (Washington, D.C.), 20 February 1830. The records for *United States* v. *Tuskinaha* are in RG 21, U.S. District Court Records, Southern District of Alabama (Mobile), Mixed Cases: 1813–1840, Box 13, Case no. 403, National Archives Federal Records Center, Atlanta.

53. Creek Chiefs to the President, 20 April 1830, OIA, LR, CA, RG 75, reel 222:285–87.

54. The Council reinstated Tuskeneah as head chief of the Upper Towns in late 1831. See Creek Chiefs to the Secretary of War, 15 December 1831, ibid., reel 222:450.

55. Eaton to King, 20 March 1830, SW, LSMA, RG 107, 12:481; Eaton to Creek Indians East of the Mississippi, [17 or 18] May 1830, OIA, LS, RG 75, 6:422–23. *Montgomery Alabama Journal,* 19 March, 9 April 1830; *National Intelligencer,* (Washington, D.C.), 6, 24 April 1830; *Niles' Weekly Register,* 38 (8 May 1830): 203–4.

56. Lieutenant F. D. Newcomb to Eaton, 9 September, 30 October 1830, OIA, LR, CA, RG 75, reel 222:374–80; Creek Chiefs to Newcomb, 27 October 1830, ibid., reel 222:381–82; Newcomb to Creek Chiefs, 27 October 1830, ibid., reel 222:377–78; Eaton to Newcomb, 10 November 1830, SW, LSMA, RG 107, 13:15; *Mobile Commercial Register,* 12 October 1830.

57. Eaton to Crowell, 4 June 1830, OIA, LS, RG 75, 6:449–51; Crowell to Eaton, 8 August 1830, OIA, LR, CA, RG 75, reel 222:319–24; Creek Chiefs to Crowell, 5 August 1830, ibid., reel 222:325–26; Jackson to William B. Lewis, 25 August 1830, in Bassett, *Correspondence of Jackson,* 4:177.

58. Instructions of Creek Council to Delegates, 7 January 1831, OIA, LR,

CA, RG 75, reel 222:425–26; Crowell to Eaton, 13 June 1831, ibid., reel 222:424–65; Philip Wager to Eaton, 28 December 1830, ibid., reel 222:402; Crowell to Eaton, 1 January 1831, ibid., reel 222:457; McKenney to Indian Agents (Circular), 18 June 1830, OIA, LS, RG 75, 6:486.

59. Tuckabatchee Hadjo and Octeahchee Emathla to Eaton, 1, 26 February 1831, OIA, LR, CA, RG 75, reel 222:413–15, 417, 432; Tuckabatchee Hadjo and Octeahchee Emathla to S. S. Hamilton, 15 February 1831, ibid., reel 222:427; Tuckabatchee Hadjo and Octeahchee Emathla to the President, 18 February 1831, ibid., reel 222:429–30; Crowell to Eaton, 2 February 1831, ibid., reel 222:470; John H. Brodnax to Hamilton, OIA, LR, CE, RG 75, reel 237:245–46.

60. Creek Chiefs to the Secretary of War, 8 April 1830, OIA, LR, CA, RG 75, reel 222:434–37.

61. Tuskeneah of Cusseta to the President, 21 May 1831, ibid., reel 222:441–43.

62. William Moor to Eneah Mico and others, 6 December 1831, SD 512, 23/1 (245), p. 709; List of names of heads of families, OIA, LR, CA, RG 75, reel 222:549–51.

63. Petition of Citizens of Columbus, Georgia, to the President, 31 May 1831, ibid., pp. 564–65; Eaton to George Gilmer, 17 June 1831, OIA, LS, RG 75, 7:279–81; Crowell to Eaton, 2 July 1831, OIA, LR, CA, RG 75, reel 222:518; Account of Dr. W. L. Wharton, 5 December 1831, ibid., reel 222:537–38.

64. Crowell to Lewis Cass, 15 December 1831, ibid., reel 222:545; Credentials of Creek Delegation, 15 December 1831, ibid., reel 222:452–53; Cass to Chiefs of the Creek Tribe now in Washington, 16 January 1832, OIA, LS, RG 75, 8:15–17; Memorial of the Head Men and Warriors of the Creek Nation of Indians, 24 January 1832, HD 102, 22d Cong. 1st sess., serial 288, pp. 1–5; Opothle Yoholo and others to Cass, 23 January 1832, OIA, LR, CA, RG 75, reel 223:79–80; Elbert Herring to Crowell, 25 January 1832, OIA, LS, RG 75, 8:37.

65. Crowell to Cass, 25 January 1832, OIA, LR, CA, RG 75, reel 222:113; Crowell to Cass, 29 February 1832, ibid., reel 222:117.

66. Opothle Yoholo and others to Cass, 19 March 1832, ibid., reel 222:88–92.

67. Crowell to Cass, 20 March 1832, ibid., reel 222:19–20; Kappler, *Laws and Treaties,* 2:341–43.

68. Herring to Crowell, 5 November 1832, OIA, LS, RG 75, 9:334–35; John Robb to Leonard Tarrant, 22 November 1832, ibid., 9:382.

69. Aiken, *Digest of Alabama Laws,* pp. 224–25.

70. Creek Chiefs to the Secretary of War, 8 April 1831, OIA, LR, CA, RG 75, reel 222:434.

Chapter 8

1. Kappler, *Laws and Treaties,* 2:341; *United States Statutes at Large,* 2:445–46.

2. Lewis Cass to Robert S. Crawford, 5 April 1832, OIA, LS, RG 75, 8:228–29; Crawford to Cass, 27 April 1832, OIA, LR, CA, RG 75, reel 223:43–44; Alexander Macomb to Philip Wager, 5 April 1832, "Report on the Death of Hardiman Owens," 3 March 1834, HD 149, 23d Cong., 1st sess., serial 256, p. 1. Hereafter cited as HD 149, 23/1 (256). *Mobile Commercial Register,* 20 April 1832.

3. Crawford to Cass, 5 July 1832, OIA, LR, CA, RG 75, reel 223:46–47; John Robb to Crawford, 20 July 1832, OIA, LS, RG 75, 9:76.

4. John Brodnax to Cass, 23 July 1832, OIA, LR, CA, RG 75, reel 223:33–39; John Crowell, Enoch Parsons, Benjamin Parsons to Cass, 29 September 1832, SD 512, 23/1 (246), pp. 467–68.

5. William Irwin to Cass, 30 July 1832, OIA, LR, CA, RG 75, reel 223:209–11; Crowell to Cass, 3 August 1832, ibid., reel 223:198; Crawford to Robb, 31 August 1832, ibid., reel 223:49–52; Crawford to Robb, 15 September 1832, ibid., reel 223:54–59; Cass to Crawford, 10 October 1832, OIA, LS, RG 75, 9:281–82. See Anne Kendrick Walker, *Backtracking in Barbour County: A Narrative of the Last Alabama Frontier* (Richmond: Dietz Press, 1941), pp. 5–7, 16–19, for anecdotal information on early Irwinton.

6. Irwin to Cass, 30 July 1832, OIA, LR, CA, RG 75, reel 223:209–11; Crowell to Cass, 3 August 1832, ibid., reel 223:198; John Elliott to Cass, 5 November 1832, ibid., reel 223:189–91.

7. Jeremiah Austill to Cass, 15 November 1832, ibid., reel 223:3–4; Crowell to Cass, 15 October 1832, ibid., reel 223;162. During 1832 and 1833, Fort Mitchell housed one company of artillery and three of infantry. The total number of men hovered at 155 to 160. See Peter A. Brannon, ed., "Distribution of Troops at Fort Mitchell," *Alabama Historical Quarterly* 21 (1959): 14.

8. Creek Chiefs to Crowell, Parsons, and Parsons, 26 September 1832, SD 512, 23/1 (246), p. 470; Crowell, Parsons, and Parsons to Cass, 26 September 1832, ibid., pp. 467–68.

9. Neah Micco, Tuskeneahhaw, and others to Cass, 20 December 1832, OIA, LR, CA, RG 75, reel 223:268; Creek Chiefs to Cass, 27 September 1832, SD 512, 23/1 (246), p. 464.

10. Enoch Parsons to Cass, 12 October 1832, OIA, LR, CA, RG 75, reel 223:299–301.

11. Neah Micco and Tuskeneahaw to Cass, 20 December 1832, reel 223:268–70; Robb to B. S. Parsons, 22 November 1832, OIA, LS, RG 75, 9:380; Robb to Crowell, 22 November 1832, ibid., 9:381.

12. Cass to Gabriel Moore, 8 December 1832, ibid., 9:402–3.

13. Elbert Herring to Crowell, 5 November 1832, ibid., 9:344–45; Cass to Neah Micco and other Creek chiefs, 21 December 1832, ibid., 9:434–35; Robb to Leonard Tarrant, 22 November 1832, ibid., 9:382.

14. Austill to Cass, 31 July 1833, OIA, LR, CA, RG 75, reel 223:515–17; Lieutenant D. A. Manning to Major J. S. McIntosh, 31 July 1833, HD 149, 23/1 (256), pp. 2–4; *Niles' Weekly Register,* 45 (26 October 1833):143.

15. McIntosh to Austill, 15 October 1833, SD 512, 23/1 (247), pp. 622–23; *Niles' Weekly Register,* 45 (2 November 1833):160–61.

16. Further elaboration on this Alabama–United States jurisdictional controversy generated by the Creek cession may be found in Michael D. Green, "Federal-State Conflict," pp. 278–89 and 289 n. 22. J. Mills Thornton, III, *Politics and Power in a Slave Society: Alabama, 1800–1860* (Baton Rouge: Louisiana State University Press, 1978), pp. 28–30, shows how the Creek removal crisis attracted Alabamians disinterested in South Carolina nullification to a less formal but equally powerful states' rights enthusiasm.

17. J. J. Abert to Cass, 14 January 1836, "Report on Indian Hostilities," 6 June 1836, HED 276, 24th Cong., 1st sess., serial 292. Hereafter cited as HED 276, 24/1 (292). This is a careful description of the execution of the provisions of the Treaty of 1832 and an explanation of the many delays.

18. Mary E. Young, *Redskins, Ruffleshirts, and Rednecks: Indian Allotments in Alabama and Mississippi, 1830–1860* (Norman: University of Oklahoma Press, 1961), especially pp. 38–39, 73–74. For a more general analysis of the policy, see Paul W. Gates, "Indian Allotments Preceding the Dawes Act," *The Frontier Challenge: Responses to the Trans-Mississippi West,* ed. John G. Clark (Lawrence: University of Kansas Press, 1971), pp. 141–70.

19. Benjamin Marshall to Cass, 26 October 1832, OIA, LR, CA, RG 75, reel 223:234.

20. Cass to Marshall, 21 November 1832, OIA, LS, RG 75, 9:374–75. Marshall was making the same recommendation in May 1833. See Abert to Cass, 15 May 1833, OIA, LR, CE, RG 75, reel 237:373–74.

21. Parsons and Abert to Cass, 3 July 1833, OIA, LR, CA, RG 75, reel 223:418–26; Creek Chiefs to Abert and Parsons, 30 June 1833, ibid., reel 223:465–66; Eli S. Shorter to Cass, 11 July 1833, SD 512, 23/1 (247), pp. 465–66. Young, *Redskins,* describes in elaborate detail the operations of the speculators in their attempts to defraud the Creek holders of reserves. For the Creek story, see especially chaps. 4 and 5.

22. Parsons to Cass, 10 February 1833. OIA, LR, CA, RG 75, reel 223:1018–20.

23. Marshall to Andrew Jackson, 16 May 1833, SD 512, 23/1 (247), p. 398.

24. The best description of this remains Young, *Redskins.*

25. Opothle Yoholo and others to Cass, 4 September 1832, "Message on the Sales of Indian Reservations, 1 July 1836, SD 425, 24th Cong., 1st sess., serial 284, p. 318. For the Texas scheme, see Grant Foreman, *Indian Removal: The Emigration of the Five Civilized Tribes of Indians,* new edition (Norman: University of Oklahoma Press, 1953), pp. 135–36.

26. Letters from Creek leaders describing various features of the fraud and speculation in their reserves are numerous. Two particularly graphic examples are Opothle Yoholo and others to the Secretary of War, 16 March 1835, HED 276, 24/1 (292), pp. 129–30, and Opothle Yoholo and others to Robert W. McHenry, 23 March 1835, ibid., pp. 131–32. The letter that Cass credited with precipitating his investigation was Neah Mico and others to the President, 25 August 1835, ibid., pp. 163–65. In Cass to John B. Hogan, 9 September 1835, ibid., p. 41, Cass appointed Hogan to the position of special investigator of the alleged frauds.

27. John W. A. Sanford to George Gibson, 14 May 1836, ibid., p. 372; *Montgomery Advertiser,* quoted in *Huntsville Southern Advocate,* in Foreman, *Indian Removal,* p. 147; Cass to Hogan, 19 May 1836, *American State Papers: Military Affairs,* 6:623. The best analysis of the "war" to date is Kenneth L. Valliere, "The Creek War of 1836: A Military History," *Chronicles of Oklahoma* 57 (Winter 1979–80): 463–85.

28. Cass to Thomas S. Jesup, 19 May 1836, *American State Papers: Military Affairs,* 6:622–23.

29. Carey A. Harris to Joel R. Poinsett, 5 February 1838, ibid., 7:952. The process of removal has been well described in Foreman, *Indian Removal,* chaps. 8–14. For information on those Creeks who remained in Alabama, see the work of J. Anthony Paredes, especially his "Back from Disappearance: The Alabama Creek Indian Community," *Southeastern Indians Since the Removal Era,* ed. Walter L. Williams (Athens: University of Georgia Press, 1979), pp. 123–42.

NOTE ON
THE SOURCES

THIS BOOK could not have been written without the rich and varied resources of the National Archives and Records Service. Record Group 75, the Records of the Bureau of Indian Affairs, contains the largest collection of documents and correspondence valuable to this study. Before the unofficial establishment of the Office of Indian Affairs in 1824, the office of the Secretary of War directly conducted most of the correspondence regarding Indian affairs. These letters are organized as Records of the Secretary of War Relating to Indian Affairs, Letters Received, 1800–1823 (Microcopy M271), and Letters Sent, 1800–1824 (Microcopy M15). After 1824, a new filing system went into effect. The Correspondence of the Office of Indian Affairs, Letters Received, 1824–1881 (Microcopy M234) was arranged by tribal agency, with a separate section of Emigration records. The Office of Indian Affairs, Letters Sent, 1824–1881 file (Microcopy M21) retained a chronological organization. These series of letters include most of the general correspondence between the agencies and Washington. Documents Relating to the Negotiation of Ratified and Unratified Treaties with Various Indian Tribes, 1801–69 (Microcopy T494), also in Record Group 75, is a valuable supplement to the agency and Indian Office correspondence. This collection includes, among other things, the journals of the negotiations of several of the Creek treaties.

Record Group 107, Records of the War Department, contains important materials on U.S. relations with the Creeks. Letters of the Secretary of War Relating to Military Affairs, 1800–1889 (Microcopy M6) includes correspondence with and reports from army officers in military contact with Native Americans. Much of the correspondence relating to Creek affairs in the 1820s and 30s remains in this collection. Letters Sent to the President by the Secretary of War, 1800–1863 (Microcopy M127) is another rich source, not so much in quantity as in quality. This correspondence provides insight into the highest levels of policy administration. Because of the political ramifications of the Georgia controversy, the letters in this series are particularly valuable.

The most useful published sources for early Creek history are contained in the various government document collections. The *American State Papers, Indian Affairs,* is a two-volume gathering of congressional committee reports and executive department correspondence that supplements, with some duplication, the National Archives material. It is particularly rich in documents relating to the Creek War of 1813–14 and the Georgia controversy. The Congressional Serial Set is a continuation and elaboration of the kinds of items found in the *American State Papers.* Commissioned by Congress, the House and Senate documents of the Serial Set provide in often extraordinary detail a wealth of information on Creek–U.S. relations. House Report 98, 19th Congress, 2nd Session, Serial 161, Report on the Georgia Indian Controversy, was especially useful.

There are no private manuscript collections equal to the Indian Office correspondence, but a few illuminate special aspects of Creek history in the preremoval period. The David B. Mitchell Papers in the Ayer Collection, the Newberry Library, Chicago, were particularly helpful in shedding light on the relationship between this Creek agent and William H. Crawford, his mentor. The Perkins Library, Duke University, hold two collections of interest. James R. Vinton's "Journal of My Excursion to Georgia, and the Creek Nation—1827," contains Lieutenant Vinton's observations of the Georgia political scene during the critical early months of 1827, as well as a description of events in the Creek Nation. The Edward George Washington Butler Papers include the trenchant comments of General Gaines's aide-de-camp during their sojourn on the Creek-Georgia frontier.

Several published collections of private papers have been useful for this study, including Charles Francis Adams (ed), *Memoirs of John Quincy Adams,* 12 vol. (Philadelphia: J. B. Lippincott, 1874–77); John S. Bassett (ed.), *Correspondence of Andrew Jackson,* 7 vol. (Washington D.C.: Carnegie Institute, 1926–35); W. Edwin Hemphill and Robert L. Meriwether (eds.), *The Papers of John C. Calhoun,* (Columbia: University of South Carolina Press, 1959–   ); and Edward J. Harden, *Life of George M. Troup* (Savannah: E. J. Purse, 1859). Finally Hezekiah Niles's *Niles' Weekly Register,* a newsmagazine published in Baltimore, is a goldmine of valuable material of the history of U.S. relations with the Creeks.

As my notes testify, my indebtedness to the published works of many scholars is enormous.

INDEX

Abert, John J., 182
Abihka, 13, 14
Adair, James, 21, 28
Adams, John Quincy, 93, 99, 114, 125, 139, 148; efforts of to remove Creeks from Georgia, 109, 128–29, 134–37; policy on execution of McIntosh, 100–102, 115; policy on 1825 survey, 101–102, 112–13, 128; policy on Treaty of Indian Springs (1825), 116, 122; policy on Treaty of Washington, 116–21; sends troops to Tuckabatchee, 153–54; trouble with Troup, 100–103, 112–14, 126–28, 133
Alabama (Creek town), 13–14, 20–21, 40–41
Andrews, Timothy, 101, 103–4, 115, 126–27
Atkin, Edmund, 29
Austill, Jeremiah, 176, 179–80

Baldwin, William, 52
Barbour, James, 93, 99, 105–6, 111, 123, 125, 130, 139, 148
Barnard, William, 59, 87
Betton, Solomon, 142
Big Warrior, 55, 84, 131, 149, 162, 164–65, 185; alliance of with Crowell, 63, 65–66, 68; death of, 95, 108; opposition to land cession, 76–78, 81, 87, 89; opposition to missionaries, 64, 66; as principal chief of Upper Creeks, 38–41, 59; as rival of McIntosh, 63, 65, 68, 72, 85, 92; role of in Creek Civil War, 41–42
Bird Tail King, 38
Bosomworth, Mary, 26

Bowles, William Augustus, 34–35
Brearley, David, 131, 148–49, 153–55
Brims, 22–24, 43
Brodnax, John, 169, 175
Broken Arrow, 38, 55–56, 84–85, 87, 90–91, 95
Broken Arrow negotiations, 76–82
Brooke, George M., 161–62
Burgess, James, 37
Butler, Edward G. W., 111, 115

Calhoun, John C., 53, 57–60, 65, 68, 72, 76, 82–83, 86, 89–90, 93, 97, 160, 180; Indian policy of, 46–50
Campbell, Duncan G., 75–76, 78–83, 85–87, 89, 92, 99, 102, 111, 114
Capers, William, 63–67
Carr, Paddy, 161
Cass, Lewis, 120–21, 169, 171–72, 174–79, 181, 184–85
Chekilli, 13–14, 24–26
Chiaha, 184
Civilization Fund Act of 1819, 47
Clark, John, 52–53, 58, 66–67, 127
Clarke, Elijah, 52
Clay, Henry, 125, 133
Cobb, Thomas, 148
Coffee, John, 159–61
Compere, Lee, 64, 66, 151–52
Coosa, 13–14
Coosa Tustunuggee, 132
Cornells, Alexander, 37, 39
Cornells, Charles, 124
Coweta, 2, 13–14, 22, 24, 26–27, 37–38, 42, 54–55, 64, 81–82, 85, 89, 98

Crawford, Robert S., 174, 176, 179
Crawford, William H., 52–53, 60, 175, 177
Creek Civil War, 41–42, 55; causes of, 39–41
Creek economic life: agriculture, 3; effects of trade on, 18–20; gathering, 3; hunting and fishing, 3, 19–20; slave raiding, 19–20; trade, 18–20, 22–24
Creek "frauds," 177–80, 183–84
Creek Nation: clans, 4–6, 8, 37–38, 70, 152; confederacy, 12–15, 22, 29; factionalism, 21–23, 27, 33, 35–36, 63–65, 68, 72, 83–85; mission schools, 47–48, 151; nativism, 27, 40–42; population, 28–29; Red-White moiety, 7, 10–11, 15
Creek National Council: adopts severalty, 170–72; appoints Opothle Yoholo prime minister, 132; code of laws, 70–72, 74, 97; decision of to execute McIntosh, 96–97, 105, 111, 150, deposes Tuskeneah, 131–32, 164; "doctrine of neutrality," 21–23, 27, 30–31; efforts of to avoid removal, 131, 136, 151–53, 155, 157–61, 165, 168–70, 177–78, 182; factionalism, 21–23, 27, 33, 35–36, 84, 165; laws against land cessions, 74–78, 82, 84, 88–89, 91, 96–97, 99, 109, 150, 163, 167; McGillivray's efforts to centralize, 33–34, 36; meetings of with Gaines, 108–11, 115–18; operations of, 73, 139; origins of, 12–13; Pole Cat Springs statement, 77–78, 80, 82; reforms of by Hawkins, 37, 69–70; reorganization of, 98, 126, 129, 131–32, 185–86; resistance to Treaty of Indian Springs (1825), 90–92; sessions of, 64–65; structure of, 149–51; tries to fire Crowell, 130, 135, 158, 161; Tuckabatchee statement, 76–78, 80, 82. *See also* Law menders
Creek Towns: autonomy of, 4, 15, 33, 149–50; councils and officers of, 5, 8–10; Lower Towns, disintegration of, 150; Upper Towns, stability of, 151. *See also* Upper-Lower division
Creek War (1813–14), 42–43, 185
Creek War (1836), 184–85
Creek-Alabama relations: Alabama interest in Creek removal, 144, 147; and Alabama legal jurisdiction, 146–47, 155–60, 162, 165–66, 172, 176, 179
Creek-Cherokee relations, 75–76, 80, 82, 120–21, 129–30, 136, 149, 151, 159, 161
Creek-English relations: American Revolution, 31–33; land, 28–30; political relations, 21–22, 24, 27–28; trade, 20, 23–24, 27, 30–31

Creek-French relations, 20–23, 27
Creek-Georgia relations: border conflict, 141–42, 169, 184–85; land, 25–30, 33–35, 73; trade, 23–24, 31
Creek-Spanish relations, 17–18, 20, 22–24, 34–35
Creek-United States relations: American Revolution, 32–33; civilization policy, 36–39, 47–48; land, 43, 73; political relations, 56–57; trade, 46–47. *See also* United States
Crowell, John: alliance of with Big Warrior, 63, 65–66, 68; appointed Creek agent, 59; background of, 59; Council tries to fire, 130, 135, 158; denies Creeks have a government, 161; dismissed as agent, 179; efforts to remove Creeks, 158, 177; provides food, 142, 169; relations with brothers, 60; and Treaty of Indian Springs (1825), 90–91, 93, 95; troubles with McIntosh, 61–62, 92; troubles with missionaries, 63–66; troubles with Troup, 67–68, 82–83, 99–100, 126
Crowell, Thomas, 60–61, 158
Cusseta, 2, 13–14, 24, 32, 38, 42, 85, 87, 92
Cuyler, Jeremiah, 62

Davis, John, 151
DeSoto, Hernando, 17–18
Dinsmoor, Silas, 50
Disease, 17–18, 29, 169

Eaton, John, 155, 158–59, 162–65, 167, 169
Edwards, William, 112
Efau Imathla, 59
Elliot, John, 164
Eneah Mico, 161–62, 170
Eneah Thlucco, 26
Eneathlocco Hopoie, 132, 164
Etomme Tustunnuggee, 89, 96
Eufaula, 14, 26, 87, 176

Factory system, 46–47
Fat King, 32, 34
Forsyth, John, 120, 142, 153
Fort Mitchell, 60, 119, 135, 142, 153–54, 165–66, 171, 174–77, 179
Francis, Josiah, 41

Gaines, Edmund P., 113, 119–20, 127, 129, 144, 150; appointed special commissioner to the Creeks, 101; relations with McIntosh faction, 106–7, 112; relations with Creek National Council, 108–11, 115–18; relations of with Troup, 105, 112, 114

Galphin, George, 32
Gentleman of Elvas, 17
Georgia, 23–24; Clarkite-Troupite factionalism, 66–67; demands Creek removal,
73; extends legal jurisdiction over Creek
cession, 103; land lottery system of, 93,
102–3; politics of, 52; role of Creeks in
politics of, 67
Graham, George, 56
Green Corn Celebration (Busk), 15–16
Gun Merchant, 27

Hambly, William, 90, 121
Hamill, Rev. A., 64
Hamilton, S. S., 167
Hawkins, Benjamin, 36–43, 50–55, 69–70,
97, 185
Hawkins, Benjamin (Creek), 96
Hawkins, Samuel, 96
High-Head Jim, 41–42
Hilibi, 14
Hitchiti, 14, 85, 184
Hopoie Hadjo, 77, 87, 118
Hothliwahali, 14

Irwinton, 175–77

Jackson, Andrew, 45, 53, 55, 77, 84, 164,
174; in Creek War (1813–14), 43; Indian
policy as President, 155–57, 160, 162–63,
165–67, 169, 171, 175–76, 179–82; views
of on treaties, 48–49; views of on Treaty
of Indian Springs (1825), 115
Jackson, James, 66
Jefferson, Thomas, 47, 54
Jesup, Thomas S., 185
Jim Boy, 156

Koasati, 20–21, 40–41

Lamar, Henry G., 92
Law menders, 37, 41, 55, 71, 96–98, 100,
131, 150
Lewis, Dixon Hall, 146–47
Little Prince, 38, 61, 76, 84, 87, 107, 124,
130, 134, 162; approves negotiations of
Treaty of Washington, 118; approves
Treaty of Fort Mitchell, 137–39; death
of, 149; explains execution of McIntosh,
109; infirmity of, 108; opposes land ces-
sions, 77–78, 80, 135–36; opposes land
survey, 130; as principal chief of Lower
Creeks, 55–57, 59; resists McIntosh, 92,
95
Little Tallassee, 33
Little Warrior, 41

Lovett, George, 64
Lower Creeks (Lower Towns), 11–12, 14,
20–21, 23, 30, 34–35, 38–39, 55, 72, 88.
See also Upper Creeks; Upper-Lower
division

McGillivray, Alexander, 33–36, 38, 40, 43,
54–55, 71, 78, 132, 139, 185
McIntosh, Chilly, 71, 81, 92, 98–101, 104–8
McIntosh, John, 54, 63, 68
McIntosh, Roly, 89, 99
McIntosh, William, 38, 64, 66, 74, 85, 91,
95, 98–99, 102–3, 105, 109, 111–12, 132,
185; alliance with Troup, 68, 83; background of, 54–56; dependence of on
Troup, 94; efforts to bribe Cherokees,
75–76; execution of, 96–97, 150; his interpretation of National Council, 84; offices of, 55–56; as rival of Big Warrior,
63, 65, 68, 72; role of at Broken Arrow
negotiations, 76–82; role in negotiation
of Treaty of Indian Springs (1825),
86–90; role in drafting law code, 71;
swindles of, 54, 56–59; his troubles with
Crowell, 61–62, 92
McIntosh faction, 90–101, 104–10, 112,
115, 119, 123, 131, 148
McKenney, Thomas L., 120–21, 124,
137–38, 143, 148, 153–55, 159–62
Macomb, Alexander, 174
McQueen, Peter, 41–42
Mad Dog, 38–39, 59
Madison, James, 52
Major Ridge, 75, 124
Malatchi, 25–27
Marshall, Benjamin, 181
Marshall, Joseph, 98, 106–7, 112
Meigs, Return, 50
Menawa, 96, 98, 124
Meriwether, James, 75–76, 78–82, 85, 87,
89, 92, 102, 111
Milledge, John, 52
Mims, Samuel, 42
Mitchell, David B., 51, 59–60, 66–68, 71,
75, 86, 97; alliance with McIntosh,
56–57, 62; corruption of, 53–54, 56–57;
as Creek agent, 52–53; and encourage-
ment of missionaries, 63, 65
Monroe, James, 46–47, 49, 52–53, 59, 76,
82–83, 86
Moor, William, 168
Moore, Gabriel, 179
Muklasa, 27
Murphy, John, 144–46, 148

Natchez, 14

Newcomb, F. D., 166

Okfuskee, 14
Octeachee Emathla, 167
Oglethorpe, James, 23-26
Okchai, 14, 27
Opothle Yoholo, 107, 133, 137-39, 149-50,
    155, 160-61, 169, 172, 184-86; decides to
    remove, 183; discredited by Lower
    Creeks, 162; emergence as leader of Na-
    tional Council, 108, 110-11, 129, 164-65;
    interpretation of laws, 109; made prime
    minister, 132; and negotiations in
    Washington, 117-25; prosecuted under
    Alabama law, 156-57; as speaker for Big
    Warrior, 87-88, 108
Owens, Hardeman, 179-80, 183

Page, John, 176
Pakana, 14
Panton, Leslie, and Company, 34
Panton, William, 35-36
Parsons, Enoch, 178, 182
Peters, Arnett S., 164
Pickens, Israel, 144
Powasee Emathla, 87
Proclamation of 1763, 29

Red Shoes, 40
Removal Act, 156, 158, 179. *See also*
    United States
Ridge, John: adviser to Opothle Yoholo,
    129-30, 132, 135-37, 139, 149, 159, 162;
    broken by McKenney, 138; payments
    to, 119, 124; role in negotiation of
    Treaty of Washington, 119-21; secre-
    tary to National Council, 111, 161
Ross, John, 75

Sawmawme Mico, 26
Sawokli, 87
Seagrove, James, 36
Shawnee, 14
Stedham, John, 87, 124
Stinson, George, 61-62, 68
Stuart, John, 29-32

Taladega, 85
Tallassee, 14, 41
Tallassee King, 32, 34, 38-39, 41
Talsee Fixico, 132
Tarrant, Leonard, 179
Tecumseh, 40-41, 45, 55
Tenskwatawa, 40-41
Trade and Intercourse Acts, 35, 46, 60-61,
    97, 133, 148, 163

Treaty of Augusta, 30
Treaty of Coweta, 25-26
Treaty of 1805, 39
Treaty of 1832: Creeks' draft proposal,
    170, 181; provisions of, 171-74, 181, 186
Treaty of Fort Jackson, 43, 62, 80, 144
Treaty of Fort Mitchell, 130, 134, 137-38,
    141
Treaty of Indian Springs (1821), 57-59,
    73-75, 96
Treaty of Indian Springs (1825): abroga-
    tion of, 116-19, 122-23, 125; negotiation
    of, 81, 86-89; protest against, 90-91,
    109, 111-12, 115, ratification of, 89-90,
    92-93
Treaty of New York, 35, 41, 79-80
Treaty of Pensacola, 30
Treaty of Washington: Creeks' draft
    proposal, 119; Georgia opposition to,
    122; negotiation of, 118-22; provisions
    of, 123-25, 141, 157
Triplett, Thomas, 148-49, 161
Triplett, William, 161
Troup, George M., 52, 53, 77, 86, 88-89,
    95-96, 106-7, 111, 115-16, 125, 134, 137,
    144, 180; and alliance with missionaries,
    66-68; attack on Crowell, 82-83, 99-100,
    102-3, 131; conflict with Adams admin-
    istration, 100-103, 112-14, 126-28, 133;
    efforts to complete Creek removal, 130,
    133, 139; efforts to protect McIntosh,
    92; efforts to survey Indian Springs ces-
    sion, 93-94, 105, 112; policy toward
    Treaty of Indian Springs (1825), 120,
    127; political needs of, 67-68, 93; re-
    action of to execution of McIntosh,
    98-100, 102-5, 108; reelection of, 127;
    and relations with Gaines, 105, 112-14;
    uses McIntosh, 83
Tuckabatchee, 2, 10, 14, 37-40, 42, 55, 59,
    64, 76-77, 88, 91-92, 153-54, 183
Tuckabatchee Hadjo, 167
Tusconah Coochee, 132
Tuskeegee Tustunnuggee, 87
Tuskeneah, 87, 108, 117-18, 124, 131-32,
    137-38, 155, 164, 170
Tuskeneah of Cusseta, 87, 161-62, 168

Uchee, 26, 87
United States: Compact with Georgia (1802),
    73, 79-80, 85, 88, 120; federal-state rela-
    tions, 73, 100-103, 112-14, 126-28, 133,
    145-48, 180; Indian agents of, 36-37,
    50-54, 62-63, 116-17; Indian policy
    (general) of, 45-51; removal policy of,
    49-51, 73, 88, 116, 123, 127, 131, 136-37,

143, 148–49, 154–56, 162, 166, 171, 181–82, 185; treaty system of, 48–50, 159. *See also* Adams, John Quincy; Barbour, James; Calhoun, John C.; Cass, Lewis; Civilization Fund Act of 1819; Creek–United States relations; Crowell, John; Eaton, John; Factory system; Hawkins, Benjamin; Jackson, Andrew; Madison, James; Mitchell, David B.; Monroe, James; Trade and Intercourse Acts
Upper Creeks (Upper Towns), 7, 11–12, 14, 20–21, 30, 33, 38–41, 59, 72, 76, 88, 129. *See also* Lower Creeks; Upper–Lower division
Upper–Lower division, 11–12, 21, 35–36, 38–39, 135–37; cultural differences, 72, 150–52; political differences, 88, 153, 158, 160, 165, 167

Vann, David, 119–21, 124, 135–39
Vinton, John R., 133–35

Wager, Philip, 155, 165–66, 174
Walker, William, 77, 82–83, 149, 152–53
Walsh, Paddy, 41
Ware, Alexander, 98–99
Washington, George, 46
Wind clan, 33, 54, 152
Wirt, William, 53
Witumpka, 177
Wolf King, 27
Wright, James, 28, 30

Yoholo Mico, 87, 109
Yuchi, 14, 184